LOCAL HEROES

The Asbury Park Music Scene

Rivergate Books
An Imprint of Rutgers University Press
New Brunswick, New Jersey

LOCAL HEROES

ANDERS MÅRTENSSON • PHOTOGRAPHS BY JÖRGEN JOHANSSON

Library of Congress Cataloging-in-Publication Data

Mårtensson, Anders, 1964–Local heroes : the Asbury Park music scene /
Anders Mårtensson ; photographs by Jörgen Johansson.
   p. cm.
   "A Swedish version of this book was first published by Accent Förlag, Sweden."
   Includes bibliographical references and index.
   ISBN 978-0-8135-4294-2 (pbk. : alk. paper)
   1. Rock music–New Jersey–Asbury Park–History and criticism. 2. Rock musicians–New Jersey–Asbury Park–Interviews.
3. Springsteen, Bruce. I. Johansson, Jörgen, 1969- II. Title.
   ML3534.3.M37 2008
   781.6609749'46–dc22
            2007029667

Visit our Web site: http://rutgerspress.rutgers.edu

Text design and composition by Jenny Dossin
Manufactured in China

Dedicated to the memory of

Bill Chinnock and Big Danny Gallagher

PREFACE

The music that truly moves you is often the music you encounter when very young. You remember where you were the first time you heard it. Your thoughts. The thrill.

Summer of 1975 was described in New York as the "Summer of Springsteen." That's when he broke through. Jon Landau, a rock critic who later became Bruce Springsteen's manager and friend, had already called the twenty-five year-old from Freehold, New Jersey "the future of rock 'n 'roll." But it was that summer, 1975, when everything exploded. That was where the real journey began.

Today we revere those early albums, *Greetings from Asbury Park, N.J.* and *The Wild, the Innocent & the E Street Shuffle*, as definitive of a generation. But the Springsteen journey would probably never have become truly lifelong without *Born to Run.*

Suddenly he ended up on the cover of *Newsweek* and *Time.* Suddenly he had gotten the entire world to listen. Over night, everyone else knew what New Jersey had known for years: that no artist would ever be able to surpass the enormous three, and sometimes four, hour concerts when Bruce Springsteen would break down all opposition, all the barriers normally built up between artist and audience.

This book is not trying to tell the Bruce Springsteen story. Instead, it's about capturing the atmosphere and the feelings, a way of recording the tales of those who were there, and those who remain there: in and around Asbury Park, this time-tested Shore town that adopted a soul-searching Springsteen at the end of the 1960s.

He became part of a community that survived on rock 'n 'roll. At the Upstage Club and the Student Prince he challenged all the other guitar slingers. And by the time the Stone Pony opened he was already the Boss.

Some three years ago in Hässleholm, Sweden: a case of beer might have been involved. This was our Upstage night. Drinking, laughing, listening to the music we love. Then finally, in the wee hours, it all seemed obvious: there has to be a celebration.

The first interviews were scheduled in the fall of 2004, the final one in the spring of 2007. Somewhere in between an initial Swedish version of the book was released.

As time went by things changed; like the Asbury Partners moving forward with their oceanfront revitalization. Also, in Spring of 2007, there was sad news of the passing of Big Danny Gallagher and Bill Chinnock. They will both be deeply missed, and it only seemed natural to honor Danny and Bill by keeping their interviews as they were originally written.

Local Heroes, in its English language version, remains a tribute to a unique club scene and its stars, its founders. Its characters: "Mad Dog," "Boom," "Phantom Dan," "Tinker," "Sugar Miami Steve" . . .

These are their stories, and our love letter for a town that breathes rock'n'roll more than any other. A town in ruins, but a town that also dares to believe in the future. A town where all roads lead to Bruce Springsteen.

We believe that you share the passion. You know this journey can only continue.

See you further on up the road.

Anders Mårtensson and Jörgen Johansson
Hässleholm, Sweden
June 11, 2007

CONTENTS

ACKNOWLEDGMENTS

The author and photographer would like to thank each and every individual who took their time to meet with us for interviews. Special thank yous: Lance Larson and Debbie Delisa, Dan Mulvey, David J. Mieras, Alison Oscar of Jon Landau Management, Nicole Barsalona of Renegade Nation, Panacea Entertainment, Tönnheim Literary Agency, Kristi Long (copy-editing), Leslie Mitchner and everyone at Rutgers University Press, Christophe Brunski of The Locution25 Group LLC (translation), Accent Förlag. Last but certainly not least: our families. Without your patience, love, and support these dreams of ours would not have come true.

LOCAL HEROES

COOKMA
KINGSLEY

PROLOGUE—A RUDE AWAKENING

October 2, 2004

There was once a time when Asbury Park, New Jersey was the place to be. To shop, lay out in the sun, and let the kids play on the carousel or ferris wheel. Maybe to catch a movie or, more likely, listen to live music in one of the many bars along the Circuit. Asbury Park has a proud history. But does Asbury Park have a future?

Can the town that was the Jewel of the Jersey Shore in the 1930s, '40s, and '50s rise again?

Who knows? New investors pour in cash, well-off New Yorkers and other upper-middle-class folk are being drawn to buy million dollar apartments in large complexes down by the boardwalk. Fresh tax money is bringing prosperity. But how do people look on everything that came before this?

Asbury Park, with its 17,000 inhabitants, offers several advantages: an hour by car to New York, an hour and a half to Philadelphia. Not to mention the beach and the waves. The history. The rock 'n' roll romance.

This is Springsteen Land, U.S.A., and what tourism still makes it here is about rock 'n' roll. It's about checking in at the Berkeley Carteret Hotel and strolling along the boardwalk, from the remains of a run down casino on past Madam Marie's, and down to Convention Hall.

But dreams meet reality in a rude awakening where everything that Bruce Springsteen wrote about at the beginning of the 1970s seems to have been left to ruin.

According to some, this is where the future starts.

Others think that Asbury Park is history. A thing of the past. A fairytale with a brutal ending.

After years of racial tension following the 1968 assassination of Dr. Martin Luther King, Jr., full-scale riots broke out on Springwood Avenue on July 4th weekend, 1970. It all lasted for four days. Lots of people were injured, stores were looted, and several properties were destroyed by fire. Asbury Park was no longer considered a safe place to live, and up until the 2000s people would call this former vacation Mecca "Sarajevo by the Sea." They would say that everything that died with the riots is buried and gone, never to be coming back.

This is a sad prophecy for those who grew up with the myths, legends, and romantic visions of Bruce Springsteen's songs. And it's something of a reality check when we finally stand where Cookman Avenue meets Kingsley Street.

The feeling changes at this intersection. Being the out-of-towners, the outsiders looking in, we go quiet. 'Cause we're here to follow that voice. Like in the Bruce Springsteen song, we'll go riding down Kingsley, like the character in that song we're chasing something in the night. It is right here, as darkness is falling, that our feeling of Asbury Park becomes strongest. Here, where our dreams meet reality.

So we go down Kingsley, past what once was the Student Prince. And then we wind back towards Ocean Avenue because we know that LaBamba's Big Band is playing the Stone Pony tonight. We know there's a party going on over in Lance and Debbie's Wonder Bar. We head over to where dreams meet reality. Chasing something in the night.

Asbury Park is a mix of feelings: Dejection, fear, sorrow, pain.

But also happiness in Tillie's smile.

And the warmth of the people who were there when it happened. When Big Bobby Williams and Vini Lopez were the house drummers at the Upstage Club. When Bruce Springsteen played the Student Prince. Night after night after night. Nothing can take that away from them. Nothing can kill the rock 'n' roll spirit. Not in this city, where hope and dreams collide with reality.

Welcome to
Asbury Park

Big Danny Gallagher

The phone rings late at night. A voice says: "Hey, Danny. You've got to go, man." "I knew that's how it would turn out, but my heart broke that night." Big Danny Gallagher tells about the conversation that changed his life. Then he sits down to play bluegrass in the lounge at the Berkeley Carteret Hotel in Asbury Park.

It's a Friday like any other, fall 2004. Big Danny Gallagher is going to play in the lounge with his bluegrass trio. Playing with friends, for friends. He comes into the warmth for a bit and, with a little luck, he'll leave a few dollars richer.

"Really need the money. So I can make it back home to Ireland. Preferably early next year. You never know how much time you have left. Fifty-seven . . . hell, I should have been dead fifteen years ago."

Asbury Park should feel like home to Danny Gallagher. He's lived large parts of his life here, and this is where he's had some of his happiest moments.

But luck changed.

"I'm not at home here any longer, not in an America run by people like Bush. Goddamn, I can't even smoke a cigarette when I want. It's fine to have smoke-free bars, but when they start putting up non-smoking signs in outdoor arenas . . .

"Times have changed. The only thing fun now is the occasional Springsteen show, but I can't even find out what time it is from those guys anymore."

Danny Gallagher has seen better days. And he believes they'll be back.

"Ireland really embraced me. Europeans are wide open to my personality."

Long ago, Danny Gallagher was proud to call Asbury Park his hometown. In the 1950s, when he was listening to Elvis, the Everly Brothers, and Danny & the Juniors.

"'Rock 'n' roll is here to stay, it will never die.' That stuff changed my life."

The 1960s: Mickey Holiday singing with the Jaywalkers. "Running Bear" and the girls. And then there was the Upstage Club, where Vini Lopez, Big Bobby Williams, Garry Tallent, Bruce Springsteen, and others were part of a musical brotherhood.

"Tom and Margaret Potter ran the place. I knew Margaret from school; she was a few years older than me and my brother had warned me about her. She was tough, Margaret. A hell of a football player, too. But my brother, he was probably one of the scariest people I've ever known."

Gallagher continues: "There were so many people coming into Asbury back then. Cars and motorcycles lined up along the Circuit. I knew most of them, but no one shady ever got into the Upstage. Tom and Margaret paid me to keep an eye on the door. And I did my job."

Gallagher tells us that the Upstage Club was open from eight until midnight for youths up to eighteen years of age. Then the night shift went from one to five.

"Two dollars at the door for non-members, one dollar for everyone who had a membership."

He laughs and says:

"We used to call the Upstage the cheapest motel in Asbury Park. Because the party lasted until five in the morning, and then, when the sun was coming up, we'd go down to the beach and sleep."

He already knew Bruce Springsteen. The first time Gallagher met the guitarist from Freehold was when Springsteen was playing the Pandemonium in Wannamassa.

"Man, in them days it was so guts. It was all guts."

"He counted in. 'One, two, three . . . ' This fucking guy. He was it."

Danny Gallagher goes quiet. He drags on his cigarette, exhales slowly, and then says: "What we had back then, with the music. I wouldn't trade that for anything."

In the beginning of the 1970s, the local music scene would undergo a change. It was a time of unrest in a segregated society that culminated in revolt and riots. Asbury Park was set ablaze.

Bruce Springsteen had been in bands like Earth, Child, and Steel Mill. Then Dr. Zoom & the Sonic Boom was a reaction, even if short-lived, to an America that was getting harder to understand.

"It was just like having a party. Dr. Zoom would be open for anyone who wanted to join in. We picked up people from the audience for the backup vocals. We had a guy fixing a motor cycle, and a few guys who played dice.

"In Dr. Zoom it was anything goes," says Gallagher, who himself challenged another Asbury legend, Upstage bouncer "Big Tiny," in Monopoly. Onstage.

There are only a few documented Zoom shows. But after Springsteen's success with Steel Mill, they got as far as opening for the Allman Brothers.

"Then Bruce started going to Richmond again, with the Bruce Springsteen Band. Garry Tallent got a girlfriend down there and he stayed behind, like David Sancious, who was working with radio jingles.

"So Bruce came home and felt that he had become stuck in Asbury Park. That's when he came up with some of the lines for 'Rosalita.'"

One day Danny Gallagher's sitting on the steps in front of his house. He feels like shit. Marriage is over, and his brother, who was just about to move in a few days earlier, had died.

"Darkness," says Gallagher. "That's all I saw. Nothing but darkness."

Bruce Springsteen comes by, feeling pretty low himself.

"Danny."

"How's it going, Bruce?"

"Not so great. You said that if there was ever anything I needed."

"Right?"

"Yeah, well I just got thrown out of my apartment. Can I stay with you for a while?"

"Make yourself at home."

Gallagher has an extra mattress, and Springsteen moves in. They get their hands on an old guitar.

"The first song he played for me in that apartment was 'Wild Billy's Circus Story.' The second was probably 'Kitty's Back' . . . no, it was 'Rosalita.' He came rushing in one night, grabbed the guitar, and said: 'Hey, check this one out.' He played a little, sang a little, acting James Brown and Wilson Pickett. Look, I get goose bumps just talking about it."

"Man, in them days it was so guts. It was all guts."

Springsteen and Gallagher partied together. They drove up and down the Jersey Shore in an Oldsmobile convertible, listening to Chuck Berry.

"We had fun. Bruce and I always had fun together. I never minded smoking a joint, but not Bruce. He never did that. Think he never even tried."

"But he tried tequila, ha ha ha. I had a bottle, and Bruce asked: 'What's this shit?' I told him: 'It'll get you loose.'"

An hour later, when Gallagher was with a woman, someone taps him on the shoulder. Springsteen is standing there with two of his own conquests. He smiles from ear to ear and says: "Hey man, this loose shit is good!"

Then one day, when Gallagher comes home from work, there's a note on the refrigerator door:

"I met with those guys and signed the deal. We're playing tonight at Kenny's Castaways in New York. There's a place in this for you if you want it."

"Bruce was going to record an album. The band went on tour, and I drove."

"We were everywhere. Up in Niagara Falls, down in Atlanta, and all the way out in California. We traveled with Chicago. We played with the Beach Boys, Richie Havens, and Paul Butterfield. Damn, one time we were the opening act for Cheech and Chong."

"That was right after *Greetings*. John Hammond, who signed Bruce, booked him as a folk music act. They didn't know that he had a rock 'n' roll band."

COVER ??

Springsteen, on his way up, continued to surround himself with friends. But new forces would come into play.

"In comes this guy, Mike Appel. He starts calling all the shots, and whatever he knew about the music business is one thing, he never understood what Bruce was about. We came from a world where everyone was equal. Bruce was the man, everyone knew that. But no one, not even Bruce, ever got any special treatment. Appel had an entirely different view of how everything was to be handled. Which essentially meant that he didn't give a shit about anyone else. And Bruce never even knew what was happening. No one said anything.

"But you know, we came home from a long tour to apartments where the rent had never been paid. The phones, the electricity. Everything was shut down. We ended up having a dispute with our landlords. So I said to Bruce: 'Can you trust this guy?' He nodded, and then I understood that he didn't know Appel at all."

Danny Gallagher says that he could never stand for any kind of injustice.

"I told Appel that I had had enough of his shit, and that I thought he was a punk."

It wasn't long after this that Gallagher realized that his behavior would have its consequences. He knew that the slight chance of becoming Springsteen's road manager was never going to happen.

Not with Mike Appel in control.

"Well, there was only one way for it to end. But I knew how hard it was for Bruce to leave people behind. He always used to say: 'I refuse to fire anyone in the band.'

"So I thought they were going to send Vini Lopez over, because Vini never had any tact. Vini could say 'take your shit and get out of here' without anyone getting upset, ha, ha, ha."

It never happened that way. When the telephone woke Gallagher in the middle of the night, it was Bruce Springsteen: "Hey, Danny. You've got to go, man. I'm sorry."

"All I said was: 'OK, I understand. Thanks for calling.'"

The axe fell. Danny Gallagher says that his heart broke that night.

played country and rock' n 'roll, had four of us on vocals. Clarence Clemons had bought himself this club in Red Bank, Big Man's West, and we weren't the house band but we were there like four or five nights a week.

"We were actually so good that Vini's wife contacted Jon Landau. Jon said: 'OK, the singer looks good. We'll dress him up in leather and give him to the girls.'"

That's when Gallagher turned to the blues.

"Well, my marriage had ended. I drank like crazy. Blues seemed appropriate."

He was going to play the blues with Dave Meyers of the Blackberry Booze Band and Billy Hector from Hot Romance. The Renegade Blues Band was formed, and later there was Big Danny & the Boppers.

"I had a great time doing it, but after a while I got tired of the blues. I got tired of feeling bad. I was kind of over my wife, but I wasn't going anywhere."

Danny Gallagher decided to get back to his roots. He traveled to Ireland in 1989, lived on a little island, and started writing songs.

"I can't hold a grudge. But it just haunts me. More than thirty years have passed, and I still haven't heard anyone who can move me like Bruce did."

"It couldn't have ended up any other way, I know. And I have no regrets, I can't hold a grudge. But it just haunts me. More than thirty years have passed, and I still haven't heard anyone who can move me like Bruce did."

Just at the same time that Danny Gallagher left the band, he also was given custody of three children. He was on disability after a work accident, went unemployed, and then started to feel depressed. Gallagher took what money was left. He bought rice and macaroni to feed the kids, and for himself he got a case of beer and what he wanted out of the music store in Long Branch.

Asbury Park had started to feel insecure. Danny Gallagher went west with the kids. He bought a little house in Colorado, opened up a submarine sandwich shop, and played bluegrass.

A couple of years later, back in New Jersey, Gallagher started over together with Vini Lopez.

"He had a band that was called Underdog. We were good,

"It was romantic in some amazing way. Living right on the shore, watching the ferry come into the harbor. And the whole time I could hear that voice: 'Drink, Danny, drink.' But I always answered by saying: 'Fuck it, I'm here to do something constructive.'"

One day, several years later, an old friend called.

"Bruce was out on the *Tom Joad* tour. I was invited to the hotel, he showed me pictures of the kids, we had dinner together, and then we took a limo up to Belfast. Bono and the Edge from U2 were there for the show, and Bruce was fantastic. Damn, I hadn't heard him play acoustic since he was living in my apartment in Asbury.

"Afterwards, a few shots of Jack Daniel's. Then we took a piss in the river. It was a lovely night, just like old times."

Danny Gallagher did fine in Ireland. He was home. But not quite.

"I had to go back to Asbury. The kids were getting into trouble, and a friend of mine got sick and died."

Asbury Park had sunken deeper into drugs and prostitution. But Danny Gallagher was not forgotten. There were still tapes floating around. There were people who wanted to listen, and Gallagher wanted to play.

"My good friend Steve Schreager and me put together a band that got better and better. Then finally there was someone who thought that we should record for real."

The problem was money. Danny Gallagher went to a loan shark who told him: "Sure, Danny. Here's the money. We're not going to charge you any interest, but remember to get it back to us on time. Otherwise there'll be problems."

In 1993 Big Danny's Lost Leader Band, including players such as Schreager and Ken Sorensen, put out *Sign of Faith.*

"I sold as many albums as I could, got the cash together, and paid it back a day before it was due. I even gave them an extra buck.

"We ourselves didn't make a dime, because everyone who had promised to help let us down. But damn, I got it done and I still think it sounds good."

Danny Gallagher says that he has never completely left his hippie days. Old ghosts still haunt him. The booze, smoking. And a back injury he got on the job.

"I try to take care of myself. Try to keep myself from drinking."

Maybe everything will turn out better when he gets back "home" to Ireland.

"It has to get better. What have I got here? I was paying a ransom in rent for a miserable apartment. So I stopped paying and ended up in court. Of course I lost, but what the hell?

"I've got my van, I can sleep in there as long as it doesn't get really cold. And I've got a cell phone, so my friends can get in touch with me."

He made an appearance onstage with Bruce Springsteen, singing back-up vocals on 'Spirit in the Night,' when the *Tom Joad* tour came home to Asbury Park. But now it's been a while since Big Danny last met Springsteen.

"I can't say anything, because what do I know what it's like to be in his position? He's been where I am, that's for sure.

"I really just mean to say that Bruce has always made me proud. For one thing I am proud to be one of those who really know him. I've even seen him naked, ha ha ha.

"And I'm proud to have been there when everything started. When Bruce was jamming with David Sancious. Oh boy, what energy! My life was definitely impacted by his songs, they showed me things I had missed earlier on."

He knows everything might have turned out different. But Danny Gallagher was never interested in choosing his own words.

"Fuck it. Money? I've gotten by. I'm sitting here now, aren't I?"

Here, in the lounge of the Berkeley Carteret Hotel in Asbury Park. On a Friday like any other.

Friends of the bluegrass trio take up a collection.

Big Danny bows, gives thanks, and hugs.

Then he does the numbers.

"What have we got tonight? Thirty bucks. God bless."

BRINGIN' ON THE POWER

Stormin' Norman Seldin

He counts as one of the originators. Known locally as the walking encyclopedia of Jersey Shore rock 'n' roll, and to the world as the first ever to get Clarence Clemons into a recording studio. But there's a whole lot more to the Stormin' Norman Seldin story.

A couple of weeks before Christmas 2006 there was a celebration at the Stone Pony. It was a night to remember a founding member of the Jaywalkers, John Shaw, and to once more enjoy the sounds of Asbury Park. Bruce Springsteen was missing in the line-up, but there were quite a few others appearing. You'd meet Doc Holiday, Nicky Addeo, Vini Lopez, original Juke drummer Mr. Popeye Pentifallo, Billy Ryan, Lance Larson, David Sancious . . .

"Garry Tallent and I anchored the whole damn show and we really had the crowd dropping back to the old harmony stuff," says Stormin' Norman Seldin. "It was a huge success, but it took a lot of work. After a few hours Garry was looking at me, saying: 'Are we gonna break here, or what?'"

Norman Seldin shouldn't actually be doing what he's doing, at least not according to the medical staff that took care of him a couple of years ago. At the time Seldin was working on a new record with Steel Breeze and while the band was performing live he had a breakdown right onstage.

"I had an aortic dissection and the doctors told my wife I would be dead shortly. But I survived and then when I was ordered to spend eight months in recovery I told them I needed to be back onstage in eight weeks. That's when the doctor said: 'Please, give this guy some more morphine.' I guess it was the bone-head move of my career.

"Anyway, they gave me a synthetic aorta and the system recovered. The voice was still there. They called me the miracle guy with the iron lung."

Norman Seldin is moving into his 60s. He never hit the lottery, never had that gold record. But Seldin had his share of success and he remained one of the area's most respected musicians.

He started out in music at age three, practicing piano on a Steinway purchased by his parents.

"You could say I was forced to play, and it was all classical. My father was a symphonic bassist. My mother was a Juilliard voice scholarship winner who was not allowed to attend by her Southern father. She became the driving force behind me and continued to be a main voice in all of the operatic arias in New Jersey.

"My first teachers were friends of my father's from the symphony. They were European and spoke either German or Italian. So I didn't really have a lot of American influences until a little later on. I got into the verge of four to six hours a day of practicing at the age of five or six. It was this five in the morning deal."

Rock 'n' roll slowly sneaked into the repertoire starting when a guy that worked for Seldin's father, in his jewelry store, took the kid off on the side to listen to Little Richard, Fats Domino, and Chuck Berry. The type of music that wasn't really going on at home.

"Then I found myself going across the tracks in most of the black sections of town in Asbury Park and Neptune. I also went to Birdland in New York. So in fact, I got the jazz and the R & B from a very young age."

"They gave me a synthetic aorta and the system recovered. The voice was still there. They called me the miracle guy with the iron lung."

Norman Seldin put together his first band at eleven and took a union card for performance at thirteen.

"Now, I was starting to hear this other music, and I began managing other groups. But to pick that stuff up and play it I needed a different kind of teacher, and I got to know a black fellow who was a jazz organist. He was the one who freed my left hand. It was technically good, but stiff. He broke that up, and said: 'You need to listen to this one and that one, see how they're having fun.'"

This is the early 1960s and Norman Seldin says that he suffered quite a bit. He was in school when starting to promote and manage, and ninety percent of his groups were black.

"That was not a good issue in those days. I took abuse from a lot of the club owners, and people were saying: 'Norman's running with the blacks.' Yeah, I did run with them beacuse they were the talent. They had what I wanted, and I only kept one white player with me. That was Billy Ryan. Billy's been with me for like forty years, always on top of his game. When you put

**"Walter Cichon, as a front man he was like Eric Burdon and Mick Jagger
in one person. I remember there was a battle going on between
the Motifs and Bruce Springsteen's band the Castiles."**

him in with all the black players who already had the jazz, that's how we got great groups like the Valtairs, and great singers like Leon Trent."

Asbury Park would see Jackie Wilson, the Imperials, and the Soul Sisters playing the club scene. Convention Hall used to have James Brown.

"You could acutally see the entire Motown Revue in Convention Hall for like five bucks. Marvin Gaye, Diana Ross, and the Temptations all came to town. Asbury Park had fifteen or twenty night clubs with bands in them."

Important times, influential times.

"Sure, Southside Johnny is an influence of Bobby Blue Bland, Howlin' Wolf, and Muddy Waters. You know, all that stuff was grabbed out of there. There was a lot of good talent in town. A lot of oldies and doo wop in the whole Asbury area."

Then, all of a sudden, there was a shift. We're talking 1964 and the British invasion.

"The Beatles hit, and that's where the black acts that were flourishing around here kind of died."

Norman Seldin, though, stayed on top of his game. He had seen the change coming and was already managing the Motifs, a band that would conquor the whole Jersey Shore region.

"Walter Cichon, as a front man he was like Eric Burdon and Mick Jagger in one person. I remember there was a battle going on between the Motifs and Bruce Springsteen's band the Castiles. And me working with a white goup was a big shock to the entire area."

The Motifs were special, says Seldin. Nothing like the local teen clubs had ever seen.

"They had all this moaning and groaning, sounding like a cross between the Zombies and the original Animals. Walter Cichon was a muscular guy who didn't sing great, but he had presence on the stage. They made quite an impact."

Norman Seldin marketed the bands as British. He worked with a Beatles cover band called the Lost Souls and he got the girls screaming for the Motifs.

"This was a New Jersey Rollling Stones and people were coming from all over to see them. They weren't the greatest band in the world, but I made them solid. Their set was two rough hours including 'This Could Be the Last Time', 'You Really

Got Me', and then there was 'Molly'. 'Molly' was the song. We recorded it on my own label, Selsom Records, and it did very well around here," says Seldin while showing one of the very few existing copies of that piece of vinyl.

Norman Seldin was a fast learner in how to get the word out. He became friends with Howard Lidell, who was head of an independent record distributor in Newark. Lidell's company was buying time on WJRL in Newark to play the records that they were selling, and this was how the Valtairs, Nicky Addeo, and Leon Trents' group the Uniques got airplay.

"Soon people would call me up, asking for not a hundred, but two hundred, and three hundred records. Then, through Howard Lidell I met Douglas 'Jocko' Henderson of WADO, Fat Daddy in Baltimore, and Rocky G of WWRL in New York. They played all the black R & B artists and they took a big liking to me. There were all these DJs hooking up in a complete five state network of radio stations, and I was the only white guy working with them."

Seldin's records were getting the airplay he was looking for, but he was still not old enough to sign checks and that's why his mother used to drive him down to Baltimore. Along the road they would stop at various stations to watch DJs turn the music on.

"When one song was done playing the guys would go: 'Oops, it skipped. We must listen to it again'. They could play the same song nine times in a row and people started calling. The next time I came through town I brought the bands. This was all the black charts and with the Motifs they didn't know what to think. Playing their music was a favor to me, and the impact was immediate."

For the Motifs it was end of story, though, as Walter Cichon was drafted.

"Walter went to Vietnam, and he didn't come back. Some still say he's the kind of guy who could probably be living over there, but I wouldn't think so."

Norman Seldin had made a name for himself all the way down to Charlotte, North Carolina. He had gotten an R & B foundation and was a sell out with his own band, the Soul Set.

He'd spent hours of time and thousands of dollars managing other artists, even teaching them dance steps and seeing that they were dressed in a proper way. Now it was time to focus on his own thing.

After the Soul Set came the Joyful Noyze.

"We played everywhere, from major venues to the smaller clubs who would budget bill to get us in. And then we got Clarence Clemons in the band."

As the story goes, Clemons had a flat tire one night outside a club where the Joyful Noyze was playing. He came in to use the phone, saw the band, told them he was a sax player, and asked if he could join them.

"The guy was huge. He was actually a football player, who'd hurt himself in an accident and had to quit the game. Anyway, I said: 'Let's put this guy up here.' And from that night on he stayed with us for a number of years."

Bringing along a black player wasn't appreciated everywhere. Seldin got to hear "don't bring your band into my place with a nigger playing."

"I said: 'Well I guess we won't be there,' and they would go: 'You just don't know what you did to yourself.' Four months later the same people would call back offering more money to have us."

With Clarence Clemons the Joyful Noyze was a powerhouse.

"He makes a focal point, you know. I was the lead singer, and up front there was also a girl singer. When we did King Curtis, Clarence got to do the strut around the clubs, just like they did it in New Orleans, and people went berserk. Clarence is a massive centerpiece onstage. He doesn't play with that much finesse, but he has his sound. The old R & B, the King Curtis sound. It's fair to say that Clarence put the sax back on the map."

Seldin was the first to record Clemons on a Joyful Noyze album around 1969. But the mighty sax player was to leave

here.' It got to a shouting match and everything, and we didn't speak for a number of years."

Needless to say, it wasn't the greatest parting.

"Because we were coming into the summer season and people were used to seeing Clarence bringing on the power. All of a sudden it wasn't there and it took a little adjusting to. The band made the shift over and kind of went to the Allman Brothers thing."

"It'd piss me off to dwell on the past. I told Clarence: 'It's gonna end up being nowhere.' Well, it ended up being something big and that was the joke for a while. Anyway, I took that part of my life to make a living and my writing didn't really come along until later."

Then out of the blue Clemons returned to the area. They were back on track and by 1994 Norman Seldin was asked to join "the big man" for the N.F.C. Wildcard playoff game's half-time show at Giants Stadium.

"We speak again, not a lot because he's sometimes in Japan, here and there. But he came back to play the Tradewinds with his band and he wanted me to be the guest singer. I went up front with him, and then Bruce came on."

There was a period when Norman Seldin not only brought back Clarence Clemons, but acutally had an album recorded with almost the entire E Street Band.

"Yeah, there were Clarence, Max Weinberg, Garry Tallent, Danny Federici, myself, and Billy Ryan. I had it released independently, on my own label. There are not many copies around, and I suppose the ones existing are worth a small fortune."

He never took his deal to a major label, 'cause it wasn't the same game anymore. It was hard to find the distributors, and he couldn't afford to press 20,000 albums.

"But we did play some great music. Actually there's one

"It'd piss me off to dwell on the past. I told Clarence: 'It's gonna end up being nowhere.' Well, it ended up being something big and that was the joke for a while."

the unit, as a certain young band leader from Freehold was making his way to fame.

"Clarence and I had our differences. It was a deal where I was booked ten months in advance which was pretty rare. He was going with Bruce and told me: 'Look, I'm gonna give you two weeks notice.' I said: 'Two weeks? You get your exposure

track, 'Misery Loves Company,' on an Asbury Park compilation album. It's the cut that stole everybody's attention, and in many ways it shows the guts of what we were doing. Now, I'm thinking about remastering twenty cuts from vinyl, for a two disc set. With a little help from the internet we would be big sellers. There are nostalgia people all over the place."

The E Streeters came into the studio, but they also became Norman Seldin's backing group as a live band for almost ten months.

"Yeah, this was during the time when Bruce had been sued by his manager. The guys would join me at this club in Fair Haven, at least three times a month. They just wanted to play while Bruce was getting everything worked out."

On his own again, Norman Seldin spent a few years down South, being one of the very few white guys playing Mississippi and the Delta. He found inspiration for his own writing listening to John Prine, Ray Charles, and Randy Newman.

"I touched that with some of the piano I really wanted to do, and they actually sent me to represent the state of Mississippi in the White House. I said: 'You're sending a Yankee Jew boy to go to the White House?'

"Anyway, as I got back to Jersey I was a powerhouse lead singer. It was a whole different ball game. I remember going to work with Clarence at Sand's in Atlantic City. He stopped the whole band and said, 'This is the guy who put me where I am. Do not sell him short 'cause he'll out sing you all.' That was a big moment, it was actually the first time I really heard him say something like that."

Norman Seldin says he's been privileged. There's some more recording in the making, teaming up with Doc Holiday and Garry Tallent in Nashville. Also, in recent years he got a job offer that was impossible to resist.

"A recruiter from Jacob's Music Company, owned by the Rinaldi family, called me up and said that someone wanted me in Philadelphia. They had six stores, representing Steinway, and now they wanted me to work the store in Lawrenceville. That way it wouldn't be all classical music. I'd be bringing in ragtime and the blues.

"It's really been great. I got my own rehearsal hall with two million dollars worth of pianos and I get to work with top instructors who appreciate what I do. Kids come into the store, and I can sit there and judge them. See if they're ready."

Meanwhile his wife, Jamey Seldin, is taking care of things at Trinket's in Red Bank, a jewelry store that's been a family matter for years and years.

"I've got a wonderful wife, you know. Jamey is the one who keeps me alive, and with all her knowledge in music she has been my greatest fan as well as my critic."

In a town such as Red Bank business stays good. On these streets it's no big deal meeting Bruce Springsteen or Jon Bon Jovi.

"Red Bank was never an entertainment capitol. We're surrounded by excellent school systems, and stores. People tend to move here 'cause it's a very solid area."

"Bruce comes from Freehold, right? Now, moving to Colts Neck and Rumson, that's money. We had Heather Locklear and Richie Sambora buy a property in this area. It was the same deal with Queen Latifah, band members from Skid Row and Monster Magnet, plus a lot of sport figures. Jon Bon Jovi is across the river in his mansion. Red Bank is close to New York City and just as close to Philly. We are near the universities;

Princeton, Monmouth, Rutgers. Yeah, money comes here, and this isn't paparazzi land. The famous people get left alone."

Norman Seldin takes us back to the late 1960s again. Remembering the Upstage Club as "kind of a coffee house Asbury still hanging in there."

"Bruce was making that his home, since he didn't have a real base. But I didn't hang around that place. I really chose the path of working, managing and promoting, and I was not too well liked for it most of the time. I knew my way around."

Seldin never made it big time, though. Not like Springsteen or Bon Jovi. Nonetheless, being among the founders of a legendary music scene, he feels that he gets the respect he's earned.

"I guess it all depends on who's looking for what credit. There are a lot of guys who never got national credit, then again they might not have been looking for it either. There are well over two hundred blues players passed away without ever getting any attention. There are plenty B. B. Kings out there, you know.

"Locally? We had a lot of good players who just didn't have the edge. They didn't get somebody's ear when they should have. Writing and playing for thirty years can make you a genius and a failure. You know, all the shoulda, woulda, coulda."

THE CARPENTER'S RHAPSODY

Billy Ryan

A van pulls up. Out jumps full-time carpenter Billy Ryan. Many, many years ago he turned down the offer to be the guitarist in what would become America's most famous band.

Scores of magnificent amplifiers. Even more valuable guitars. Billy Ryan collects stuff, and memories.

His teenage daughter looks into the living room. She says: "I'm going out for a while. I'll be back in a few hours." Her father replies: "Sure, honey."

Billy Ryan laughs and then he says:

"A few hours? Sure. Does she think I've forgotten what it's like to be that age?"

That was a while ago, of course, but back then, in the 1960s, Billy Ryan knew the wild life. The carefree life. Rock 'n' roll, beers, girls.

"And here we are, 61 years old. No, actually. I'll never get old. It's the same thing with the other guys: Southside, Vini Lopez, Stringbean, Bobby Bertelson, John Luraschi, Nicky Addeo, Norman Seldin. Norman had heart surgery, but he's still around. We're doing the same thing now that we were doing forty years ago. That whole thing about growing up, give me a break."

Billy Ryan lives in Tinton Falls, New Jersey. But back then, Asbury Park's neighboring town, Allenhurst, was home. Here was a kid who listened to his mother sing jazz and who started to cry when Gershwin's 'Rhapsody in Blue' was put on the record player. He cried because the music stirred his soul, and he brought the record to school thinking that the other kids would react just like him.

That was years before Bill Haley and Elvis Presley.

"My parents probably dreamed of having me become a doctor or a lawyer. But they couldn't really figure out what my brother was doing so they got him a guitar for Christmas.

That's how we both picked up the guitar, and I was the one who kind of took it over. I was the one who became obsessed with it, listening to records by Jimmy Reed and B. B. King and then trying to copy what they did. That's what everyone did. We all played honky tonk and blues."

At fourteen Billy Ryan had his own band, and soon enough he'd become the guitar player for a band that backed up the Coasters. Ryan would also be working with all the singing groups from Atlantic City, because they were managed by his friend, Norman Seldin.

"This was like 1959 and we were very young. There were just a whole bunch of people around and Norman would put on the shows. I think he was twelve or something but already a great promoter."

There weren't really that many rock 'n' roll records out yet. That stuff hadn't been made, but come the mid-1960s things had changed. Rock 'n' roll ruled, and after playing with locally famed singer Nicky Addeo, Billy Ryan would join the Jaywalkers. This was by far the most popular cover band in and around Asbury Park, and certainly the biggest thing to hit the clubs along the Jersey Shore.

"Yeah, God. There was no other band that attracted as many people and no other as well played. John Shaw sure made some money because it was his band."

The Jaywalkers—Shaw (drums), Ryan (guitar), Billy Lucia (saxophone, vocals), and Mickey Holiday (bass, keyboards, vocals)—dominated the local scene. Billy Ryan talks about a Top 40 band doing all the American music: soul and R & B. Then came the British invasion. The Beatles.

"Mickey was a soul singer, so we did Ray Charles. We sounded good, but we could have been even better. It was never the real thing, you know. The Jaywalkers never practiced, and as I see it we were never for real. I always wanted to play B. B. King."

Still, looking back, there's no denying that Billy Ryan had become a rock star.

"I think I was in that band for three or four years but at the time it felt like an eternity. Then what happened? I guess John Shaw just got disillusioned."

During that eternity Billy Ryan did seven nights a week at Mrs. Jay's in Asbury Park.

"The first club in this area with go-go girls. We made thirty-five dollars a night, and that was really a lot of money back then. I played a cherry-red Gibson and everyone in the band had new cars. In 1968 I bought a Pontiac LeMans, even though by then I was already married."

That year, 1968, Billy Ryan was known as the area guitar hero. That was also the year when Carl "Tinker" West showed up to sell surfboards and put together what he considered to be the best rock band around.

"He always had a goal in mind: to manage the best rock band ever. He discovered me first and Bruce later. So 'Tinker' was on the road to success, he really could have been king. But everyone knows how things turned out."

"Tinker" West was nonetheless the one who got Billy Ryan out of Asbury Park. He was friends with Gordon Kennerly, who managed James Cotton and had all these connections—Columbia Records and the Albert Grossman Agency which signed the likes of B. B. King and Paul Butterfield.

"When Elvin Bishop left Butterfield I got a nod to audition for the Paul Butterfield Blues Band. I think I did great 'cause I had already learned all that stuff. So I was picked for the job and traveled up to New York every week to play with the band, doing all of Bishop's parts."

Back in Asbury Park, after quitting the Jaywalkers, Billy Ryan played with Tom Wuorio's band, the Moment of Truth.

"When I joined the band Tom was playing bass and they had Garry Tallent on guitar. But we couldn't have two guitar players so Garry started doing the bass, Judy White and Tom would be singing, and I was the guitar player.

"Tom was a bit nuts, you know. Then after some time he and Judy quit, and that's when I kind of took over the band and brought in my people: guys like Garry Tallent and Donnie Lubitz."

The Moment of Truth morphed into Speed Limit 25 and there was a new house band at the Student Prince and the Upstage Club.

Billy Ryan says:

"We were fantastic, but the drugs ruined so much of it."

By this time, a new guitar player was making his first appearances at the Upstage Club: Bruce Springsteen.

"I was told by 'Tinker' to check him out and I remember that Bruce played this song called 'Season of the Witch.' He grabbed the microphone, said two or three words, and everyone ran up to the stage. I'd never seen anything like that. The guy was a genius, he could get the guitar to sound exactly how he wanted. Bruce had all the charisma and as a guitarist

he was definitely in the same league as Jimmy Page. By then we already knew that if Bruce Springsteen couldn't make it nobody would make it."

It wasn't that long before Speed Limit 25 was over. Billy Ryan was broke and his first marriage was finished. He talks about too much alcohol and years of anxiety that resulted in a nervous breakdown.

"I put down the guitar and didn't play for a long time. Then Norman Seldin called and wanted me to be part of a benefit in Red Bank. Sure, OK, it was time to move on. Besides, I needed the money."

In 1969, Billy Ryan, along with Clarence Clemons, had been in the studio when Seldin's band, the Joyful Noyze, recorded their first album. Years later, when some old friends wanted to get together, big things were to happen. That was the plan.

"Norman had some stuff going on with the guys from Bruce's band: Garry, Clarence, Danny, Max. But then Bruce decided to back a record by Gary U. S. Bonds and he wanted to bring in the E Street Band. So what chance did we have? I mean, we didn't even have a label."

Billy Ryan shrugs his shoulders and then confirms the story that he had already said no to being Springsteen's guitarist.

"John Shaw put together a band that he called Moses. John's brother was program director at a radio station in Kansas, and he hyped our single so hard that it became a number one there. Damn, we were ahead of Michael Jackson. I was a star again. Smoked weed, drank way too much, and looked like a hippie.

"The first thing they had to do before they could show me anywhere was get me a haircut. Then there was someone who bought a pair of pink corduroys and a pink shirt."

Back from Kansas, Shaw decided to turn the band over to Billy Ryan. The music was for real now. Ryan was on the road to glory, doing his own thing.

Bruce Springsteen was, of course, already the big fish in the small pond. The struggling local hero with all the ambitions. And one night in the early 1970s, when Billy Ryan had been jamming with Springsteen's band at the Tradewinds in Sea Bright, the offer came.

"I think I was in that band for three or four years but at the time it felt like an eternity. Then what happened? I guess John Shaw just got disillusioned."

"Billy, I want you to be in the band."

"Sorry, Bruce. I've got my own thing now."

Ryan laughs before he continues:

"Yeah, but I really did have a band and a hit. Bruce and the other guys didn't even have cab money."

Through the years he's heard the same talk over and over again, but Billy Ryan says that it's really no big deal. After all, he's not the only player who said no thanks to Bruce Springsteen.

"Bruce is a genius, but I didn't have a crystal ball and who knows, I may have never survived the trip he took his band on? I've played with all those guys and their success isn't what surprises me. Because Bruce is a songwriter of the same caliber as Dylan, and as a performer he's bigger than Elvis."

Eventually, Springsteen's old pal Steven Van Zandt got the job. Billy Ryan said no thanks, and survived. The fight against

**"Bruce is a genius, but I didn't have a crystal ball and who knows,
I may have never survived the trip he took his band on?"**

alcohol was won, and Ryan has been sober since 1997. He worked as a photographer for a while, but today he earns a living as a full-time carpenter.

Then there's this little thing called the blues. In recent years Billy Ryan hooked up with Ronnie Earl. He's also been frequently seen with his own band, the Bluescasters, at the Crossroads Bar in Asbury Park and other clubs along the Jersey Shore. Friends like Vini Lopez and Bobby Bertelson sometimes sit in.

"We're still out there," says Ryan. "I think I paid my dues to play the blues."

In the 1980s there was a tour when Clarence Clemons got his Red Bank Rockers together.

"All I knew was that Clarence wanted to do his own thing. I thought we were a blues band or an R & B band."

Billy Ryan never got to be on the album, but for a year and a half he traveled America with Clarence Clemons. He remembers that on the back of the Red Bank Rockers t-shirts it read "the no product tour," and he still thinks that the band sounded amazing.

"As a unit we were unbelievably tight, and Bruce's way of working, using strict arrangements, was always the model. Everyone knew exactly what they were to do. I have to give Clarence credit for what he did with this band and I think it's great that he's still living off of the music, playing with his new band in Florida."

Billy Ryan says that there are mostly fond memories and very few regrets.

"I went my own way, regardless of what happened with Bruce or anyone else. I trusted my own choices and I don't intend to apologize for it.

"A second chance? No, thanks. I'm not so sure I would be as lucky next time around."

Sonny Kenn

It's common knowledge. Sonny Kenn was the first rock star along the Jersey Shore. But the greaser never felt at home in the hippie culture of the 1960s. He took another path, and if you travel through Monmouth County on any given evening you can bet that he's playing somewhere nearby. In a small town, in a small club. That's where you'll find Sonny Kenn and the blues.

The hair is slicked back. He's wearing dark sunglasses, a denim jacket, and pointy boots. Sonny Kenn, once a greaser, always a greaser.

The grand old man of the Asbury Park music scene seems to be living the legend. But Sonny Kenn is not all about attitude, nonetheless. This is his everyday look, this is the life he leads. Small town charm in Red Bank by day turns to a string of smoky clubs once night falls along the Jersey Shore.

Sonny Kenn was born in Colorado Springs, Colorado. His father wanted to be a musician, but earned the family's bread and butter by teaching. When the kid was eight, his family moved to Newark, New Jersey. Shortly thereafter, his father died, and his mother then chose to move a few miles farther south.

Kenn grew up in Belmar, a stone's throw from Asbury Park.

"I started playing guitar while my father was still alive. He performed as a singing cowboy, a sort of Gene Autry or Jimmie Rodgers. I remember thinking how cool it was when he would talk about his little radio show, the one he had back home in Colorado Springs in the 1930s."

Country & western was never Sonny Kenn's thing. And he doesn't see his father as the guitar teacher.

"Nah, but I guess his musical interests meant something. I remember when he let me practice on a ukulele because my hands were too small for the guitar. I think we played a little boogie woogie together.

"And I have done what I could to keep a bit of him alive in me. I dug out a few old demos about twenty-five years ago or so, and made my own recordings of the same songs."

Sonny Kenn's music career began in Belmar. His best friend, Ritchie, played guitar and when Sonny told that he still had his father's old Gretsch and Martin, Ritchie offered to tune the instruments.

"Cool. Ritchie taught me a lot. And we started a little band together."

Two guitars and a snare drum. It was a start. A repertoire built on instrumental rockabilly songs.

"We made up our own stuff, and we got pretty good. We actually won a talent show in eighth grade. People applauded. Girls screamed. It was a big deal for a young kid."

His friend Ritchie quit after a while. But not Sonny Kenn.

"Anyone who wasn't good at sports needed music to get the girls. Quarterback or guitarist. It was just a matter of choosing between the two."

The Electrons became the Teen Beats. After the Blazers, Sonny & the Sounds was formed, and finally, the Jersey Shore was ready for Sonny & the Starfires. The girls screamed even louder. Sonny Kenn was the guitar hero everyone was talking about.

"You don't notice so much yourself. Not more than that people want to hear the band play and that you start making a little money. The part about being a rock star was something I never understood. But one thing I understood was that I made as much every weekend as I would have made working entire weeks at a gas station or by cleaning people's offices.

"That's an easy choice, wouldn't you agree?"

> **"Hippie culture was taking over. The drugs, people sitting around cross-legged on the floor. I was a greaser who never really fit in."**

Another Jersey Shore music legend came into the picture around the same time that Sonny & the Starfires were working their way towards being launched as the hottest act in Monmouth County. Two drummers had left the band and Sonny Kenn stayed behind one night at a dive where Buzzy Lubinsky was getting kids to dance to the latest Top 40 hits.

Lubinsky, who himself played drums, backing up the songs on the jukebox, was used to letting different local talents take his place. And on this special occasion it was Vini Lopez's turn to show what he was made of.

"Buzzy had taught Vini to keep a backbeat, and that was just the sound we were looking for. So after an audition of no more than two or three songs he got the job."

Vini Lopez also brought Sonny Kenn something else that he had been looking for: energy.

"For Vini it was always important to keep the audience entertained. Not just to play as well as possible. We had a manager for a short time, who was himself part of a really successful band, the Aztecs, and he would always point out that people pay to see the band. Really to see the band. Not just to listen to it.

"So we worked hard to always give the best show, and we looked at what the Beatles were doing. We knew that differ-

ent girls had their own favorites in the band. So they would scream even louder if we took turns singing and fronting."

Sonny Kenn says that the Beatles were not just a popular band. They started a movement.

"But what they were doing was not so exceptional. We knew that we would be able to do the same thing here. Right here in New Jersey."

The Beatles meant a lot to Sonny Kenn. Jerry Lee Lewis meant even more. Kenn got to meet him, and they even played on the same stage.

"This was back in 1965. We had won a talent contest where the prize was to get to play for the whole summer at a shopping center in Eatontown, the same place that today is known as the Monmouth Mall. There were two stages, one built just above the other. We did two shows every day, at one o'clock and four o'clock. Always as an opening act for bears or chimps."

Or Jerry Lee Lewis?

"Ha, ha. Exactly, that or Jerry Lee Lewis. There has to be a song in there somewhere: Bears, chimpanzees, and Jerry Lee. . . .

"Anyway, he hung around one day. We got to meet him and be his opening act. Jerry Lee was one of my biggest idols, musically speaking, anyway. He was not exactly a father figure. But I think that it was right then and there that I understood: 'OK, this is what I want to do, and what I am going to do.' That's how it works with a passion. It doesn't leave you any choice."

Sonny Kenn was number one in Monmouth County. A role model. But fame, other than the screaming of girls in the middle of the 1960s, is unknown to him. On the other hand, he doesn't seem to care very much about the fact that it was those who came later, Springsteen, Lyon, Bon Jovi, that reached national and international fame.

"Who wouldn't want to have a little more money? But seriously: I am glad that my life didn't turn out like theirs, because I know I wouldn't have been able to handle the success.

"That's one of the reasons I have to give those guys credit. They survived success, and I can still respect what they are doing."

He met the young Springsteen at the Upstage Club in Asbury

Park, but already at that point, during the latter half of the 1960s, Sonny Kenn had changed his sound.

"Yeah, I started playing the blues. But the difference is actually as slight as could be. Listen to early Stones, Kinks, Animals, Chuck Berry, or even Little Richard. Their roots are in the blues, and once you understand that, you can also sct out on a pretty magical trip.

Now and then he goes to New York City to play a another kind of blues, at B. B. King's on 42nd Street.

"Down here, in New Jersey, people know who I am. They come to every show 'cause they know what this band is about. Here I always play what feels right for the moment, not what I think people want to hear. I play what I play, what feels most meaningful for the moment.

"To get the feeling of having really moved someone, and to see the same people come back the next night with that smile on their faces. That's when you know you're on the right track."

"The blues is an emotion. A sense of freedom."

Sonny Kenn hit the Upstage Club with a power trio: Maelstrom. This was Kenn, Vini Lopez, and Southside Johnny, developing their own style somewhere between Muddy Waters and Led Zeppelin.

"It was interesting, at least for a while. We did two shows every night, one with a set list and one as a jam session."

But he would grow tired of it:

"Hippie culture was taking over. The drugs, people sitting around cross-legged on the floor. I was a greaser who never really fit in."

Kenn moved out, and never looked back. He played through four decades, beginning in the 1960s, and has found his place in today's scene as well. But without ever compromising his music. The unstoppable Sonny Kenn Band, with Vic Bayers on drums and Dan Mulvey on bass, works its way up and down the Jersey Shore. And if you're driving by Belmar on any given Sunday, you'll find him at this charming Creole restaurant called the Ragin' Cajun.

Sonny Kenn will be sitting there among friends, most likely with a glass of red wine within reach, playing the blues with Ken Sorensen's band, Stringbean & the Stalkers.

"B. B. King's is a totally different thing. Tourists come there from around the world because they are fans of B. B. King and they just want to hear the blues. The real thing, no matter who's playing it. It's all about the upbeat standards, and if everyone stays on to enjoy the second set then I know that we've been able to deliver."

Sonny Kenn has stopped dreaming. He may, of course, harbor a longing for Europe, as he knows that Tony Amato and his Boccigalupe & the Bad Boys have made a couple of trips across the Atlantic.

Kenn wouldn't mind traveling the world himself.

He would also like to finish the next album. And he will, as soon as there's money to pay for the recordings.

But more than anything, Sonny Kenn just wants to keep on playing. 'Cause even though the girls aren't screaming any more, standing in front of an audience is still among the things that matters the most to him.

"To get the feeling of having really moved someone, and to see the same people come back the next night with that smile on their faces. That's when you know you're on the right track."

Says Sonny Kenn. The first one.

THE KID AND THE STRATOCASTER

Bill Chinnock

"My stuff was always rooted in the blues. Bruce's godspark, I think it really came more from Dylan, and, later, Spector. There were big differences, but we had the same approach. It was one, two, three and God help the ones who follow us. If you're gonna die, die after the show. We played on the same stages with the same musicians. So I understand why people make the comparison. But I wish that someone, years ago, would have asked: 'Who is this guy Bill Chinnock?' I would have gladly told 'em how it all began, in Asbury Park."

His hair has some touches of grey. The eyes he hides behind dark sunglasses may seem a little tired.

"Otherwise, I am the same guy as that fourteen year-old with a Stratocaster," says Bill Chinnock.

Greetings from Asbury Park, N.J. was the album that put the Shore town on the world map. Bruce Springsteen would eventually become the leading figure on the rock scene, while Bill Chinnock counts as part of the same community. One of those who was left standing in the shadows.

"I have to hand it to Bruce. I celebrate his success. But nothing started with him. Vini Lopez and I painted the walls of the Upstage Club. We jammed there, we had bands that were close to breaking through. To me, it seems like the gods of music have had their fun. But I swear that there was never any competition between Bruce and me. I'd like to consider us friends. Two musicians with similar backgrounds who definitely respect one another."

It's early March, 2005. Bill Chinnock arrives at Logan International airport in Boston, Massachussetts. He's on his way to a business meeting in Dallas, Texas.

Still, there's time for coffee and a talk. He leans back and starts telling about life after moving to Maine. Up north he secured one career in music and another in filmmaking. Chinnock's production studio, The Artist Group Inc., became

successful in documentary films and music videos. His records, from the 1970s onwards, have sold in modest numbers, but they did establish his name as a revered regional artist, and in 1987 the song "Somewhere in the Night" brought Chinnock an Emmy Award for musical direction and composition.

It's only fair to call Bill Chinnock the first Boss. He had already been rockin' the Shore for a couple of years when the long-haired guitarist from Freehold started to make his way up towards fame. But Springsteen and Chinnock would never travel the same roads.

"The years go by so fast. I had played all the clubs around Asbury Park when Bruce showed up. He was an unknown guy from Freehold, and there were some of us who had already given Asbury a sound."

It was the early 1960s when Chinnock, born and raised in Newark, put his first band together.

"When we started there was no scene. It was the beginning of it, an era influenced by Elvis and Bill Haley. Then us kids growing up in Jersey started listening to Sam & Dave, Ray Charles, and all of the R & B that poured out of the Shore.

"When we put the first band together there was no rock scene, as we know it today. Most of it came from the bunny-hops that they used have on the boardwalk. Buzzy Lubinsky was playing and Vini Lopez set up his drums with Buzzy at the Belmar

Pavillion. I was like twelve or thirteen, and just had the spark to become a musician."

Chinnock's first effort was called the Nightriders. Later came the Storytellers.

"There wasn't even a keyboard around so I brought in this young fellow from Flemington who played accordion: Danny Federici. His mom used to drive him up to my parents house and she'd sit in my mother's living room while Danny was playing with the band.

"We had a drummer named Chippy Gallagher and we got Bill Wolf from Newark on bass guitar.

"It was the genesis of the band and we recorded a single in Newark. We finished it up at Bell Sound in New York and got our first little record deal. We probably weren't even fifteen years old."

"New Jersey, at that time, was a culturally mixed environment. To me music was about something entirely different from the Beatles. The first time I heard the Beatles I thought: 'My god, who are these guys kidding?' The Beatles were light, like the pop version of Peter, Paul, and Mary."

Bill Chinnock's school was the blues. James Cotton's harmonica, Paul Butterfield, Mike Bloomfield. The voice of Ray Charles.

"This was our church. How could you not want to sing like that?"

Then the Upstage Club opened in Asbury Park. Chinnock and Vini Lopez painted the walls and helped install the loudspeakers. Friends remained friends, but Downtown Tangiers couldn't survive.

**"I had played all the clubs around Asbury Park when Bruce showed up.
He was an unknown guy from Freehold, and there were some
of us who had already given Asbury a sound."**

Chinnock remembers how his mother supported his musical interests. His father seemed the most surprised, but came home from his job in New York with the first guitar for Bill nonetheless.

"It was just a time of magic. A whole new era. We were definitely number one in the Hullabaloo clubs. We even had the chance to go on Zachary's TV show in Newark."

As the Storytellers grew, Chinnock and Federici wanted to go further.

"Chippy, our drummer, was a wonderful guy, but perhaps not a career musician. I had heard Vini Lopez play at the bunnyhops and I used to go down to Asbury to hear him practice with Buzzy. I knew that he could turn the band into a phenomena. So Vini came with us, Wendell John replaced Bill Wolf on bass, and things started to happen for real."

The Downtown Tangiers Rockin' Rhythm & Blues Band was formed around a new kernel of musicians. Their popularity on the rise, Downtown Tangiers became the Electric Circus house band, and got to go on the same stage as Jimi Hendrix.

"We were truly a force of nature. It was, in many ways, the essence of the music we had grown up with. We played a rhythm & blues that captured our angst. Music became our religion.

"Holding that band together was like trying to contain a hurricane with band-aids. 'Cause there was Vini on drums, and once you found his on switch there was no way back. His nature on the drums was magnificent, but off the drums he was a pain in the neck. There was no way of taming him.

"Downtown Tangiers toured and even recorded an album, which was never released. If it had been released, then I think everything would have been different. But all of that never happened."

Bill Chinnock talks about a time of big social changes.

"Wendell John was black, and a smart guy who wanted to do something else. Wendell gave up music to go study at Harvard."

Once more, the band reshuffled.

"That's when Garry Tallent came along. Garry had always been a steady hand and Danny was already the virtuoso. Vini was explosive, and I guess there was something I brought to the picture. The music was written in my school. I was the creative force, pushing everybody in the band. The circle was complete. We were all childhood friends, and the music was sensational, but we just had to take a break."

The Upstage Club turned into a jam scene. It would become home to Chinnock, Lopez, Tallent, Federici, Big Bobby Williams. And soon Bruce Springsteen.

"But all of that was starting to put me under. I got hepatitis from eating little lobsters. Got sick as heck for about six months, and when I finally came back Danny was playing with a buddy in Flemington and Vini had teamed up with Bruce. Not such a strange thing, really. There weren't that many band leaders in Asbury Park. It was really just Bruce and myself."

Bill Chinnock was joined by Garry Tallent, the mighty Big Bobby Williams on drums, and a very young David Sancious on keyboards.

"I remember going over to David's in Belmar and appealing to his mother, who was heavy into the church. Mrs. Sancious probably thought, 'that Billy is such a nice boy.'

"This was Glory Road, and we rehearsed at the Danelectro guitar factory. Everyone knew Garry and David, but Big Bobby

was also a strong player. Not a virtuoso trained at Juilliard, but he had a beat that would shake the room. Vini and Big Bobby were the same model."

He talks a while about life on the Shore. About the carnival town Asbury Park, with Harleys parked up and down Kingsley.

This is where Bruce Springsteen comes in and takes over.

"The Castiles were a Freehold band that never played our circuit. But I used to go to the Upstage and hear Bruce play. He was definitely something else, but he didn't sound anything like the Bruce we know today. It was more Grand Funk or something, he had hair down to his waist. I think he had Child, or maybe Steel Mill, with Vini and Danny.

"Sometimes we'd play together. I would say it was a relationship that wasn't warm, but definitely acknowledging. 'Cause you could not deny I preceded him by several years."

Chinnock has had to live with the comparison.

"It was inevitable since we all came from similar backgrounds and had the same attitude about music. But I already had a history. I had played with everyone else who would later play with Bruce, with the exception of Steve Van Zandt and Clarence Clemons.

"Musically there were big differences. I was rooted in the blues. Bruce's godspark, I think, it really came more from Dylan, and, later, Spector. That big wall of sound, I love it."

There was never any competition. Springsteen was a worldwide hit, Chinnock moved north. Slightly stung, but never defeated.

"Earlier on in my career, I saw it as a bad thing to always be compared to Bruce. It was never a problem in Europe, but here at home it was almost ridiculous. It seems like everything that ever came from the Jersey Shore is measured with Bruce. A strange feeling, especially for me who always celebrated his stardom. I mean, we all came from humble beginnings. That's the beauty of it."

Bill Chinnock thinks that Southside Johnny, and even Steve Van Zandt, have had to live in the same shadow.

"We're good at our games, but we've all been measured in terms of his success. Sometimes I can imagine that my albums would have gotten more air time if people just bothered to realize who came first. Maybe I would have been taken more seriously? Being one of the founders of this music scene, I think I have earned it."

Now Chinnock laughs. It's about *Badlands*.

"Yeah, God. I recorded an album for seven thousand dollars. We called it *Badlands*, and this was back in the day when you could still get some radio play.

"Now, I had no idea that Bruce was working on something with the same title. Not before I found out that he was going to take new cover shots and change the name of the album to *Darkness on the Edge of Town*.

"I believe to this day that he thinks it was a manipulated act on my part."

Anyway, *Badlands* became, in one way or another, Chinnock's way out.

"It exorcised the demons. All the angst, the neon lights. After *Badlands* I was more free to pursue my own vision. I stopped looking backwards and became a lot happier. The next album, *Dimestore Heroes*, marked a big change. I like to think of it as a progression."

Bill Chinnock found his new home base in Stephen Kingland, a five or six-hour drive north of Asbury Park. He ended up in Maine on the invitation of the legendary John Hammond, who had once signed Bruce Springsteen to Columbia.

"John wanted to do the same thing for me, but the director at Columbia said no. So when my first album came out on Paramount Records, it was John who wrote the liner notes. John believed in the written word. He was influenced by Allen Ginsberg.

"Holding that band together was like trying to contain a hurricane with band-aids. 'Cause there was Vini on drums, and once you found his on switch there was no way back."

"I had developed this huge committment to the blues. I moved to New York and ran John Lee Hooker's band for a while. There I was, walking with giants like Willie Dixon and James Cotton. I sat back listening to Sonny Terry and Brownie McGhee.

"But John wanted to get me out of the city. He told me to focus on my songwriting. So I got hold of a tourist brochure about Maine, loaded the guitars on the VW and went on my way."

Asbury Park was exploding. It was set to end and Bill Chinnock didn't care. Not any longer. He has often returned, played at the Stone Pony and other clubs on the circuit. But Maine became home, except for a period when the Downtown Tangiers Band was reunited in Nashville.

"Bruce had fired the E Street Band. Huge mistake. It's like Fonzie firing the street gang. You don't fire the E Street Band.

"Garry had already moved to Nashville, I spent some time there, and Danny was on a flight. I guess Vini was caddying or something in Florida so we used Roger Cox on drums. Three songs were recorded, an album was on the way. But the record company wanted a new E Street Band and we wanted to give them Danny, Garry, and Bill. That was it."

Bill Chinnock says that nothing of what happened is a big deal. The music is what's for real. It's the things around it that are out of control.

"Anger and resentment, I carry none of that. I just play. I am not like Bruce, and never have been. But I can still write songs and I get to go on tour with great musicians such as John Kumnick and Tony 'Thunder' Smith. They have been with me for well over twenty years. They are my brothers."

He finishes his breakfast, smiles and says:

"You know what I really want to do? I want to write music that can influence other peoples' lives for the better. There's no greater reward. There's a gold record."

WONDE

R BAR

TEQUILAS, RED HATS, AND FISHING REELS

Lance Larson

"What's making it? I was down, but I survived. That's my success. That's why I can say: 'Yes, I made it.'" Lance Larson feels blessed. He got the chance to start over. Life smiles and Larson smiles back. "Sometimes I think my father is sitting up there pushing things around. Anyway, God showed me that he wasn't ready for me just yet. He must think that I've got something left to do down here."

"Lance has his own bar. Things really are starting to happen in Asbury Park."

Says Bruce Springsteen onstage during the holiday shows in 2003.

Almost one year later we find Lance Larson right across the street from Convention Hall, sitting in the bar that got its revival once Larson and his girlfriend Debbie Delisa took over business.

The Wonder Bar, like Larson, an Asbury classic.

"A dream come true. Hey, Deb! Hurry up that cocktail!"

Lance Larson laughs: "That's a start, don't you think?"

Then he wonders how much space we have on the tape.

"So much has happened in my life. I probably shouldn't be sitting here today. But I am. I got my own bar in Asbury Park, with the world's best girlfriend, and I've got good friends. What have I got to complain about?"

This comes from the heart of a man who had almost been taken out of the game. Who was as good as dead.

The lights went out when Lance Larson was on the way home from work, in the beginning of December 1993. It was pay day at the building site, and Larson was attacked by some people who figured that he was the one carrying the cash. They grabbed the hammer and smashed it against his skull. Time was almost up when help got there. Larson was forced to undergo a series of operations, and suffered a temporary memory loss. But he survived.

"The nurses all used to wait around for Bruce to call on the telephone and they thought it was funny that I didn't know or even remember who Bruce was."

Slowly, but surely, his memory returned. Slowly, but surely,

Lance Larson came back to life. Not everything would be like it was before, but that may not have been his wish, either.

"My earlier years in music was a time filled with so much shit that I had to put behind me anyway. I'm taking it easier today, and I am writing better songs than ever."

In order to understand what has been Lance Larson's life, and all that could have been, we have to go back in time, to the 1960s and a childhood in Shrewsbury, New Jersey.

"I was going into sixth or seventh grade when the British invasion hit. That was when I started taking lessons on keyboard."

Larson says that he listened to Paul Revere & the Raiders and the Animals.

"You had the Farfisa organ, that happy organ. That's a great sound for a band, and in Shrewsbury there was no one else my age who played the organ."

Halfway through the 1960s he was still too young for clubs that served alcohol. So was Bruce Springsteen. But Larson saw Springsteen and his band, the Castiles, at different teen clubs, the so-called Hullabaloos, such as Le Teendezvous, the Left Foot, and the Fort Monmouth Teen Club.

"I lived in Shrewsbury, directly up the street from Le Teendezvous. So that was my hangout."

"The Castiles was probably 'the band.' But there were others, such as Black River Circus and the Mods. Those guys, the Mods, were almost stars, because they had recorded the theme song for *Candid Camera*."

"But then came the Motifs. Vinnie Roslin, who later played with Bruce, was in the band. They were guys from Jersey, but

"My earlier years in music was a time filled with so much shit that I had to put behind me anyway. I'm taking it easier today, and I am writing better songs than ever."

their manager, Norman Seldin, would tell everybody that the Motifs came from England. Then he had them appear at a shop in Red Bank and the street outside was packed with people. The rest of us, the other musicians, realized what was going on, but we sort of kept our mouths shut."

The Mods, the Motifs, the Castiles. And then there was Sonny Kenn.

"Sonny was rolling. It wasn't like with Bruce, not the same star quality. But at the time, Sonny was really up there."

Like that summer when Lance Larson's band, the Spartans, also got the chance to play in the shopping center in Eatontown.

"We had talent shows, Battle of the Bands. Sonny's band won. His Starfires got a whole season that summer. They opened for acts such as Jerry Lee Lewis and Beau Brummels."

Lance Larson slaps his forehead and laughs:

"But Muggs was always the star."

Muggs?

"Mm, Muggs the chimpanzee. He had been on the Ed Sullivan show. Muggs and the Beatles.

"Anyway. Muggs was really a star. He loved being onstage because then he knew he would get his treats. As soon as the curtain went down and Muggs knew that the show was over, he would get really pissed. It took three or four men to get him back into the truck.

"Sonny Kenn and I usually have a good laugh about that. The biggest star in Monmouth County? No damn way it was Bruce Springsteen. It was Muggs."

Those days often come back to Larson.

"Famous? Seriously, the only people from around here who became truly famous are Jon Bon Jovi and Bruce Springsteen. Yeah, and the guys who played with Bruce, of course. But these scenes have witnessed so many good bands. From Billy Chinnock's Downtown Tangiers Band to the Cahoots."

And the Lord Gunner Group?

"And the Lord Gunner Group."

But Lance Larson needs to take his story for a few more turns until we get to Lord Gunner. He returns to the Hullabaloo clubs, where the audience was made up of either surfers or greasers.

"Then we grew into hippies, all of us."

Springsteen?

"He started getting some real writeups when Steel Mill was opening for Grand Funk Railroad at the Ice Palace. He kicked the shit out of those guys. That was when Bruce really proved himself."

"After that 'Tinker,' his manager, just had to put up a couple of posters and the rest was word of mouth. 'Tinker' would set up a stage, and wherever Bruce showed up the place was packed."

In the mid 1960s Lance Larson moved to Tinton Falls. But he was almost never there, because everything was happening in Asbury Park. A couple of years later, Larson got a job as a bartender at the Student Prince, across the street from the Sunshine In where Bobby Fischer was booking the big acts.

"Bobby was a man who always had the same deal with the bands. Fifty percent was to be paid prior to the show, and the other fifty percent before they were going onstage. So while bands like Slade and Joe Walsh was playing Bobby would come over to see me at the Student Prince 'cause he was short like 1,500 dollars. He'd say: 'Lance, I need two grand. If I can't pay you back, you can have the bill of sale to my car.'"

Larson liked the deal, since Fischer was the owner of a nice Cadillac Eldorado.

"I'd lend any kind of money because I knew one day he wasn't gonna be able to pay me, and then I'll have the Cadillac.

"A few days after Slade's show, Bobby was gone. We started to get a little worried. This guy comes into the Student Prince and asks if anyone has seen Bobby Fischer. I'd go: 'Yeah, who ain't looking for him?' Then the guy says: 'He owes me a lot of money, but I ain't too worried about it.'

"And guess what? He picks up the same bill of sale that Bobby had given to me!"

Did Fischer ever return?

"Yeah, Bobby came back and he ended up paying everybody."

We're moving forward, to late 1960s Asbury Park.

"Every band who was anybody would come to Asbury. The Doors, the Stones, Yes, Emerson, Lake & Palmer . . . they all played the Convention Hall.

"Growing up in this town, we knew how to sneak in. We

slept underneath the Convention Hall, we knew how to get through the Paramount and upstairs to an exit door. Then we'd go across the roof and come down in the Convention Hall to see the bands. Nobody ever knew, and we never got caught.

"Besides the Convention Hall we had the bars, like Bruce playing the Student Prince five or six nights a week."

Larson says there was no place in the world where he would rather have grown up.

"Bruce was always the star and everybody was proud of him. We were all still kids, just fucking around, and while the rest of us were having some beer and thinking about who's the nicest girl to pick up, Bruce was writing, and writing, and writing.

"It wasn't like he didn't have his good moments, but he was really into his own music, and I think that was good because he gave us all a kick in the ass."

In the beginning of the 1970s, Lance Larson tried to go his own way. He lived in California for a few months, but was back in Asbury in 1972. He moved into an apartment on Fourth Avenue, and took a construction job.

"After I left the Spartans I wasn't in a band for quite a while. Meanwhile, I got back to writing songs on an acoustic guitar, but being a keyboard player I was never good enough on the guitar. So I figured if I can write the songs at least I'll know how to play them. And it worked.

"At the time there was a band called the Fireball Kids. They released two albums, and everybody from New York or New Jersey had heard about them. I got to open for them, by myself, and it was a really good learning experience. Opening up for a band as an acoustic guitar player is tough since everybody is there to see the band. But I did pretty well in winning the audience over, and in the end I got a lot of publicity."

Years went by. Larson moonlighted as a bartender and a sound guy. And among his friends was this kid called Bruce.

"'Wow,' he said. 'Am I actually on that list? And do you really think that Warren Zevon is number one?'"

Time passes, then one day there's a phone call. It's Springsteen's road manager saying: "Lance, I can't get into it, Bruce just told me to call you. Get out to the house right now. It's really important."

"I didn't know what the hell all this was about. I might have been thinking that Bruce had listened to my material and that he wanted to produce an album."

Larson walks into the living room. Springsteen is sitting there, half-watching an old movie: "Lance, what's up? Have a seat."

"Then he doesn't say anything else, and I'm starting to wonder. What's going on?"

That's when the doorbell rings.

"Hey Lance, can you get the door?"

"This is your house. I ain't gonna answer your door."

"But you're closer."

Larson goes over. He answers the door, and guess who's coming to dinner?

"Holy Christ, Warren Zevon. He was my goddamn Elvis!"

Larson was in shock. Zevon doesn't understand any of it. Springsteen is doubled over laughing.

"Bruce said: 'Warren, meet Lance. He's your biggest fan. He writes his own music and whenever he plays anyone else's, it's yours. '"

Lance Larson continues:

"Zevon was there to write 'Jeannie Needs a Shooter' with Bruce. I sat out by the pool while they worked. The window was open. It didn't sound right, they kept going to this one minor and I wanted them to play in A-minor. After a couple strawberry daiquiris, I got a bit louder. Bruce threatened to shut the window.

"But what a gift that was. What are the chances of getting

"Sonny Kenn and I usually have a good laugh about that. The biggest star in Monmouth County? No damn way it was Bruce Springsteen. It was Muggs."

It's time for Lance Larson to give us the best of Larson and Springsteen.

"Ok, this is a good one. Bruce asks me: 'Lance, who are your favorite songwriters?' I replied: 'Number one is Warren Zevon, I love Zevon's stuff. Number two, Smokey Robinson, I would guess. And then, number three, that would have to be you, Bruce. As a songwriter you are definitely up there.'

to meet the person you admire most? Bruce broke the ice, and Warren and I became friends. He always used to call whenever he came to Asbury Park to play the Stone Pony or the Fastlane. I got to open for him on a few occasions. That's a pretty good dream come true."

Let's continue on the same theme.

"You know the red hat story?

"We'll take it from the beginning. We were on the way with the Lord Gunner Group, and things were starting to happen. After a late show in Jersey, with Graham Parker, we were going to go to Woodstock, New York. A hell of a long way up to Levon Helm's house. People had invested time and money."

Larson had a problem.

"My old man always loved a party, and I let him come along as long as he didn't argue about what I was up to. But sometimes he drank entirely too much. That evening, everything got derailed. Bruce's road manager was there telling me: 'Lance, we're gonna send the band up ahead in a van. Your father can't go.'

"We dropped him off and left for Woodstock. Then, after a few days in the studio, when we had really been sweating with the recordings, the phone rings. They're telling me my father's had a stroke and he's in a real bad shape.

"There I was, sitting in the studio with the band, while my father was dying down in Jersey. I was so burned up inside worrying about everything, I just collapsed."

Larson checked into a hospital, and when he came out, everything was over. His father died, a week before Father's Day.

"They spread his ashes without me."

Larson went downhill. He'd be sitting at the Stone Pony drinking straight tequila from the moment the bar opened. People knew who he was, and the rumor spread.

"One night Bruce comes into the bar and picks me up. 'Come on, buddy. Let's take a ride, he said.'

"He puts me in the car, we start driving around. We talked about everything that night, Bruce and I. His father, my father. We talked about life. I just wanted to drink or do a line. Do anything at all, just to forget. Bruce lifted me up. He said: 'Lance, you can't do this to yourself.'"

When Springsteen drops off a happily sobered Larson, he says:

"Lance, I love that red hat you're wearing. Can I have it?"

"The hat? Sure Brucie, but why?"

"I want to remember this night. You'll see, Lance, this ain't over yet."

One year later Lance Larson is sitting at the Xanadu in Asbury Park. In runs Springsteen, who had just released *Born in the U.S.A.*

"Lance, come here buddy."

"What is it?"

"The hat, Lance. The hat, do you remember what I said?"

"The hat, what are you talking about?"

"That red hat. It's history, Lance."

Larson still understands nothing.

"We stayed at the bar, had a few more cocktails, and then I went home. I turned on the TV. MTV. It was about Bruce, about *Born in the U.S.A.* And there, for God's sake, there was the hat, in the back pocket of his jeans. The image on the cover."

"But wait," says Larson. "Here comes the best part."

Time passed, the album sold, and Springsteen became a superstar. A video was filmed for "Glory Days," and he still has the hat on.

It says Rembass on the hat. So everyone starts talking, because the thing is that Bruce Springsteen never wanted to sign any advertising contracts. Everyone wonders: what does Rembass mean?

Lance Larson is down at the Stone Pony, talking with a couple of guys who worked for Springsteen.

"Bruce comes in. He says: 'Everyone's talking about the hat. Rembass, what does Rembass stand for?'

"'Oh boy, Brucie. I never thought about that. Tell me, that Chrysler deal, how much was it worth? Fifteen million or something?'

"'What's that got to do with it?'

"'Well, Rembass is a product. It's a condom, a rubber. It was made by a company I used to work for. Ain't it funny, those guys were offering you fifteen million, and now you're advertising rubbers for free.'

"'It's a what?'"

Springsteen looks up, walks away, mumbling:

"This fucking Lance. I'm walking around with a rubber on my forehead."

Larson continues:

"I can tell that he's really pissed, and I let him go for about an hour. Then I tell him: 'Listen, you know the whole thing with AIDS. You can be like a big spokesman for a safe-sex campaign. People need to protect themselves, don't they?'"

"Lance, shut up."

Larson backs off. He lets Springsteen have another drink and then says:

"Let me tell you something. Rembass doesn't make rubbers. It's a freshwater fishing reel."

Springsteen perks up, and Larson is laughing:

"My friend, I really had you. You were about to have a heart attack."

The red hat became a Jersey classic. As did a few of Lance Larson's bands. One, Cold Blast & Steel, was pretty much built around players from the up-and-coming Cahoots.

"I was doing sound for the Cahoots around the time that George Theiss, their singer, songwriter and guitar player, decided to leave the band.

"As George was leaving the guys in the band were looking for a replacement, so they asked me if I wanted to join them. But I wasn't that sure, I was more into the songwriting thing. Anyway, I joined and then it was all downhill."

Larson is laughing while moving on to Cold, Blast & Steel. Here you would find an Asbury all star lineup including Lance Larson, John Luraschi, Ricky DeSarno, Steve Schreager, and Vini Lopez.

"It was really a variety of different players. 'Boom' Carter was there sometimes, so were guys from the Jukes horn section. Anyone home played. We went all over New Jersey, playing seven nights a week.

"It was a cover band, but a good one. And we never played Top 40 shit. If we were gonna do a copy song it was gonna be a kick ass copy song. Graham Parker stuff like 'Hold Back the Night' and 'White Honey.'"

"I just gotta tell you a good story."

"We were playing this place in Somers Point. Disco was really big, it was also the Summer of Sam, with a serial killer running around blowing people away on discos in New York. Everyone was afraid. But there was a joke among rock 'n' roll people saying 'ah, what the hell, he just don't like disco people. He's not going to hurt us.'"

Cold Blast & Steel came to Somers Point, New Jersey with "Boom" Carter, Lance Larson, John Luraschi, Ricky D, the saxophonist Tommy LaBella, Tony Pallagrosi from the Jukes, and Michael Scialfa on the keys.

"This band was ready to rock, and the ones playing before us, a disco band called Doc & the Operators, was nothing great. But the place was packed and the audience went wild, so we were thinking: If people can get into this music, then OK, no problem. We were there to kick ass."

Cold Blast & Steel goes onstage. "Boom Carter" counts in "Hold Back the Night."

"By the end of the second verse nobody was doing nothing. It was so quiet you could hear a pin drop. So I asked the audi-

ence: 'What's wrong with you?' They answered: 'We're into disco.'"

Lance Larson can't handle it. He grabs the mike and says: "Listen, I really don't wanna say anything, but where the hell is the Son of Sam when you really need him?"

"Christ, they started a riot. We got hit with more bottles than anyone could count. And poor 'Boom', that did it for him. He was usually with David Sancious in Woodstock. Just this quiet guy into the peace thing. 'Boom' quit the band, and who could blame him?"

Cold Blast & Steel had good times at the bars. They did the Stone Pony with the Jukes, and went to Atlantic City. They went all over the place, and worked really hard for three or four years.

"But I was still more into original music. The bar scene was a lot of fun, but it wasn't getting anywhere. I just felt it had to be worth something to me, artistically."

Larson and Ricky DeSarno left to form the Lord Gunner Group. "Boom" Carter wanted to play again, and Steven Rava became the bass player.

"Lord Gunner was the closest I've ever been, that's for sure. We did real good," says Lance Larson.

He wanted his music to mean something. The first song he

running out to stop the ladies, saying: 'I gave him the wafer. If you're going to beat anybody up, beat me up.'"

The mission was all original music, and soon enough there were a dozen or so Larson-penned songs.

"That's how we started out, and that's why a guy like 'Boom' wanted to be in the band.

"Then we were getting so many bookings, like from the Pony. But I didn't have enough material so I felt that we were up against the wall. I had songs for a forty minute show and realized that we had to do some other stuff as well, just as long as those cover songs would be written by an artist that I admired and who wasn't that well known. There was only one guy that fit the picture, and that was Warren Zevon.

"Warren had been played a little on the radio, and a few people here and there had already heard 'Werewolves of London'. We added eight of his songs to the set list but most of the people who came to our shows thought everything was written by me."

Lance Larson says that the Lord Gunner Group was lucky: "I have always thought of Lord Gunner as a successful band.

> ## "I have always thought of Lord Gunner as a successful band. We didn't make it on the music market, we didn't become millionaires. But we were good, and we got to rub elbows with artists like David Johansen, Warren Zevon, and Sly Stone."

wrote for Lord Gunner, 'Sacred Heart', was autobiographical. It was about living a lie, where two brothers in South Amboy, New Jersey were put in Catholic school without being Catholic. How the boys' mother told them to keep quiet and how one day the younger of them had had enough.

"I got to a point when I couldn't take it no more. Then, one Sunday at mass me and my brother was going up to get Communion. I just said: 'To hell with it, I'm going up there, and I'm tired of lying'. 'Cause all this time we were making up excuses for not taking Communion or going to confession."

He received Holy Communion and after the mass the shit hit the fan. Larson thought nobody knew he wasn't Catholic, but everybody knew. And as he's walking out of church three Polish Catholic women grabbed the boy on the stairs.

"They wanted to crucify me. They said I was a pagan, a lost soul. I really felt like a piece of shit. This is when the priest is

We didn't make it on the music market, we didn't become millionaires. But we were good, and we got to rub elbows with artists like David Johansen, Warren Zevon, and Sly Stone."

The Lord Gunner Group also had a nice opening act: John Bongiovi & the Wild Ones. (John Bongiovi later became known as Jon Bon Jovi).

"Yeah, we took Jon with us, and we had Tico Torres as a drummer. Later Tico started playing with Jon. Those guys are fantastic. We're still friends."

So what actually happened?

"Well, there was never a record deal because I was a complete idiot."

Lance Larson says that he went to every show as sober as a choir boy. Only to end up acting like a nut.

"The transformation was a part of the show. I went crazy, but I never lost control. Not onstage."

Larson says that he had created a monster. He doesn't have any regrets, though, since he did what seemed right at the time.

"But it went too far. The booze, the drugs."

One night, when Lord Gunner went to Georgetown, Larson knew that the *Washington Post* was there. He was desperate to draw attention to the band, for the sake of the music.

"I was prepared to do whatever it took just to get people to listen."

He ended breaking glasses, ashtrays, and bottles over his own head. The white shirt was covered in red.

The *Washington Post* published an interview with Lance Larson saying: "Basically it's an expression of art. I do what I have to do to get attention for the band."

The audience came for the blood. They were out for the monster.

"And I had a lot of white shirts, but only one skull."

The Lord Gunner Group could not survive. Lance Larson couldn't survive that life. Ricky DeSarno went with Carolyn Mas, Tico Torres joined Bon Jovi. End of story.

Or was it?

Lance Larson, who finally, after all these years, got to release an album under his own name, *The Lost Asbury Tapes*, says that the Lord Gunner material is still around waiting to be put on record.

"I want to do something with the same guys who played on the *The Lost Asbury Tapes*—Garry Tallent, Jon Bon Jovi, Richie Sambora—but mainly with the original musicians from Lord Gunner.

"I always thought the Lord Gunner material was a bit dated, but when I see people these days they say: 'What, are you nuts? Songs like "Angel with Broken Wings" are never gonna be dated.'

"We've waited twenty years, but I really want people to get the taste of what that band was all about."

After the Lord Gunner Group Lance Larson hit the brakes, cleaned his act up, and wrote new music for a band called Larson. He got a recording contract as a songwriter, and has done music for the film industry. And then in 1993 he was nearly killed on his way home from work.

Lance Larson fought his battles and won. He got to run his own bar, formed his own Wonder Band with Ricky DeSarno bending the strings, and found new backing in Days Awake (which later morphed into Paperback Radio).

Finally, at the 2005 Asbury Park Music Awards, Lance Larson was honored for a lifetime achievement in rock 'n' roll, and on top of it all he returned to a recording studio alongside Jon Bon Jovi.

"I've been through a lot, but I'm not gonna be a cry baby about it," he says. "I still have the craziness of rock 'n' roll in my soul.

"And I'm sitting here, aren't I? I've been blessed.

"Cheers."

THE LAST OF THE MOHICANS

Richard Blackwell

"Freehold," says Richard Blackwell. "All towns send out different vibes. People were crazy in Freehold. Completely crazy. And you know why? There were almost no girls there."

Memories get blurry as time passes. Then again, exact dates are perhaps not the most important thing as Richard Blackwell is telling a story. It's been a long time since the days of youth in a town that was not among the most open-minded. What Bruce Springsteen described early on in his songs was a reality for him, and for Richard Blackwell.

"'My Hometown,' the part about two cars at a traffic light and a gun in the back seat. That really happened. My buddy Bootsy's brother, Dean, had an eye blown out one night. Guess someone said something to someone. Bootsy knows why that whole thing happened, and how it went down. I guess it was something like a gunfight at the OK Corral. Something you think you're only gonna watch on TV."

Freehold, New Jersey in the 1960s.

"Yeah, there was a lot of racism, but I was a kid, and kids don't think that much about black and white. I hung out on the street corners with my friends, singing doo wop songs. Then we'd play hooky from school, jump on the bus going to New York, and stand up there in Times Square singing the same doo wops."

Nowadays, Richard Blackwell lives in Asbury Park. But he grew up just a few blocks away from Bruce Springsteen's home in Freehold.

"Bruce was a bit of a loner. But cool. Bruce is still cool. Maybe a little more serious now that he's getting older. But back then, me and him never were serious. It was always about a joke.

"The first thing you have to understand when it comes to Bruce Springsteen's music," says Blackwell, "is that it has an origin.

"Freehold was a small country town. The white cats were digging the same stuff as we were digging. Everybody listened to R & B. That was where it started, for all of us, with the '60s R & B. All the black people in the world, over fifty years old, know where that stuff came from."

Springsteen's teenage band, the Castiles, was among the top local acts. This was common knowledge.

"Sure, people were digging them. But I guess I noticed early on that Bruce was driven by the same things as everyone else in Freehold. Everybody wanted to get out of that town. We all wanted to be somebody, someplace else. That's why there was no other place with so many egomaniacs.

"I remember George Theiss in kindergarten, first day in school, with a guitar on his back. He wanted to look like Elvis Presley. Hell, everyone wanted to look like Elvis. Even the black kids. It was all about being seen, and getting some kind of attention. Getting attention was your only chance of getting out of Freehold."

On top of all this, Freehold was, as Blackwell describes it, a town where there weren't enough girls.

"Man, you really had to fight for them. We used to come to

"Freehold was a small country town. The white cats were digging the same stuff as we were digging. Everybody listened to R & B. That was where it started, for all of us, with the '60s R & B."

Asbury Park or Red Bank to find girls, 'cause in Freehold the older guys had the fancy cars. You got a fancy car, you get the girl."

Finally, Richard Blackwell got out. He left Freehold and ended up on the West Coast in Berkeley at the height of the hippie explosion. He met musicians playing with Tower of Power and Santana. Blackwell was supposed to work with some of these guys, but things never really turned out that way. Still, he chose to stay out west for a few years, for better or for worse.

"Those were my hippie days. My black power days. Black people were trying to be even blacker. I'm black and I'm proud, blah blah.

"In any case, I'm out there playing a gig at Big Sur and a friend of mine comes up and says: 'Hey, Richard, there's a cat at the door asking for you. He says he knows you from Freehold, New Jersey.'

"I remember George Theiss in kindergarten, first day in school, with a guitar on his back. He wanted to look like Elvis Presley. Hell, everyone wanted to look like Elvis."

"Shit," said Blackwell. "Quit tripping. There ain't nobody from Freehold way out here. This is Big Sur, California."

But his friend insisted:

"I'm not lying. He's standing down there now, he says his name is Bruce Springsteen."

This story is available in a slightly different version, as recounted by Bruce Springsteen at the Paramount Theatre, Asbury Park, during the *Tom Joad* tour. Springsteen explained how he had driven the entire way from New Jersey. Three days and three nights, without any sleep, mile after mile. Finally he makes it to Big Sur just to find himself lost in the big redwood forest.

All alone in the woods Springsteen hears something that sounds like the beat of a drum. Following the sound, he comes up to a clearing, where he finds: "Richard" who looks up, equally surprised, and says "Bruce. . . ."

Towards the end of November 1996, the story ends with an intro to 'All That Heaven Will Allow,' and a laughing Springsteen who waves to his old friend: "So we meet again."

Richard Blackwell smiles and says:

"Bruce has a tendency to take a simple story and make it interesting. It's OK, he's an entertainer."

But there was a point to the meeting in Big Sur. Springsteen said to his old pal from Freehold: "Rich, when you come home, let's get together."

"Next thing I knew I was doing an album with him. And then, a couple of years later, the guy's a superstar."

In the spring of 1973, Richard Blackwell entered the studio with Springsteen and laid down some tracks for *The Wild, the Innocent & the E Street Shuffle.* On the back cover it reads: "Cameo appearance: Richard Blackwell, congas and percussion."

"You know, I never toured with Bruce, that's why it says cameo appearance. But I sure felt like one of the guys in the band. If I had just been around on the day they took the cover shot . . ."

Richard Blackwell remembers the recording sessions as relaxing.

"It was just a matter of going in and do it. Bruce knew what he wanted, and I just made up a beat on the conga drum to go with what he was singing.

"For me it was very special, because I was in the middle of learning to understand my instrument. And I still think some

of that stuff is really cool. Bruce just wrote some beautiful songs, but who knew that he was going to be this big star?"

Any live gigs?

"Sure, there were shows. My friend Alan Emmons, a.k.a. 'Empty,' booked us in places like Rova Farms near Jackson, New Jersey. Me and Bruce used to come out first and do a couple of acoustic tunes. After that the rest of the band would go onstage. I guess today people don't know that. 'Empty' has a trunk full of stuff from those days."

Richard Blackwell finishes a cup of coffee and then continues:

"One night, when Bruce came towards me with the guitar, I lost everything and ran out. He never could figure what happened, and many have wondered. There are those who still say: 'Richard Blackwell. The guy ran off stage, what the hell happened?'

"Many remember, many wonder, but nobody to this day knows. I've never talked about it. Not until now."

California had left its marks, Richard Blackwell's hippie days were not yet over.

"When Bruce started coming towards me, getting closer, looking bigger and bigger, I just freaked out. I was imagining things, hallucinating."

The Wild, the Innocent & the E Street Shuffle sold in modest numbers, like its predecessor, *Greetings from Asbury Park, N.J.* Many people in the Springsteen community, including Richard Blackwell, seem to be uncertain in what order albums were actually recorded.

"I have been told that I was on some of the *Greetings* recordings. Well, I don't know. I guess I always thought that *The Wild, the Innocent* was recorded first, but then they decided to put out *Greetings* instead."

A couple of years later, as Springsteen took his giant step forward with *Born to Run*, sales of his first two albums also picked up speed. Richard Blackwell was proud of being part of something that special, and many years later he wanted to hang a gold record on the wall.

He put in a request. There was a delivery, and for a while that gold record could be seen among the collectibles at the rock 'n' roll museum in Asbury Park.

In 1996, when Bruce Springsteen was doing his acoustic *Tom Joad* tour, Richard Blackwell was one of the guest performers. He came to the Paramount Theatre in Asbury Park and went onstage to play the *Tunnel of Love* song 'All That Heaven Will Allow,' with Springsteen on acoustic guitar.

"Interesting. I had never heard the song before and I couldn't figure out where it began. It wasn't like Bruce counted in. So I got started with my shit, and I thought I would mess things up. I tried to just feel where he was coming from.

"Afterwards Bruce was asking me what kind of beat that was. I had no fucking idea so I just told him it was the Freehold beat."

Blackwell continues:

"I guess I had something to give Bruce, in the same way as David Sancious. David is amazing, he can play everything. I remember that Bruce enjoyed listening to me and David jamming, but that wasn't what he was trying to do himself.

"You've got to respect the man. Bruce and me, we both grew

**"What happened to Latin music, R & B, or doo wop? Where is that shit?
What happened to everyone who came to Asbury in the 1960s and '70s
to listen to the Cadillacs, Smokey Robinson, or James Brown?"**

up in Freehold with the R & B music. But when he turned to rock 'n' roll, I would still be more into Latin and doo wop."

Looking back is just fine with Richard Blackwell. He calls Springsteen "a good guy, like other good guys from Freehold" who, among other things, co-signed for one of Blackwell's first cars.

"I don't see him that much anymore. Don't always know what he's up to. But people keep asking me about Bruce. I just tell 'em: he's a homeboy."

Still, over the years Springsteen and Blackwell have run into one another on a few memorable occasions. Richard Blackwell describes various encounters, like the reunion in the Paramount Theatre, as whims of fate.

"I used to be a piano mover in Manhattan for a long time. One day we went to the Power Station, what's now the Sony studios. They had this large concert piano, and we were getting ready to set the thing up. I couldn't resist asking who was going to use it.

"Bruce Springsteen, they said.

"And I go: 'Bruce! What the? Bruce is up here?'

"So we met, I left the truck and took a ride around town with Bruce and Jackson Browne. He told me he had to change hotels because there were always too many groupies hanging around."

On another occasion Richard Blackwell slipped into this place in Red Bank called the Downtown Café.

"I'm just sitting there talking with the bartender. It's just me, him, and one more guy left in the bar."

The third person is sitting with his back to Blackwell.

But he turns around and. . . .

"It's something about our life cycles. The way it flows, the vibes from Freehold."

We leave the lobby of the Berkeley Carteret Hotel in Asbury Park, and cross the street. Past Convention Hall, down towards the boardwalk. Richard Blackwell stops at the entrance to the Paramount Theatre.

"Here," he says, "I'd like to do some kind of Apollo-type thing to tap into the abundance of talent in all kinds of music, not just Jersey Shore rock. What do you think? An *American Idol* thing in Asbury. I'll wanna do it, it will be my new thing."

Then Blackwell says that the music scene in Asbury Park has become one-note.

"Now it's all about Jersey Shore rock 'n' roll on this side of town.

"I have this band, Cocoa Suave. It ain't no Santana, it's Latin jazz. This music makes the crowds go crazy, but still you can't book us down here, at the Stone Pony or the Wonder Bar. There just ain't no place for my music.

"My point is that in this town, right now, you can hear blues or rock 'n' roll, but nothing else. And if you don't mix things up we're all going to poopoo creek.

"What happened to Latin music, R & B, or doo wop? Where is that shit? What happened to everyone who came to Asbury in the 1960s and '70s to listen to the Cadillacs, Smokey Robinson, or James Brown? Where are they now? Wouldn't they like to relive some great music in Asbury Park?

"I'd like to see Asbury honor its full musical heritage with opportunities in town to hear all kinds of music. If I can't bring back old style Latin jazz I guess I'll just be the last of the Mohicans."

Delores Holmes and Barbara Dinkins Gunter

Delores Holmes and Barbara Dinkins Gunter hug each other outside that very special house on Kingsley Street. They lean against the facade of what was once the legendary Student Prince. It's a thin line between laughter and tears when Holmes and Dinkins Gunter talk about a time that made them lifelong friends.

Barbara Dinkins Gunter says she's going to improve. She is longing to get back onstage, and she will. Delores Holmes says nothing, but judging by the expression on her face, she's thinking: "I want to believe what you're saying. I want to, but can I?"

So this is a promise one friend to another:

"I have already booked a few jazz nights downtown. And Dee, that's not something I can back out of."

These ladies are unknown to the average Springsteen follower. But anyone who looks back into the music history of Asbury Park knows how painfully close Delores Holmes and Barbara Dinkins were to taking a big step forward.

Holmes grew up in Matawan, no more than a fifteen minute drive from Bruce Springsteen's Freehold. Her mother was an organist for the high school, as well as the local Baptist church.

"I have early memories of singing. The first one goes back to when I was four years old and so scared that I couldn't pick my eyes up off the floor. So my roots are in gospel music. I sang in church. I had breakfast, lunch, and dinner in church. My whole life was in the church, and then Bruce Springsteen came along, ha ha ha."

Something happened in between, of course. Like jazz, during her teenage years.

"I was totally into that stuff, but then everything changed when I saw Joe Cocker with 'Mad Dogs and Englishmen' on TV. Oh man, that was it. That music was so hot!

"I wasn't looking to join that kind of a group, I guess I was just trying to expand my horizon."

Delores Holmes lowers her tone a bit. The story takes her back to a childhood that was not always so sunny.

"Mama died when I was twelve, and two weeks later Dad took off. We were four kids left alone, two girls and two boys, for about three years. My sister and I were the youngest, but we had to take turns cooking for the others."

Music was the way out. The school choir came first, but later Holmes joined a sextet and a vocal group, where she also fell in love with a boy who would later become her husband.

"The marriage lasted a year. One day he went out to buy a pack of cigarettes and he didn't come back for a week. So I said to him: 'Do that again and I won't be here when you get back.'"

Delores Holmes stood by her word. The next time her husband took a week-long walk for cigarettes she packed her bags and left, taking the couple's baby, Layonne.

"I know now that I made the right decision, but back then I wasn't so sure. I had to go find my father, forgive him, and ask for his help. But he had started over with a new family in Asbury Park, and didn't seem very interested in solving my problems."

One day, as Holmes was reaching bottom, she ran out of gas in Asbury Park. She went in the first open door and met a woman who let her and the baby stay. Asbury became home, and Delores Holmes soon met Barbara Dinkins, who would become a friend for life.

"I met Barbara at my babysitter's. These girls were sitting there singing in the living room. We said hello and soon I was in the group."

This was the Darcelles, a vocal group that also included the late Lizzy Smith.

"It was great just doing all the fun stuff. Then, as the group broke up, Barbara and I had gotten so close that it was no matter what, we're gonna make music to the end."

Barbara Dinkins Gunter talks about her own upbringing more fondly. She grew up in Asbury Park, and lived there until she was twenty-three. Like Delores Holmes, Dinkins started singing in church when she was four years old.

"There were six kids in the family, I was the youngest, and everyone sang. My brother, who's a year older than me, was the one who inspired me most of all. He's a smooth balladeer."

Dinkins Gunter says that music has always been an important part of her life. But that what happened during the short time with Bruce Springsteen was the only time she allowed herself to be truly focused. That was when she ended up on a big stage for the first time. That was when she came so close to fame.

She turns to her friend:

"Do you remember that show at Lincoln Center in New York? When we got to hear our voices on the radio. Do you remember? Wow, what a feeling."

Delores Holmes laughs and says:

"Hmm, and do you remember the pictures? With our huge afros? Oh, mama!"

Holmes and Dinkins Gunter are living proof of how everything can change in an instant. Like when a singer picks up the local paper and finds an ad that says: "Wanted: two singers with a gospel sound."

The young woman calls her friend: "Delores, I think this is us."

Bruce Springsteen had placed the ad, and answered when Barbara Dinkins called about the job.

Dinkins and Holmes came to the factory where "Tinker" West made surfboards. Steel Mill had broken up, and now Springsteen wanted to organize rehearsals for what would become the Bruce Springsteen Band.

"Bruce put on Van Morrison and said: 'This is what I'm looking for.' He played a few songs, and we sang. After a while Bruce says: 'OK, OK, you guys got the job!'"

Delores Holmes laughs before she continues:

"I didn't even know who this person was. Had never heard of Steel Mill or the Castiles. He could have been just any guy from the streets. That was great, it really made me humble before the job."

Barbara Dinkins Gunter also remembers her first meeting with Springsteen:

"He was out for a soulful sound, and we were the back up singers with the gospel roots."

The Bruce Springsteen Band, with Holmes and Dinkins, started rehearsing in January 1971. Six months later they came well-prepared to their first show, in front of 3,000 people at Brookdale College. It was then that Delores Holmes realized that this guy had something special.

"Energy. There's something that jumps off of the man. I remember one time onstage, as we were still learning, still making our mistakes. Bruce was playing his guitar and he came towards us. All of a sudden it felt like something had just hit me. It was kind of like being on drugs, but I wasn't. There is an energy field around Bruce, but I don't know if he himself is totally aware of this.

"What's amazing is that I experienced the same thing when I met Patti Scialfa for the first time. You see I'm in this volunteer group, the Holiday Express, and Bruce comes and plays with us every now and then. We did a show at the Tradewinds. Bruce got onstage and he brought Patti with him. There's definitely something about this woman. I can see why Bruce married her. Patti is what Bruce needs. Down to earth, an excellent mother. And believe me, she would never take no stuff."

The Bruce Springsteen Band turned into a large and costly live production. "Tinker" West would take care of business and at times they had to realize there wasn't enough money for backing vocals and horns.

"That was understandable," says Holmes. "I was doing a lot of other sessions, and when we worked with Bruce he paid us well. Very well, if you think of the fact that this was more than thirty years ago."

Holmes continues with another story about Springsteen's generosity:

"The band traveled to Virginia and I brought this no good boyfriend with me. The guy got mad at me and beat me up because I didn't give him the money to buy a gun. He really hurt me. When Bruce found out what happened, he held up the concert and took me to the ER. He stayed there with me until they'd stitched me up, and then he took me back to the hotel."

The Bruce Springsteen Band appeared without Delores Holmes that night, but Springsteen made sure that Holmes got the same pay as the others.

"I had a torn background, low self-esteem, and even worse experiences with men. I just made some bad decisions. And here there was someone, a man, who protected me. I didn't think that sort of man existed."

Barbara Dinkins Gunter and Delores Holmes describe what was a happy period. But soon there came an inevitable split.

Dinkins Gunter on her goodbye:

"I called Bruce after a show at the University of Richmond, Virginia, and told him that I couldn't stay in the band. He asked why and I explained that I wanted to go back to singing in the church. He understood and wished me luck. Bruce was always a gentleman. He wanted to play happy music and he wanted everyone around him to feel good."

drinkers. I was kind of the corny type. I never got comfortable and I didn't want to sing on Sundays.

"No, I don't regret anything. I'm a firm believer in that God has a plan for each of us. When you regret, you miss out on joy. Suddenly something positive would have passed you by without a trace. I miss that time with Bruce, it meant a lot. But I made my choice after that concert on October 23, 1971, and I would make the same choice today."

The money?

Barbara Dinkins Gunter:

"We've just always focused more on a spiritual wealth."

Delores Holmes:

"We didn't come from money, and we've gotten by OK. No one knows what a ton of money would do to us. It never felt like a million dollars would make me happier."

Holmes describes her own departure from Springsteen, partly with a lasting trace of low self-esteem:

"It was very easy for me to sabotage myself. If something looked like it was going to get good, I would stop it. So I was convincing myself that this guy was never gonna make it.

"Then, all of a sudden, it wasn't that much singing anymore. Barbara had left and I asked Francine Daniels to take her place, but Francine didn't work out as well as Barbara did. It started to be not as exciting. It started to be work. I think that Bruce understood too that Francine wasn't cutting it. So he goes in another direction. He tries his best to hold on, but he still has to follow his heart. There were fewer shows, and I realized it was all going to end."

The story was about to take another turn, nonetheless, one night when Delores Holmes visited the Orchid Lounge, a club where Garry Tallent would often hang out.

"Clarence Clemons, who had played with Bruce for a while, noticed me there and said: 'I've been looking all over for you.

"I sang in church. I had breakfast, lunch, and dinner in church. My whole life was in the church, and then Bruce Springsteen came along, ha ha ha."

Many would question that decision.

"Bruce already had a vision and I knew he had the potential to be a multi-millionaire. But I have always needed to stay close to home. That in combination with the fact that my background was singing in churches, for non-smokers and non-

We're getting ready to take off.' Clarence gets Bruce on the phone and he says: 'Dee, we're having rehearsals tomorrow, can you make it?'"

Delores Holmes went to the studio the next day. But she never got out of the car.

"I didn't really understand what was happening, that *Greetings from Asbury Park, N.J.* was about to come out. And I wasn't sure that this was right for me. Then, after an hour in the car, I pulled off.

"It might seem strange, but I have never regretted it. When I think about how I felt at that time, I would never have been able to handle everything that happened with Bruce's band. The way my head was, I probably would have become a drug addict or an alcoholic. There was no foundation. I wasn't strong enough to handle it, either in success or failure.

"You should know that some of the guys in the band started acting really silly when they were first successful. It would have been the same, if not worse, for me."

Music would nonetheless remain a passion of Delores Holmes. When she looks back on the more than thirty years that have passed since that day in the car outside the studio, there is a sense of satisfaction.

Holmes retired after twenty years at the *New York Times*

advertising department. Today she sings full-time in the band Rain, together with her daughter Layonne, and they are also among the artists behind Tim McLoone's volunteer group Holiday Express.

She is also one of those who's stayed in touch with Bruce Springsteen.

"Bruce is unique in many ways. Several years have gone by, and I guess I'm not still in his phone book, but he'd come in and out of my life. Then, one day there's a call. He says: 'We're hav-

"Sheryl Crow pulled out her new black credit card. I just laughed and thought: 'You go girl!'"

Delores Holmes and Bruce Springsteen remained friends. They don't talk often, but it happens. Barbara Dinkins Gunter, on the other hand, has not been in touch with Springsteen since October of 1971, when she made the decision to leave his band.

"We didn't come from money, and we've gotten by OK. No one knows what a ton of money would do to us. It never felt like a million dollars would make me happier."

ing a barbecue at the ranch, why don't you and your daughter come?'

"It was so cool. They had a rodeo and a mariachi band. Some of the B-52's were there, and all of the E Streeters. Just a lot of Bruce's good friends.

"He had a stage set up and called Layonne and myself up. Then he told the story of how Layonne, my baby, would lay in her carriage and cry as the band was rehearsing at 'Tinker's'. After that Layonne sang 'In my Life' accompanied by Bobby Bandiera on guitar. Bruce leaned over and said: 'Dee, the baby. . . . '"

9/11 happened. Springsteen wanted to show the American people his support. He calls Delores Holmes and says: "I can't forget those harmonies. I wrote this song for Asbury Park, but it really is appropriate for this occasion. I'd love for you and your daughter to sing it with me."

So in fall 2001, Delores Holmes again shared the stage with Springsteen when he played "My City of Ruins" for an emotional vigil in honor of the fallen heroes of 9/11.

She describes something at once both exciting and sad.

At the following banquet, Delores and Layonne Holmes ended up sitting at the same dinner table as Paul Simon and Sheryl Crow. Needless to say, mother and daughter Holmes didn't reach for the check.

Today, Dinkins Gunter has a divorce behind her. She says that she's walked down forgiveness avenue, and she has made a new start. After some marketing courses she came up with two different business plans. One involves music production, the other will launch her as a sculptor.

"It's music and art. I really found my true calling."

Dinkins Gunter pauses, and then she says:

"I know I haven't done much singing in the past few years. Dee, I was always the shy one. But you've been encouraging me and I promise to get better. I miss the stage, I really do."

She also mentions a valuable piece of paper. A handwritten draft of a gospel song, signed Bruce Springsteen and dedicated to Barbara Dinkins.

"People have offered me a lot of money for it, but I would never think of selling it. I am not even going to reveal what the song is called. It's Bruce's creation.

"On the other hand, it would be fantastic to record it together with him."

"Who knows," says Delores Holmes, "there may come a day when Bruce calls and asks us to go on tour."

Barbara Dinkins Gunter looks at her friend and says:

"Dee. I would be right there. That would be the first time I'd get on an airplane. Brucie would be the only reason for that."

DELAWARE RIVER
KITTATINNY CANOES

A MAN AND HIS TRUCK

Carl "Tinker" West

"Take a look around," was all he said. "Take a look around." Nothing else was needed. The rest is rock 'n' roll history.

He has almost made a career out of avoiding interviews, and likes being photographed even less. But Carl "Tinker" West eventually comes around.

"I like you guys. You're Swedes and look like Vikings."

It's been some thirty-five years, and there's not much that's rock 'n' roll about "Tinker" West these days. In the little house in the Atlantic Highlands, overlooking where the ocean meets Raritan Bay, there are only two things that reveal his past. One is a Steel Mill poster from 1969.

"An original. Not many of those around."

The other is a photograph of "Tinker" himself. He's leaning against the truck that took the band on tour, the same vehicle that is still in his shop. The picture is signed: "A man and his truck //Bruce."

He is one of those who had the greatest impact when it came to building the rock legend we know as Bruce Springsteen. He is proud of this, and he starts his story. But not without pointing out:

"I hate the entire groupies thing. Someone succeeded in tracking me down on the Internet and now I keep getting tons of emails from insane Bruce fans. So I am thinking about writing a book myself to avoid all this. To tell what really happened. There are far too many people trying to make a buck on the Bruce Springsteen story. People who were not there when it all began. People like yourselves."

"Tinker" West laughs and then he says:

"OK, here's the deal. We're not talking about my early years. I grew up in California and studied at UCLA. That's all you need to know."

He came to New Jersey in the middle of the 1960s.

"I was building surfboards, and 67 percent of the market sales was in the Northeast. People out here . . . well, if one person has something his neighbor has to have it, too. They don't know why, but they'll go get one.

"So, I had a partner out here and I said to him: 'You run this shop and I'm gonna take some guys and some surfboards over.'

"Me and this really good surf team jumped into a truck with twelve boards. I turned the guys loose on the beach and everybody went 'oh . . . , ah . . . '"

There was, of course, a master plan:

"New Jersey was a good place to start the business, centrally located between Boston and Richmond. It had low state income tax at the time and a decent school system. With the twelve surfboards we picked up some dealers. One in Rockaway Beach, one here in Belmar, a guy in Atlantic City, and another guy in Virginia. Later on all that expanded to other dealers.

"Then, by looking at the demographics: Why should I be shipping things all the way from California when I could set up a shop out here? I decided to open it in the spring of 1966, and then go through the season which ends in August. I told my partners that this was gonna work and we succeeded. We became the largest surfboard manufacturers in the Tri-State area for quite a while and put everybody else out of business."

"Tinker" West was already acquainted with Gordon Kennerly, the tour manager for Quicksilver Messenger Service. In California he'd also met people around the Grateful Dead.

"I got turned on to music through these guys. Then, in Jersey, I started going to night clubs and realized that nobody did originals. There was no way you'd get hired unless you played cover material.

"But Asbury Park had this after hours place called the Upstage. Tom Potter and his wife Margaret ran it. I became friends with the Potters and the Upstage bouncer, Jim Fainer, who was this cool biker guy. A more-or-less 'don't mess with me guy' who used to hang out with Danny Gallagher and a few others.

"The Upstage was different from all the other clubs. Everyone would jam, but it was mostly blues songs 'cause the chords were easy enough. There were different guys playing, you'd hear a lot of different licks. I used to fiddle around with some folky stuff myself at the little coffee shop downstairs. I could write songs, but not lyrics. Either way I was too busy. I had a business to run, and a bunch of employees. It was pretty hectic."

West had found the place he was looking for, and he also made a number of new friends.

"Sure, I met Mr. Lopez at the Upstage. Danny Federici was there too. We were just hanging out and I said to them: 'If you ever put a band together, and you wanna do some original material, I got this big building. You're welcome to play there.'

"So they kicked it around and finally one night there's 'Stringbean.' The kid, Bruce that is, wasn't that good a guitar player,

but he had great stage presence. He was and still is the best live performer in the world. I told him right there and then: 'You're gonna be bigger than Bob Dylan.'

"Bruce had conviction. You know when people are sincere about what they are doing. He was so into it."

At first this was just kids meeting, jamming at the Challenger Eastern Surfboards in Wannamassa, New Jersey.

"When Lopez got Bruce we had four guys and that's really all you need. Four players. It was Lopez, Federici, and Springsteen. Plus Vinnie Roslin on bass. Vinnie's a great guy. Not as flashy as Van Zandt, but he filled it in."

"Bruce had had his three piece band, Earth, that never took off. 'Cause they didn't do what happened next."

It was the spring of 1969 and after a few months as Child the band changed its name to Steel Mill. Steve Van Zandt was to replace Vinnie Roslin on the bass, and Carl "Tinker" West became the manager.

"They all got into surfing. Springsteen actually worked in my shop, you know. He didn't do much work, but he'd putz around."

"This was the start of something new for all of us. Me, I hadn't been playing around with audio professionally until I got involved with these guys."

A band, supposed to be on the move, would need their own PA system. Danny Federici was the one who pointed this out.

colleges. There were a couple of little gigs here and there, but if you only play for 200 people you gotta play ten nights in a row to get the same exposure as doing one college show in front of 2,000 people. That was one of my theories.

"Then I met some other guys, playing in bands called Odin and Sunny Jim. They were a lot like King Crimson, did some great stuff but nobody would hire them. So we all started working together. A lot of the other bands, the regular bands, didn't like me 'cause I wanted original material. But since I owned all the shit there was nothing they could do. I had this forty-foot tractor that would drive up with a stage in it."

Steel Mill, fronted by Bruce Springsteen, grew into a heavy rock 'n' roll force, influenced by acts such as Cream and Jimi Hendrix. It was all about a raw energy.

"We were trying to get markets up here, but I didn't want to play bands more than once a month in one area, because that would burn them out. Plus there is an anticipation amongst the troops. It becomes a scene."

Steel Mill had established a reputation. The fan base was growing. Soon "Tinker" West was managing the hottest act in the area.

"I suppose you've heard about the Clearwater Swim Club episode? Well, there was a riot. The cops came in and started beating people up. There was no reason for it, but they tried

"So they kicked it around and finally one night there's 'Stringbean.' The kid,
Bruce that is, wasn't that good a guitar player, but he had great stage presence."

"Well, I was making a lot of money so I went down and bought all the things and started putting it together. Having a physics background I had no trouble building all the stuff I couldn't buy. It's all an apprentice thing."

The musical skills were honed at the Upstage. Now, the songwriting's a different deal. "Tinker" West knew it was up to Springsteen to supply the original material.

"He was doing a lot of covers stuff and said: 'What am I gonna write about?' I said: 'Just take a look around. There's enough stuff [worth] writing about just walking up the street.'

"So he started working on all those songs that Vini Lopez is still using with Steel Mill. It's been more than thirty years but I still think they're some of the best stuff Bruce ever did."

The remaining trick was to spread the message:

"Clubs wouldn't hire us. But I had built this PA, and at the time it was the biggest thing around. So we started working

to shut us down. Everybody was pretty well behaved, I think. It was just joints and the normal shit people used to do. Human nature. Anyway, they turned the power off, so I climbed the pole and turned it back on.

"We had over 2,000 people, at two bucks a head. That was a lot of money. It was wild, I still have clippings in some pile of crap.

"You know, we did all this without a record label. Didn't have tapes or anything. It was all a live performance."

Now that Jersey was conquered "Tinker" West started looking for new markets.

"Billy Alexander, a surfer kid who worked for me, went to school in Richmond, Virginia. So I made him a tape and he got it played down there.

"It was what it was. Just a small crew. The hardest thing to move was Federici's B3 organ."

Virginia became a second home front. Steel Mill played a number of legendary shows, several with the Richmond-based Mercy Flight as the opening act. Bruce Springsteen also recruited a new Steel Mill member. Later it was said that Mercy Flight singer Robbin Thompson got the job because Springsteen wanted to focus on his own guitar playing. "Tinker" West can neither confirm nor deny:

"That might have been the case. Still, I never understood why Bruce wanted Robbin in the band. Nothing wrong with the guy, he was, and still is, a strong singer. But, my God, we already had the best."

After winning Virginia over, the band started doing some serious touring. "Tinker" West tells about gigs as far away as Knoxville, Tennessee.

"One night we rented another truck, did a show at Richmond University, then drove straight to Knoxville, and came back to play VCU the third night. I was the guy that drove."

Steel Mill reached the first level of success. It was time to approach the industry.

"I went to some record companies, met all these A & R guys. I would have the books, and everything had been paid in cash. No taxes, I just gave them the wrong security numbers. Anyway, these guys were arrogant, trying to act so cool. I said: 'Look, we made 30,000 dollars in the last few months, without an album.' They said: 'Sure, fine. But we need to redo some things.' I said: 'No, this band don't need any work.'"

Steel Mill was to remain a live attraction, able to blow Grand Funk Railroad off the stage at the Ocean Ice Palace in Bricktown, and soon ready to cross the nation.

"One day I got a call from Gordon Kennerly, in California, who said: 'Come out here. I got a rehearsal studio for you, and there are some people who will put you guys up.' So we did a benefit concert in the surfboard shop and got about a thousand people stuffed in there. Took all the money, jumped into that flat bed truck, and drove west.

"Gordon knew everybody. He got us plugged in with Bill Graham at the Matrix in San Francisco. That was a lot of fun, but there were so many bands, and no money. Jersey today is no different. But back then, between the Highlands and Asbury there used to be lots and lots of places that had bands several nights a week."

Out west, "Tinker" West set up a meeting with Clint Wilson of Paramount Records.

"I had gone to Paramount at the Gulf & Western building in New York and they gave me this song and dance. I had actually gone to a lot of companies. But I didn't wanna give up the publishing. I felt if I'm managing a band I want the best deal for the band.

"Wilson was the first guy really willing to work a deal on the publishing where they'd only take a percentage to promote us. And being a hard nose I demanded to see how they would spend that promotion money."

There was a connection. For the first time West felt that he might actually be able to get the band a recording contract.

"After San Francisco we came back here, and played a gig at Monmouth College. It was sort of a homecoming. Wilson came out to offer a deal. He was the first guy in the record business to see Springsteen for what he really was. To this day, I would say Wilson was right on.

"So, this was it. But you know what? Bruce didn't want to do Steel Mill anymore. He'd seen Leon Russell and Joe Cocker and that big ten piece thing. From there I didn't know what to do. Jesus Christ, finally the door was open.

"I told him: 'It's not my problem. Do what you want to do.' I couldn't stop it. Besides I never needed Bruce to make money."

As Springsteen got ready to make a new start, "Tinker" West felt that this might be the beginning of the end.

"Everybody just sat around doing nothing for about a month, and finally there was no money. So they put together this goof band, Dr. Zoom & the Sonic Boom. This was around

**"There was no Pony when we started out. We played the Stupid Prince,
that is the Student Prince, and some crazy shit went on in there.
It was like the alcohol Upstage."**

the time we'd heard David Sancious at the Upstage and that kid was phenomenal.

"Dr. Zoom did a couple of gigs for Bobby Fischer at the Sunshine In. But Bruce was still just fucking around and I thought that someone was gonna screw him off. So through this friend of mine, Pat Carwyn, I got introduced to Jim Cretecos and Mike Appel.

"I didn't know anything about Appel but Cretecos was a great guy, and I didn't wanna see Bruce flounder around down here for another ten years. I brought them a tape and told Bruce: 'I think we got someone here who can actually do something good.'

"Bruce goes to see these guys and the next thing was John Hammond. You know the rest."

West wanted Springsteen to move forward, but not without paying attention to all that was going on around him.

"I sat Bruce down and told him: 'What you have to do is get an accountant, and tell him you want every record of everything that's done.'

"He never did it, and that's why it went to shit. Those guys were really screwing him around. That's pretty common knowledge."

Springsteen became a recording artist. He signed for Appel/Cretecos, and for Columbia. There was nothing to say, nothing "Tinker" West could do.

"When Bruce was talking about his ten piece thing, the Bruce Springsteen Band, it wasn't as easy to make deals. The band was so big nobody would sign it."

"The time after Bruce, I had to prove to myself I was a good manager. So I was helping out a country rock band, with George Ott writing the greatest songs. We made over 300,000 dollars with no overhead. That's always been my thing: how to get things done without spending a lot of money."

West and future E Street Band members just went their separate ways. Some people became world famous, others stayed behind.

"What the hell. I knew he was gonna be big. Once you've opened the door . . . the kid was it."

"Tinker" West laughs as he continues:

"Bruce told me the last time I saw him: 'It's amazing. I write a song and there's a quarter of a million dollars.'

"Well, good for you. What else is there to say?"

People keep asking about the old days, but not many have gotten their stories straight.

"The Stone Pony . . . ," says West in a tone that reveals frustration.

"I get so sick of hearing that stuff. There was no Pony when we started out. We played the Stupid Prince, that is the Student Prince, and some crazy shit went on in there. It was like the alcohol Upstage.

"And you know what? There's no Asbury Park music scene. It was cover bands in the '60s. Later everybody tried to copy Bruce, but the original guy is the original guy.

"It's still that way. You could put together a small four piece band and Bruce would still be a killer. The best stuff he does is when he sits by the piano. There's just too much bullshit onstage."

Asbury Park today. Does Carl "Tinker" West believe in a successful revitalization?

"Nah, after the riots it was all over. The state came in, they built this and built that. Finally they ran everybody out of business, and taxed everybody to death."

"Tinker" West doesn't mind talking about what used to be. He actually says he "enjoys bullshitting about it."

"But I think if you dwell always on the past, you don't go into the future."

10
A
S
V

E Street

You won't find it in Asbury Park. So we get in the car and drive south. From Main Street, Asbury, past Ocean Grove, Bradley Beach, and Avon-by-the-Sea.

In a little more than ten minutes we end up in Belmar, New Jersey, and we're told that a few blocks from the marina we'll find the concrete signpost where E Street meets Tenth Avenue.

Late nights in Asbury Park, at the Upstage Club on Cookman Avenue and the Student Prince on Kingsley Street, were what created this legend.

But these streets in Belmar, this neighborhood once home to David Sancious, holds just as a strong symbolic value when it comes to telling the story of one of the greatest bands of all time.

CREATING SOMETHING FROM NOTHING

Steven Van Zandt

It's been a couple of years since he was last traveling with the E Street Band, and Steven Van Zandt says he's hungry for the energy input. "Sure, you can get burned out on the road, but all that energy coming from the audience fills you through the tour. You get a little bit of it here and there, but not that much anywhere else."

Renegade Nation headquarters in Manhattan, April 2, 2007. You won't find Silvio Dante between these walls, at least not in a physical manifestation. Still, the deadly mobster is all over the place, making his statement. Looking suspicious on that poster, like he's thinking: "You wouldn't wanna mess with me."

That's when reality strikes back. Steven Van Zandt enters the room, looking like you'd expect him to. All rock 'n' roll. Van Zandt is in the house checking out the troops. This is where he's running a small empire, including radio's last true rock 'n' roll station and a record label ready to pave the way for a number of up-and-coming bands.

"We're still talking to European distributors, so that's not settled yet. If the deal goes through we'll be in Europe this fall. Hopefully that'll happen," says Steven Van Zandt.

Wicked Cool Records was created as an extension of *Little Steven's Underground Garage*, a radio show that's getting airplay in various parts of the world. Van Zandt says that the message is straight ahead garage rock.

"Which is really traditional rock 'n' roll, and we're gonna keep that identity for a while. Maybe at some point we'll expand to other types of music."

Van Zandt is known as creator of a bar band sound that was first heard in the early 1970s Asbury Park club scene. He rose to world fame producing and arranging Bruce Springsteen songs and taking care of guitar playing as well as hitting the high vocals in the E Street Band. Some thirty years later, Van Zandt finds himself on a mission, fighting for the survival of rock 'n' roll.

"Well there's nobody else to take care of the bands we're working with. Half of them don't have any distribution in America. It seems that nobody's really responding to rock 'n' roll, record-company-wise. The industry wants indie bands and hard rock. It wants pretty much everything but straight ahead rock 'n'roll."

That's the industry way. Kind of confusing, considering that Van Zandt has had 165 new bands played on his radio show over the last five years.

"Right now we're probably playing ten bands from Sweden. Stockholm is the rock 'n' roll capitol of the world."

He speaks enthusiastically about a movement founded around 1979, fronted in the U.S. by acts such as the Chesterfield Kings, Stiv Bators, and the Dead Boys. He wants this music to get a lot of airplay.

"With the radio station we're quite consistent, and we're trying to get tours paid for by sponsors. The thrust of the company this year is to direct the bands from clubs to high schools. I want to reach younger people."

It's obvious that Steven Van Zandt is one of the hardest-working men in show business. He admits that sometimes there's too much work, and that without getting any help from the business world, it's a drag spending time chasing money.

"I'm barely making it. There are things I should be doing, but I'm not. I should be more creative. Maybe do a little more writing, co-writing, or producing bands on our label. That's certainly fun.

"Then again I have to do some work for the schools. There's

"I can tell you that the Beatles showed us a new world. If right now a spaceship landed in Central Park the shock to this culture would not be greater."

this project on the history of rock 'n' roll that I need to finish. Also, I should be setting up a TV show for our station, and chasing sponsors for the touring radio show. It's really a pain in the ass, just constantly fighting."

Without even mentioning shooting the final season for worldwide TV success *The Sopranos*, where he stars as mafia consigliore and strip club owner Silvio Dante, Van Zandt goes on about reaching an even broader audience with *Little Steven's Underground Garage*.

"We need ten more people, 'cause today we don't manage to dedicate our time in the creative way we should. Radio has been so devalued. We have the most popular show in America but it's expensive to produce, you know. I'm not here to make a profit, just trying to achieve my lifelong goal of breaking even. Ha, ha, ha."

Steven Van Zandt was born in Boston, Massachusetts in 1950, and moved to New Jersey at age seven. He got turned on to rock 'n' roll at thirteen, experiencing what he refers to as "the big bang." That's the Beatles playing *The Ed Sullivan Show* on February 9, 1964.

"That was the birth of everything. Prior to that moment I had been playing guitar for a couple of years, just learning some songs that my grandfather taught me. I was kind of a lost kid. Not really depressed or unhappy, but I didn't fit into society. Played some sports for fun, but I was too small. I didn't want to go to college, didn't have any ambitions to be anything."

The Ed Sullivan Show was watched by almost every family in America.

"Yeah, like 72 million people or something, and I can tell you that the Beatles showed us a new world. If right now a spaceship landed in Central Park the shock to this culture would not be greater."

Not even the original birth of rock 'n' roll ten years earlier had a greater impact, according to Steven Van Zandt.

"Elvis was freaky too, being the first white guy to perform like a black guy. He was radical and unique, but not so unique that he didn't look like other people from the '50s. Elvis was a good looking guy, with a pretty wild style. Still, he wasn't from another planet. You could see guys that were similar to him."

Presley was no threat to society, says Van Zandt. "At least

not a threat other than the implicit threat of liberation brought on by rock 'n' roll.

"The Beatles were really a bit more shocking. The long hair introduced androgyny, the confusion of the genders. Guys who look like girls, what does that mean to the society? Clothes were different, speech was different. And there were four of them. This was the first time anyone had ever seen a band."

Within just a few months everything was different. That's when the Rolling Stones hit America and the Beatles stopped being the number one threat. The Stones, on the other hand, stayed threatening.

"The British invasion brought ten different bands here, and they were all successful. For me, this was the beginning of life."

Steven Van Zandt joined various teen bands in Middletown, New Jersey, including, the Source, the first group of his own.

"We played the circuit, and actually managed to get out of Middletown. We went as far as Freehold, where Bruce was playing with his band, and we went to Asbury Park. There was a triangle between these towns and back in the day the distances seemed big. We had teenage night clubs built just for teenagers and we had the high school dances. There must have been fifteen to twenty regular places you could play, before you got to the club world."

He says that it was the greatest time to grow up.

"And everything that was happening was one hundred percent because of the British invasion. There was nothing else. The Beatles ended almost everybody's career. The Beach Boys, the Four Seasons, and Motown survived, but all the solo singers were gone."

Around 1968 he got to hear about a new place in Asbury Park, a club called the Upstage.

"Bruce came to a show my band was playing at Le Teendezvous in Shrewsbury. We talked for a while and he told me to check out this new club in Asbury. So I went down there and it really was something very unique.

"It was so important and so cool. We were, believe it or not, living off of the music. When you played the Upstage you got five dollars, and if you ran the jams you got fifteen. There was really only me and Bruce, and maybe one other guy, who actually ran them.

"Today I really hate jamming, 'cause I did nothing but jam for three years. A guitar solo shouldn't last any longer than thirty seconds. Just the other day I went to see Cream and even with them, without a fourth instrument providing a rhythm structure, the guitar solos just aren't the same."

Steven Van Zandt tells of an inner circle. The Upstage attracted players from all over Monmouth County, but there were no more than ten to fifteen regulars. Some, but really not that many, became famous.

Springsteen and Van Zandt became friends in 1965, and by staying friends the two players influenced each other.

"In those days it wasn't hip to be in a band. In fact, it wasn't socially acceptable. My parents would probably have preferred me being a thief, 'cause that was more respectable. Rock 'n' roll was just weird, and long hair was even weirder. I was the only one in my town, and Bruce was the only one in his town."

In spite of the Beatles' influence on millions of American teenagers, there were no more than ten bands from the local scenes that actually got out there and played.

"Everybody knew everybody. Then Bruce and I would go up separately to Greenwich Village in New York City on weekends, and this was a big deal. Other kids didn't do that. We were fifteen or sixteen years old and the Café Wha had bands playing all day. I ran into Bruce at this place, and since we were both going up to see what was going on we became even friendlier. The Village was about a year, maybe two years, ahead of New Jersey. So we would steal what we could steal and use it in our own bands. That's why we had the best bands, and then we started playing in each other's bands."

David Sancious. The three of us were playing in Virginia. I think I moved there for a while, but I'm not sure. It gets a little hazy after all these years."

This is around the time Bruce Springsteen got signed as a folk singer and started calling everybody up again.

"But the manager didn't like me, so I got rejected and told Bruce: 'That's alright, don't worry about it.' I just split, and soon after that I quit playing."

For two years Steven Van Zandt earned a living in construction, working a jackhammer on the New Jersey Turnpike.

"I'd be playing flag football on weekends, and this one time, as I grabbed a flag, I broke my finger. I had some on-the-field surgery, and then to exercise the finger I started playing piano in a bar band. One of the guys' cousins was related to a player from an oldies band called the Dovells. We became the Dovells band and went to Las Vegas to play the oldies circuit."

"My parents would probably have preferred me being a thief, 'cause that was more respectable. Rock 'n' roll was just weird, and long hair was even weirder."

Asbury Park saw various constellations, including Funky Dusty & the Soul Broom, the Sundance Blues Band, and Dr. Zoom & the Sonic Boom. But it was Steel Mill that became the first real touring force.

"My first experience on the road had been playing with a band from Boston. I was just out of high school and hadn't heard of the Upstage yet. One of those guys stole my grandfather's guitar . . . I swear I'm gonna find it someday."

Steel Mill was a whole different ball game, a tight Asbury Park all-star unit, and by replacing Vinnie Roslin on bass, Steven Van Zandt would join Bruce Springsteen, Danny Federici, and Vini Lopez.

"An odd sort like Allman Brothers, early Deep Purple, and Rhinoceros. Bruce and I were both big on Rhinoceros. We had the B3 organ and to me it sounded a bit like southern rock. It was heavy, but in those days heavy wasn't that heavy. It had R & B, it was melodic, but still intense."

Steel Mill got big along the Jersey Shore and in Richmond, Virginia. But Springsteen would decide to break up the band, and Van Zandt was moving in new directions.

"I was doing a country blues duet called Southside Johnny and the Kid. It was me and Southside, and then we added

Steven Van Zandt describes this period as interesting, because he liked to gamble, and for gamblers Vegas was like Mecca. More importantly, though, he got to meet his heroes; Little Richard, Gary U.S. Bonds, the Drifters, Ben E. King.

"I started writing because I wanted to write a song that would bring Ben E. King back. Guys like him are so good and the Beatles put them all out of work. I wrote 'I Don't Want to Go Home' and it was the first of my own songs that I was proud of, kind of Leiber-Stoller style. But I didn't have the courage to give it to Ben E. King, so I gave it to Southside Johnny the next year."

The tour with the oldies circuit, run by Richard Nader, ended in Miami, Florida. Ironically, it was at the Deauville hotel where the Dovells had gotten their name in 1960.

Van Zandt wound up the tour and went back to Asbury Park with all short-sleeved flowered shirts, and a Frank Sinatra-style straw hat.

"I kept wearing that stuff in January in Asbury where it's snowing and freezing cold. I said: 'I'm never going to acknowledge winter again.' That's when Bruce started calling me Miami Steve.

"Later I gave the whole look to Jimmy Buffet and he made a hundred million dollars."

Giving that song, "I Don't Want to Go Home," to Southside Johnny and helping Johnny Lyon to assemble the Asbury Jukes became one of Steven Van Zandt's major efforts in creating the Asbury Park sound.

"Yeah, we invented that, and we changed what a bar band was. A bar band up until the Asbury Jukes were people who copied the Top 40 music. No horns, since horns became unfashionable when the Beatles hit. We reintroduced that. By 1973, when we started the Jukes, the renaissance was over. We had missed all the good stuff. So, now what do we do? We'd try something original by combining straight-ahead R & B, like Stax and Motown, with rock 'n' roll rhythm section arrangements. Kind of what Stax was already trying to do when Steve Cropper was co-writing with Otis Redding.

"We didn't know it at the time, but this revolutionized the entire bar band world. It became the sound of a bar band that was very different from the sound of the Top 40 music. It was

that sound. It's not good, it's actually fucking terrible compared to what you're used to live. Eventually, once you're doing it right, and by the time you mix it, everything's great. But the early stages of recording . . . I thought: 'If this is the business who needs it?'"

Success came, but not immediately. It took years and years of struggling, and when finally making it to the top Steven Van Zandt responded to fame by quitting the band.

"Yeah, after working very hard for like fifteen years. I was really an asshole, ha, ha, ha."

He tells of how the band would slowly build audiences, by playing the same towns three or four times a year.

"The first thing I produced was 'Hungry Heart' for *The River*, and that became our first hit single. With *Born to Run* there was sort of a temporary splash of publicity which turned out to be mostly bad in a weird way. In some cities it was the first time people heard the name of the band, and then Bruce got

<blockquote>

"I wrote 'I Don't Want to Go Home' and it was the first of my own songs that I was proud of, kind of Leiber-Stoller style. But I didn't have the courage to give it to Ben E. King, so I gave it to Southside Johnny the next year."

</blockquote>

always an insult to call a band a bar band, 'cause it meant that they couldn't make it in the real business, even though those gigs played a very important roll. I'm afraid people are skipping that today, to their own limitation.

"Anyway, after the Jukes started there came Graham Parker, Elvis Costello, Mink DeVille, and Nick Lowe. People started calling them part of the bar band genre, and they meant it in a good way. It was a big moment."

Another big moment was Van Zandt's reentry in the musical world of Bruce Springsteen, arranging the horns for "Tenth Avenue Freeze-Out" on Springsteen's breakthrough album *Born to Run.*

"It was just one song. You know, I was so naive and not intelligent enough to be nervous or diplomatic. I just laid on the floor saying: 'This sucks. What are you doing?' They told me: 'Well if it sucks, then go ahead and fix it.' So I went in and fixed it.

"I didn't understand the business or the studio. When you first go into a recording studio it takes a while to get used to

on the cover of *Newsweek* and *Time*. Everybody thought it was hype, not real, like manufactured. Which it wasn't.

"I think that record got to number twenty or something. Then *Darkness on the Edge of Town* basically got no airplay. Now, this is probably his best collection of songs. I mean, they all became classics just from playing live. Unfortunately, that album is produced very badly and that's the reason I wanted to start producing the records. It was just a shame on all those great songs. Anyway, we made up for it on *The River*."

The band was drawing good attention, and with help from legendary agent Frank Barsalona they were playing not only across the country but also going to Europe.

"Then all of sudden we sold three million copies of *The River*, and everybody thought that's the most you can sell. It was amazing, like complete success. An odd feeling after all those years."

Steven Van Zandt explains how he had this tunnel vision where rock 'n' roll was all he could see.

"Then that started to fade away. When coming to Europe

in a more proper way everything became different. People in all those countries were singing your songs, even though they couldn't speak English very well. Still, they knew every word. That was a revelation.

"I realized that we can speak to each other around the planet, not just through our governments. That had to mean that this medium could be more important than just entertainment."

As the tunnel was fading, Steven Van Zandt wanted to learn more about what was going on in the world.

"I didn't know anything about anything, except rock 'n' roll. We came to Germany and this one kid said: 'Why are you putting missiles in my country?' At first I didn't think anything about it, I just told him: 'Check my guitar cases. Nothing in there but guitars.' But I couldn't forget what he said and eventually it hit me. When you're overseas you're not looked at like a guitar player, a Democrat, a Republican, a lawyer, or a doctor. You're an American.

"Suddenly, I was getting hit with all these revelations.

Well, the kid was right. I guess if I live in a democracy I am putting missiles in his country. So what else am I doing with my tax dollars, if I ever had any in those days? I started studying foreign policy after World War II, and it was just so shocking. I mean, America is the birthplace of democracy, but still we're supporting every fascist dictator in the world. OK, Russia and China have a few, but we got most of them. Learning about all this made me quit the band."

Steven Van Zandt co-produced *Born in the U.S.A.* He worked on the album for three weeks, cutting a number of songs. Then the process went on for two more years and they added three songs.

"Over the next two years I put out two albums of my own and I think the first song on the first album, 'Lying in a Bed of Fire,' got me introduced as a political artist. Peter Garrett of Midnight Oil stole it for their hit single 'Beds are Burning,' but that's OK. I introduced Peter to the world with the 'Sun City' record. He's a great guy, wonder what he's doing now? I heard he was running for office."

Van Zandt saw his first album, *Men Without Women*, as an introductory record. Then came *Voice of America* and everybody knew that this was a political guy.

"As I was doing research for the third record, traveling all over the place, I eventually came to South Africa. It was just gonna be a song on my *Freedom No Compromise* album, but the situation down there was just so bad I pulled it off of the record. Then I added some other artists, and when the song, 'Sun City,' got successful . . . well, that's when I really got banned. Nobody wanted to know me anymore. It was like: 'Oh, this guy. Who's next, who could be next?'"

A fourth solo effort, *Revolution*, got released in Europe and the fifth album, *Born Again Savage*, was recorded ten years later. Steven Van Zandt spent most of the '80s in Europe, because America didn't want to know anything about politics.

"The journalists here are much less sophisticated. European rock journalists are just as politically aware as the political journalists are here. I would do press tours in Europe, twelve interviews a day for months. I even had a few hits over there. But after writing the fifth album I just walked away. I had learned what I needed to learn, I got to know how the world works. I said what I wanted to say. Now I'm ready to think about what I want to do with the rest of my life. You know, the basic things, including a career and just making a living."

By the time there was an E Street reunion, eighteen years had passed.

"Everything went surprisingly smooth. It was just the original band plus the two people who had replaced me. Bruce had gotten Patti to sing my parts, and Nils to play my parts. It was like an orchestra at that point, and it still is. We didn't rehearse that much, it was just learning stuff on tour. That's the nice thing about a ten piece band. It doesn't matter if you don't know the song, ha, ha, ha.

"First of all, it's fun playing with those guys. They're really quite good, and you forget that. More than that, your brain does not remember that sort of excitement and energy that comes from the audience. Right now I'm in an all-time low from energy input. All my energy is going out, nothing's coming in. On tour there's an extreme amount of energy going out, but it's a flow and pretty much of it stays with you and fills you through the tour."

Steven Van Zandt calls the E Street Band audience the most enthusiastic in history.

"Yeah, I would say it's the most loyal crowd ever, and it's not only aging. It's really nice coming to places like in southern Europe and half the audiences are young people. Basically teenagers. I guess some of them weren't even born when I left the band, and still here they are singing every word, even in the obscure songs. That's a remarkable thing. If we did lose a few fans over the years we sure made up for it by bringing along new ones."

Asbury Park, New Jersey. That's where it all began. But time passes and Steven Van Zandt says he's not all that familiar with what's going on in the Jersey Shore town these days.

"I haven't really followed it, but maybe things will turn out OK. You never know with a place that has a history like this.

"In Liverpool they rebuilt the Cavern Club after they paved it over. There are lots of geniuses. . . . The first thing I did when we got to England in 1975 was to go to Liverpool. And you know what? There were no signs that the Beatles ever even existed. I was looking for statues. I mean, what does it take to get a statue in that town?

"Asbury Park? I don't know. What I do know is that we created something from nothing, and sometimes when you do that, those roots go deep."

"THANK GOD FOR ROCK 'N' ROLL"

Danny Federici

Bill Chinnock was waving a recording contract in front of his eyes. That's why Danny Federici, at age sixteen, dropped out of school. The long journey began in the middle of the 1960s, but Federici has not yet seen the end of it.

In 1985, Danny Federici received the E Street Band's lifetime achievement award. Onstage, in the Los Angeles Coliseum, the Boss showed his appreciation.

"Bruce had a little house in L.A. at the time. Earlier that evening he had sent over a couple of roadies to pull out the washer and dryer with hoses and everything."

Danny Federici laughs. Known as "the Phantom," he's the longest standing E Streeter. He was also one of those who reacted most strongly when Bruce Springsteen let the band go after the Amnesty tour at the end of the 1980s.

"Seriously, it came as a shock. Because Bruce called at a time when I was expecting him to talk about new songs, a new album, and maybe a tour."

Danny Federici says he wasn't prepared. He was enjoying his role as a rock star. As money was flowing in, Federici bought a Corvette and invested in real estate.

"Then everything changed. It was hard to stay behind in New Jersey once the band broke up. We lost a lot, the magazines stopped writing about us. It's funny how people at some point think that they are a part of your life. Then, suddenly we were no longer of interest to them."

Federici got to learn a good deal about ups and downs.

"I found out who my real friends are, more than anything else."

There was really no choice but to get away, to change environments.

"My then-wife and I moved to California. The point was to write music for TV and movies, but it has to be said—I wasn't successful. I guess the break up of the band wasn't really favor-able. It was like starting from scratch. I thought my name still meant something, and it probably did. But not enough."

After fifteen years on the West Coast, Danny Federici is back home again. He's been living in New York, together with his new partner in life, Maya, who owns a gallery in the fashionable Chelsea district.

Federici seems relaxed as we meet at the gallery. Life's good, not just because the E Street Band got back together. He's made a fresh start with Maya, the second solo album was signed to V2 Records, and he is working on a book about his long life on E Street.

"I am more put together today. More prepared, whatever happens with Bruce and the band."

Danny Federici grew up in Flemington, New Jersey. He describes a sleepy community, working class. The locals used to work in town, in the various businesses and companies. Nothing was ever open past nine at night.

"Just fifty miles away from New York. But in those days fifty miles was a big trip."

Music would take Federici a long way from Flemington. Much farther even than to New York.

"I started playing early. Classically trained. Accordion, piano. My mother took me to New York, my mother took me all over the place and was always putting me up on some stage or another. Her dream was for me to be a concert pianist, Las Vegas-style. Thank God for rock 'n' roll."

Flemington: one hour to New York City, one hour to Asbury

Park. A friend of his had heard about a hot music scene in the town on the Shore. So the Volkswagen bus took young hippies to the club on Cookman Avenue.

"A lot of people give credit to the Stone Pony, but Asbury Park was always more about the Upstage. The Upstage is where everything got started. That was where all the musicians ended up after they were done with the Top 40 gigs in other clubs.

"It was a great melting pot. People went there to jam. The way it was set up made it very easy. All you had to do was plug in and play."

Danny Federici says that the place had a certain hierarchy.

"I don't know who did it really, but there was like an order who got to actually play. I try to remember back in those days, but it gets a little sketchy. The great thing about it was that you could make all the noise you wanted."

Federici continues:

"This really bohemian couple, Tom and Margaret Potter, ran the place, and it was probably Margaret who made those decisions. She had her own band, the Distractions."

The word was guitarists against guitarists, pianists against pianists.

"I can't say there was any real contest. On the other hand, everyone had different attitudes. I came there trained. I was quite the virtuoso compared to a lot of them. After playing classical, rock 'n' roll was easy. I considered myself the best in town."

Bill Chinnock had built up a reputation in and around Asbury Park. The recording label Kama Sutra wanted to sign him.

"I quit school for Bill. I was sixteen years old when my mother realized that my musical career progressed and she couldn't hold

"Sure, I still don't have a diploma, even though something did get sent from the school not that many years ago."

It was nothing in the form of a credential, but rather proof that fans could be of any age.

"My old principal called and asked if I could get him tickets to a concert. So I said: 'Sure, but you know it would have been cool to have a diploma.'"

Bill Chinnock, Danny Federici, Vini Lopez. Local heroes in Asbury Park, even before the kid from Freehold came to town.

"Vini and I had had it playing Top 40 songs. We met 'Tinker' West, told him what we wanted to do, and then we went to the factory where he made surfboards. 'Tinker' meant a lot, but I think he never really knew how he would work with us. That was pretty much why he later had to give up the band to Mike Appel."

Federici and Lopez were looking for a singer, and they found one: Bruce Springsteen.

"We were tired of Beatles tunes, tired of sounding like everyone else. We wanted to play original material. Then we saw Bruce at the Upstage. Real skinny, long-haired, with a Les Paul in his hands. His whole body language, his attitude! Where did he come from? Who the hell was this guy? He just blew us away."

The first band would be known as Child, followed by Steel Mill.

"I remember Child as an easier, more melodic band. Steel Mill was completely different. Heavy organ, heavy guitars. Almost heavy metal. Only four guys, but we really kicked butt. Like the time we opened for Grand Funk Railroad at the Ice Palace.

"It was always hard for anyone who came after us. And that's

"It was a great melting pot. People went there to jam. The way it was set up made it very easy. All you had to do was plug in and play."

on to me any longer. We recorded a single, 'Cry with Me,' but for some reason we didn't get to use Kama Sutra's name, so we released the record on a label called Tristereo."

The contract was the thing. Who needed school?

"There was no hesitation, and I dropped out. But a couple of years ago I went back to my old school. I played there with a jazz band, and I spoke to the kids. I told them it took me four or five years to really get my career anywhere."

Danny Federici had time to reflect. And regret.

just how it was when we went on tour with the first album, whether we were opening for Stevie Wonder or Chicago."

Big things were in store for Steel Mill. Danny Federici really believed so, and Bill Graham, the promoter in San Francisco, also thought so. Graham signed the band, and they recorded three songs. Then Springsteen said no thanks, and Steel Mill was back to square one.

"Everything ended after a show at the Clearwater Swim Club. We were doing a benefit for Vini, who'd been in the wrong place at the wrong time, and was held up down in Virginia. Things got crazy that night; it was a total riot. The cops came in and said they found guns and other stuff under the stage. I didn't think it would do us any harm, since bad publicity is still publicity. But Bruce and 'Tinker' took it seriously. So the band broke up. Bruce had new ideas, and he put together the Bruce Springsteen Band."

Danny Federici was off the train. Disappointed, hurt.

"I didn't play rock 'n' roll to impress the girls. Music was my whole life. So what happened with Steel Mill hit me really hard."

Springsteen tracked down his friend some years later.

"I was someplace on Long Island with Bill Chinnock. It rang, and Billy handed me the phone: 'It's for you, it's Bruce.' Too bad for Billy, he realized what it was about. Bruce said that he was going to be recording his first album, and I think in the back of my mind I knew there was no other choice."

Federici remembers the years before the breakthrough as exciting times. Success first came in 1975, with *Born to Run*, but:

"Hey, we had a real contract. We were touring with our own roadies, doing gigs around the country. It's funny in retrospect, but I thought we had definitely made it. Steady money was coming in, and even if I already knew that there is no security in this business, that's how we felt nonetheless—secure.

"We toured, came home, took some time off. Then Bruce did his thing, he wrote new songs. After that it was time for the next tour. It was a very interesting way to live."

It was also an easy lifestyle to get used to. But not at all crazy, almost bizarre, like in the mid-'80s when Danny Federici found himself in the middle of a circus called *Born in the U.S.A.*, with paparazzi and screaming fans outside the hotels.

"I guess we were the biggest band in the world. Or, more correctly: Bruce was the biggest and the most sought after. Sometimes it was a rude awakening. Especially when we went to Europe.

"I remember *The Rising* tour, waking up after a flight, and there were kids against the window of the car. It was like leaving normal life behind."

Perhaps the breakup was inevitable. The quiet years that followed could be hard for several E Streeters. But the reunion came.

"It was almost unreal. Here each of us dropped into the studio. We hadn't worked together in ten years. It had been even longer than that for Steven. Nonetheless, he sat down and played everything automatically. All of us did."

Danny Federici continues:

"The thing is this: we know these songs. Today, when a tour is over, everyone goes off in their own direction. In the early days, everything was so different. We spent so much time together. We lived on busses, ate together, did everything together. We got really close to one another. That's why we no longer need to talk as often in order to be able to communicate in the music."

There's a leader, and that's how it has to be, thinks Danny Federici:

"These are Bruce's songs, and he always knows what he wants. If I forget something, or choose to play it differently, he immediately says: 'That's not how it goes, is it . . . ?'

"But there always comes a time when he gives everyone their space. I think there are a few songs where I really get heard, like 'Kitty's Back,' 'Sandy,' and 'You're Missing.' 'Kitty's Back' in particular. Playing that lead is one of my favorite things to do. It's great to get that look from Bruce: 'OK, it's time for somebody else.' When we get our moments we try to pack everything in there for a couple of minutes."

Federici says that Springsteen has been more open to influence since recording *The Rising*.

"Something definitely happened when Brendan O'Brien came in as producer. Brendan has, without a doubt, an influence on the sound, and he has taken a lot of time with us individually. For example, he might dedicate an entire weekend to working with me."

The studio is one thing, playing live is another altogether. That's when Springsteen can throw out any surprise at all without warning.

"I remember an outdoor show many years ago. Bruce came over to me: 'Get out the accordion.'

"Then he pulled a song out of his hat, an obscure old song that I didn't even remember the title of. He said to the audience: 'Ladies and gentlemen. If anyone screws this one up, it's Danny.' But I had a sense about it, a perfect pitch, so it was pretty hard to stop me."

Federici speaks highly of his employer:

"There should always be something negative to say about the Boss. But I don't know. Looking back and looking forth the guy keeps on making points with me. Bruce has perspective, more than anything. He knows who he is. He knows his job.

"He separates us as individuals, tells us not to step on each other. But he also gives freedom, and that's why there's no jealousy or big egos in the band. There's never any fighting over guitar parts or keyboard parts."

With his own album, *Out of a Dream*, we discover another side to Danny Federici. Jazzier, more sensitive.

"Yeah, I'm playing a contemporary jazz. And I think that anyone who doesn't know my background will be fairly surprised. With the E Street Band we have so many members, it's a small window to show your own style. But this is my music, the music that comes from my earlier inspirations: Jimmy Smith, Jimmy McGriff."

Danny Federici can do what he does, simply because he wants to do it. The guy with the lifetime achievement award in the E Street Band doesn't need to think about money.

"The record companies are funny. They give you a deal, but still there are difficulties getting distribution in Europe, and in the U.S.A. there are maybe a hundred radio stations that play my music."

Danny Federici knows about the game. He is independent, and feeling secure.

"There will come a day when it's all over, but I hope it takes a long time to get there. There have always been speculations around Bruce and the band. I probably get more information from other people than Bruce. But that's OK. Speculations come with the job."

Garry Tallent

Garry Tallent is not a man of big words. He doesn't give away any of the secrets that made the E Street Band one of the most powerful rock 'n' roll machines of their time. "That's because there are no secrets," says Tallent. "It's all time, material, and experience."

The Upstage Club in Asbury Park. Fall of 1968, perhaps. Garry Tallent says that, after all these years, it gets a little blurry. He played with so many different bands and was a part of so many things at that time that exact dates have become impossible to figure. But we'll stick to the Upstage Club and assume Tallent follows the timeline from there.

"I'd been away from Asbury for a few weeks, out touring with Little Melvin & the Invaders. But others, like Danny Federici, were talking about the new guy. The new guitarist who had come into town. 'Bruce,' they said. 'Bruce Springsteen.' 'Good,' I thought. 'Let's check him out.'"

Springsteen, the new guitarist, is standing on the stage that is home to Tallent and Federici, Big Bobby Williams and Vini Lopez, Bill Chinnock, and Ricky DeSarno.

"When Bruce started to play, people moved away from the dance floor, and I was left sitting there on my chair. He was good, I really dug him. But I guess from the stage he just saw this guy from a rival band checking him out. He might have felt uncomfortable, thinking I was dissing him. Of course, that's not how it was, but this was our first encounter and we just got off on the wrong foot. Bruce didn't like me after that, and I always had the feeling that he was looking for another bass player, just to get rid of me."

"If I've asked him about it? No, he'd just deny it. But deep down? Ha, ha, ha."

Garry Tallent has another cup of coffee. The evening flight from Florida to Tennessee was delayed. Tallent landed in Nashville at around four o'clock in the morning. Now it's ten, and the coffee is a lifesaver.

Nashville has been his home since the end of the 1980s. Garry Tallent came here to start over. To build a normal family life and work with other artists. Nashville was the way out of E Street.

"At that time,1987–88, I was fairly unhappy with the way things turned out. I don't wanna go into the negative, but there was a change. Everything became so big. Too big, almost out of our control. It just wasn't the same band it used to be. I felt it, and Bruce felt it. So when he said that he wanted to break up, my immediate reaction was: thank goodness."

Tallent recalls that the change was called "for now," something temporary.

"But it felt definitive. Bruce fired us, that's just the way it was. And who could blame him? It was time to move on. I remember when Paul Simon had his *Graceland* album come out and I thought: 'Phenomenal. This is what Bruce should be doing. Look beyond the horizon, see something entirely new.'"

It never really happened that way. Springsteen recorded the simultaneous releases *Human Touch* and *Lucky Town*, and was touring with a band of younger rock musicians. The criticism mounted, but Garry Tallent takes a diplomatic approach.

"It worked, I guess. I mean Bruce's songs were still Bruce's songs and he is doubtlessly one of the greatest songwriters of our time. OK, it wasn't the E Street Band any longer. The experience was not there, and experience is something that can't be replaced. We'd played together for so many years. We'd worked right alongside Bruce, both in the studio and onstage. He could make a choice that hadn't been played for twenty-five years and we'd pull it off."

Garry Tallent is the E Streeter in the background. The backbone. The security.

"I have never really been comfortable having the spotlight turned on me. It's not my thing. With *Born in the U.S.A.* on the charts, it was hard to feel secure. We went to Australia for the first time, landed in Sydney, and the paparazzi were chasing the band the entire way to the hotel. I remember thinking: Is this really what we've been asking for?

"And looking back now after so many years, yeah, I guess so. I guess we were after fame."

Garry Wayne Tallent was born in Detroit, Michigan, in 1949. His family moved around a lot. Virginia, Tennessee, and then New Jersey, via Wilmington, Delaware. His school was in Neptune City.

"We came to Jersey in 1964. I started playing in the school orchestra. And it was the same instruments as everyone else: clarinet, violin, flute. Then the tuba became the first instrument I wound up liking."

Teen Clubs were the scene in towns all over Monmouth County, like Middletown and Sea Bright. Garry Tallent and Vini Lopez often played in the same bands. Southside Johnny was part of the same circles.

"The three of us, Vini, John, and I, graduated in the same class. As a matter of fact, how I got to know Southside is a funny story. I was working in a music store and he came in with his dad to buy a bass guitar and an amplifier. But John didn't really know how to play it, yet. I played bass in a band, but I didn't own an instrument. The band I was in had fired the previous bass player without telling him and I was using the gear he had left behind. Finally he got wind of it, and came to pick it up. We had a gig that same night, so Southside lent me his brand new rig which I practically blew up and brought it home broken."

"We've been friends ever since."

Tallent, Lopez, Lyon. The guys from the same class were part of an emerging scene.

"People knew who we were. Famous? No, never. But like I said, I always played with the best bands in my neighborhood. I was able to learn from guys that were better than me. Guys

"It was totally uncool to play in a band from New Jersey. Tourists from New York came down to the Shore for the summer. They laughed at us, and we'd make fun of them. That was just the way it was, we kind of kept it that way."

"It went on from there, through high school. My mother would play and sing country songs on her acoustic guitar. We laughed at her, but that didn't stop her. Eventually she started showing me a few chords."

At first Tallent was solo. The new guy who saw that a rock 'n' roll band was the best way to make friends.

"This was about the same time the Beatles became a hit. Everyone wanted to get into it, and everyone wanted to play guitar. Me too, and I was no better or no worse than others."

"But I also realized all the English bands had bass players. Nobody in my neighborhood knew what a bass did, but since I was a tuba player I could easily figure it out. So whatever band that won the Battle of the Bands this or that week wanted me, because I was the only one who really had a clue what the bass could do."

Garry Tallent throws his arms out wide:

"No lessons. I just took it from there and faked the rest."

like Ricky DeSarno. He was a fabulous guitar player, the first one I ever met who knew how to bend the strings."

After high school, the Moment of Truth was formed: Lopez, Tallent, DeSarno, and singer Tom Wuorio.

"Tom was a very natural musician, great voice, a bit of a nut. We played the Student Prince in Asbury Park five nights a week. I would say we were the hottest band in Asbury Park. A band with a big following. But we weren't so different from the others. Just a Top 40 band. Sometimes we'd hire a female vocalist to do Jefferson Airplane, sometimes we'd play 'Sgt. Pepper' and 'A Day in the Life'. Vini could sing all that high harmony stuff."

Garry Tallent talks about a circle of friends.

"But we were living in a vacuum. It was totally uncool to play in a band from New Jersey. Tourists from New York came down to the Shore for the summer. They laughed at us, and we'd make fun of them. That was just the way it was, we kind of kept it that way.

"We were the locals, we had our own scene, and no one from any record label would ever take us seriously. We lived in our own microcosm and as I recall we were happy."

Then something else happened when Tom and Margaret Potter opened the Upstage Club on Cookman Avenue in Asbury Park.

"Yeah, this was a whole different animal. A psychedelic teen club, or really more like a coffee house. People came in after doing God-knows-what before they got there. Everyone was free to try new things with other musicians at the Upstage. We never played as full bands. The concept was more like: welcome, grab an instrument and let's see what happens."

There were hundreds of guitarists. There were several bassists as well, but none of Garry Tallent's caliber. Tom Potter paid Tallent and drummer Big Bobby Williams fifteen dollars a night so that the different guitarists would always have a secure beat.

"Them guitar players? Basically a bunch of gunslingers. One trying to outplay the other, almost like a live karaoke."

The Moment of Truth was in the course of breaking up. Musicians drifted around from band to band. Garry Tallent would work with Speed Limit 25 for a while, and then he replaced Speed Limit band mate Billy Ryan as a guitar player in the already established Jaywalkers.

"I started playing guitar with the Jaywalkers, but then became a bass player again when the slot was open. I can't really tell you how it all went down, I can only tell you what was playing on the jukebox.

"But there were still no original bands. The Jaywalkers were probably just the big deal of the area at that time, and it also became my first real studio experience. I was like eighteen or nineteen years old and we were recording in New York and Philadelphia. But nothing happened. So everything went on as usual. Business as usual."

Garry Tallent says that he played wherever there was work to be had. Sometimes blues, sometimes rock 'n' roll, sometimes soul and R & B with Little Melvin & the Invaders.

"I was ten years younger than the rest of them, and the only white guy in the band. A great experience. By the way, it was through Little Melvin that I got to know Clarence Clemons.

"I even played country. It's true, I was a drummer in Albee Tellone's band, the Hired Hands. I don't know if you could call it work, but this was life back then. You'd play a show and earn five bucks. And then everyone went back to the Upstage."

Bill Chinnock was a big name in Asbury Park. Tallent took care of the bass in Chinnock's various bands: Downtown Tangiers Rockin' Rhythm & Blues Band and Glory Road.

"Then Bill got sick. He got hepatitis, I think, and was away from the scene for a few months. That's how I started to travel with Little Melvin, and that's when Vini started to play with Bruce."

Bruce Springsteen had become the new guitarist in town. The one who, after the misunderstanding at the Upstage Club in the fall of 1968, avoided Garry Tallent.

"We didn't know much about Bruce. His high school band, the Castiles, were hot in Freehold, but not in Asbury. Then there was Earth, if I remember correctly. After that he put Child together, which would later become Steel Mill."

Child and Steel Mill were initially made up of Springsteen, Lopez, Federici, and Vinnie Roslin, a bass player from the Motifs, who were known as the hottest band from the Freehold area.

"Bruce didn't like me, that's a fact. Because when things weren't working out with Roslin any longer, Steven (Van Zandt) got the job in Steel Mill. And Steven was a terrible bass player."

Here, somewhere, Lopez had picked up Danny Federici from one of Tallent's bands.

"I was starting a band that was supposed to do something in the style of Procol Harum and Spooky Tooth. You know, the two keyboards, both piano and organ. We had Donnie Lubitz and Danny Federici. But it always turned out being Donnie against Danny, it was like oil and water.

"Danny didn't like that there were two of them so he went with Vini and I actually think that it was the two of them who asked Bruce to join what was supposed to be a reformation of the Moment of Truth. I remember me and Vini having a big

"Them guitar players? Basically a bunch of gunslingers.

One trying to outplay the other, almost like a live karaoke. "

fight. I'm not sure about what, we had lots of big fights over the years."

Tallent was working with Little Melvin, Glory Road, and the Jaywalkers. His friend Steve Van Zandt, who played piano with the Jaywalkers for a while, never got on well as bassist in Steel Mill.

"Here's my theory: Steven wanted to play guitar again, since he is, after all, a guitarist. He replaced Vinnie Roslin in Steel Mill, but like I said, Steven was never a bass player. So when Bruce ended Steel Mill, I'm sure Steven pretty much insisted that I should be the bass player in Bruce's next band. That must have been how it happened. I have Steven to thank. He must have assured Bruce that I could handle the job. That I was OK, and that I would show up sober. It can't have been Bruce's own idea, that's one thing I'm sure of. But he called, anyway."

That phone call came the night before Tallent was going to go to Kansas City and do some promoting with another band.

"I feel very fortunate. I mean, how many people have had this opportunity? But I regret I didn't enjoy it as much as I should have. It was always about work. Get out there and do it. Keep your eye on the ball."

"No big deal. But we, the band was called Moses, had been played in the Midwest, and that seemed almost unreal."

Tallent never hesitated, though. Springsteen had gotten a new bassist, and at the same time, Danny Federici had to accept another keyboard player in the circle: David Sancious.

"One hit in Kansas City. So what? I knew that Bruce was a major talent and if I was gonna get anywhere in this thing I'd really like to give it a try with him."

Steel Mill had become the Bruce Springsteen Band, with female backup singers and horns.

"We played a few gigs, but it was not enough to keep us busy. Then Dr. Zoom & the Sonic Boom became a side project. Dr. Zoom was never Bruce's band. Bruce, Steven, and Southside all took turns singing."

There were a lot of followers in Richmond, Virginia. Springsteen and Steel Mill had become a cult down there. Then the whole band moved there, because there were clubs and colleges around Richmond. The audience potential was greater.

"One day Bruce was gone. I still don't know what happened. He just disappeared, and the rest of us stayed behind. I played in a band with David Sancious and his friend 'Boom' Carter. We did some things at this studio called Alpha Audio. Steven was also there. I guess we kind of moved the whole Shore thing to Virgina for a while."

"Bruce was . . . I don't know where he was. I've just read about it."

Garry Tallent guesses that six months must have passed, during which time he'd gotten married and found a job in a music store. Then Springsteen called.

"Bruce told me that he'd been signed in New York by John Hammond and Columbia Records. He wanted me to come back to Jersey to make a record.

"He presented a ton of songs that I had never heard. Less R & B, more folk. I think he was living at Danny Gallagher's in Asbury, and I remember that we rehearsed in Point Pleasant. 'It's Hard to Be a Saint in the City' and 'Growin' Up' were among the first songs we did. It was all cool and very different from the songs we had done before."

Tallent also remembers that he went to pick up John Hammond in New York City on several occasions.

"I got to drive him up to Blauvelt, New York, and it was just entertaining as hell. He would tell stories and I would get us lost just to make it last a little longer."

The job was done. The album was recorded and released.

"Then nothing happened until the next time Bruce called. My wife was very understanding, so I quit my job in Richmond and moved back to New Jersey."

Tallent knew that Bruce Springsteen had been doing some gigs with a different bass player in his absence. He wasn't surprised. Springsteen playing with others never bothered him, and as he came home to rejoin the band there were a number of new songs. Songs like "Rosalita" and "Wild Billy's Circus Story."

"Cool to have the tuba along on 'Wild Billy's'. We'd had a gig in Boston, at Paul's Mall, and we were staying at Jim Cretecos's mother's house outside of Boston when Bruce tried the song out. I remember him saying: 'There's a line about an elephant. I want to have some elephant noise.'"

Garry Tallent confesses that it gives him chills to look back.

"We had a few tough years. We traveled, we played. And we were truly a band."

On the way to something bigger?

"Those albums sold 17,000 copies or something. You still meet a lot of people who say: 'Wow, I remember when those early albums came out. I bought both of them right away.'"

"Well, if that's the case . . . the truth is we sold almost nothing before *Born to Run*."

1975, then. Nonetheless, Garry Tallent claims that the E Street Band never was on top of the world. Not until 1984.

"To me, what happened in '84 was like an overnight sensation. *Born to Run* might have been a number one record, and a big hit in New York. But *Born in the U.S.A.* brought something that was never there with *Born to Run*, *Darkness*, or *The River*. Up until *Born in the U.S.A.*, everything was still a struggle. Bruce was famous, he'd been on the cover of *Newsweek* and *Time*. The rest of us were fairly known, but none of us had any money to show for it. I always had the feeling that we were chasing after an audience."

Those legendary nights at the Bottom Line in New York, 1975, were, says Tallent, a local phenomenon.

"We broke New York. But it was still the hometown crowd that lined up outside. It was still a Jersey thing."

All along there was another feeling of greatness. Greatness in the music.

"Like when we rehearsed 'Born to Run' for the first time, in my dad's garage. Then I knew: This is it. This is the song that's going to pay the rent."

Spring of 2005. Garry Tallent is sitting at home in Nashville. He's doing well here, and enjoys watching his kids grow up. Family life has given him perspective. Tallent has played the biggest stadiums around and seen the world.

"Of course, all that was enormous. Shocking, I would even say. I feel very fortunate. I mean, how many people have had this opportunity? But I regret I didn't enjoy it as much as I should have. It was always about work. Get out there and do it. Keep your eye on the ball.

"On the other hand, none of that means anything in comparison with picking up your newborn daughter. I chose not to become a father before we had settled down in Nashville, because I didn't want to be an absentee father. There's nothing more important or better than being with one's family."

So when Bruce Springsteen called again, halfway through the 1990s, to record "Blood Brothers" for a compilation album that was the upbeat to the reunion of the E Street Band, Garry Tallent hesitated.

"The band had made it through a separation, and I was happy. I'd produced different artists in Nashville, started my own record label, and I was proud of that. I was not really sure I wanted to start over.

"But when it came to taking the family along on the road, the choice became much easier."

Garry Tallent tells that, during the hiatus, he actually went for an audition with the Rolling Stones:

"They hadn't played together for like three years, and all I can say is it was a good thing I was the one doing the audition, because they really stunk. But I definitely would have taken the job. After the Amnesty tour with Bruce, I was ready to do just about anything. Just to get away."

But the road wound back. To E Street.

"Apparently it never ended. We did 'Blood Brothers' and I was in California to play with Bruce on his *Tom Joad* album. I'm not going to say that we've talked much through the years, Bruce and me. We live different lives, in different parts of the country. But we have a job to do together."

Nor was the reunion anything that surprised Tallent.

"I've never been one of those who definitely thought that Bruce would take us back. I never really believed that would happen. But it turned out that way, and I guess there were always people who knew a lot more about what Bruce had in mind than I did."

The future?

"Let's not talk about that. Talking about the future is scary. I work less these days, because I want to be with my family. I love helping singer/songwriters here in Nashville, but I have my own children to take care of. My own children's hands to hold.

"I don't have the label anymore. We had a bit of success with a Greg Trooper album, but when you can't pay the bills despite having an album climbing the Americana charts, you know you're swimming with sharks."

A BLUES FOR HEAVY LOUISE

David Sancious

Bruce Springsteen's breakthrough came without David Sancious. But the general consensus is that something was lost when this masterful sound architect decided to leave E Street.

We follow the jeep up winding roads. David Sancious has a magnificent view from his home in the Catskills. He could have taken the long journey with Bruce Springsteen, but there is no question that Sancious has made it on his own. The walls in his home studio are covered with gold records, from the early years with Springsteen and through collaborations with Sting, Eric Clapton, and Peter Gabriel.

Springsteen recognized that he had lost a unique artist when this original E Streeter took his bow. He also knew and understood that Sancious had to go his own way. All of this makes perfect sense as we're visiting David Sancious at his house near Woodstock, a couple of hours' drive north of New York City.

David Sancious was six years old when his family left Asbury Park and moved to the neighboring town of Belmar, to the house that stood where E Street meets Tenth Avenue. As part of the move, he started taking piano lessons, initially from his mother, who was a school teacher with musical talent. He then became the inspired son who would go on to study under a classical virtuoso.

"I stayed with him until I was thirteen or fourteen. But I already knew by the time I was seven or eight years old that I didn't want to be a classical pianist. I loved the music, but I was always after an experience. I have never fitted very neatly into any category."

David Sancious says that he becomes uncomfortable without the variety he finds necessary.

"There was so much music in the kind of household where I grew up. It was such a broad variety that way before I was a teenager I got grounded in the idea that music is open for who-

ever has the skill to do it, and whoever has the taste for it. In other words, the blues is for anybody who can play the blues. You don't have to be black, and born in Mississippi. The same goes for classical music. It's free. It's wherever your heart and your skills are.

"I grew up liking and hearing a lot of different music every day. My mom and dad had very different musical taste. Father liked jazz and R & B, while my mother was into classical music and popular music. Her taste was probably a little more sophisticated.

"My two brothers also had very different taste. The oldest was heavy into avant-garde jazz, and my middle brother was a fan of rock 'n' roll, jazz, and Eastern music. So as a result of this we heard everything from Beethoven to James Brown, and a lot of things in between."

He became the different guy on the block. Because in America at the end of the 1950s and beginning of the 1960s, there were not many kids from Sancious's neighborhood playing classical music.

"But the impression that was made on me was by music and not by people telling what I should be liking and not liking. Lots of times I took ridicule and criticism for being involved in things that others couldn't understand. But again: I fell in love with the music way before I had a chance to be impressed by other peoples' ideas. So when I would come up against that kind of attitude, I thought it was funny that they had such a small mind. I just went about my task."

He would, nonetheless, experience an interesting development of the local music scene.

"There was a lot of jamming going on. A lot of interaction with different musicians and different types of music. Basically there was just a lot of music. The whole thing was to keep yourself involved."

"It was exciting. There was a lot of jamming going on. A lot of interaction with different musicians and different types of music. Basically there was just a lot of music. The whole thing was to keep yourself involved."

David Sancious was no more than nine years old when he formed his first band.

"It was a little jazz band. We had a piano, a vibraphone, and drums. Desmond Norman on the vibraphone was ten or eleven and Michael Lee, the drummer, was about the same age as Desmond. We wanted to have a bass player too. But we didn't know anyone in our own age that could handle the bass."

The youngest in the band was also the youngest kid at school.

"I started when I was four years old, 'cause there was a test you could take in New Jersey at the time. I took the test, and I passed it. So they let me start school before I was five. That's why I always ended up being the youngest one in my class.

"It was actually more of an advantage, socially. Kids do a funny thing, you know. When older kids realize that you have a talent that they don't have they'll kind of let you in. If the eleven year old can pick up the guitar and do something that the fifteen year old can't do; sounding like Jimmy Page or Jimi Hendrix, the older kids will respect him. I spent most of my time with kids two or three years older than me."

The keyboard whiz was blossoming into brilliance on a second instrument, and people are still talking about how Springsteen and Sancious would show down in duels at the Student Prince in Asbury Park.

"I started playing the guitar when I was about ten or eleven. I was very interested in folk music, and begged my parents to buy me a guitar. After some time they broke down and got me a very inexpensive acoustic guitar. I carried on with that for a while, but then I got to a certain point when I figured out that I wanted an electric guitar. So I had to ask my parents again and finally my dear mother, God bless her, agreed to buy me this Japanese guitar in a pawn shop.

"I wanted to be on a certain level before showing up at a jam session, and after about a year I had made pretty good progress. I guess Ernest Carter was the only one who knew that I was working on it. Ernest and I grew up together and did a lot of musical things way before playing with Bruce. We had different soul and R & B bands.

"I think we were among a handful of musicians on the Jersey Shore who used to work both sides of the tracks. We would work in the black community of Asbury Park, but we would also cross the tracks and play with the white guys. There were a few others, like Clarence Clemons, doing the same thing.

"It was very vibrant and there were a lot of opportunities to play."

In his early teens, David Sancious started to visit the Upstage Club in Asbury Park. At first just to dance and have fun with his friends.

"On the first level there was a coffee house and a folk club, and when you'd go upstairs it was like a disco with day-glo painted walls and psychedelic music. We'd spend all night there and then walk back home.

"I always wanted to play and sit in, but there was this hierarchy and a whole list of people trying to get onstage.

"But what happened was that one day I had done a session where I somehow ended up with Garry Tallent. Garry and I hit it off, and a week or two later I'm walking into the Upstage. Bruce and Garry are standing at the top of the stairs. They're organizing a jam session. Garry sees me and introduces me to Bruce who asks: 'Do you feel like sitting in?' I think I played the organ all night, and it ended up being a very long jam with a lot of people coming off and onstage.

"Bruce had this blues song called 'Heavy Louise.' It was pretty much a basic blues tune but he would improvise the verses with whole long stories that got locally very famous. I think we played from one o'clock in the morning until the place closed at five. The Upstage had very odd opening hours."

Springsteen told Sancious that Steel Mill was over and that he was getting ready to start something new.

"I don't remember it to be very formal. This band, the Bruce

Springsteen Band, had some different configurations. It was always Bruce though.

"He had a couple of things, like Dr. Zoom & the Sonic Boom, with just a lot of craziness going on."

Sancious continues:

"Bruce has always been famous, you know. Even before he was famous. Locally, way before he had a record contract, he was the most popular musician on the Shore by far. There was no contest.

"So when I met him, he was already a big deal. I was aware of his music, and I thought he was fantastic. You could not have watched him back then and not recognize what a talented guy he was."

Bars, colleges, clubs, theaters. David Sancious joined the touring machine.

"It was still a cult thing, but a huge cult popularity that

hadn't reached the national level that it got to later when Bruce got the cover of *Newsweek* and *Time*. That was some amazing stuff."

Nonetheless, Sancious chose to leave. He wasn't around to ride the wave of success, and long-time E Street Band followers would agree that without him something was lost. The sound of the band was changing.

For David Sancious, though, the parting from the band was the most natural thing, even considering Springsteen's commercial breakthrough.

"I wasn't looking at it like that. When you're in a time period, week after week, month after month, you don't think about getting successful. I just had an agenda of what I wanted to do musically.

"And if anybody had an agenda back in those days it was Bruce. He was dead set on getting all that music written and getting it out there to be heard. In a way he actually inspired me to go ahead and do my own thing by setting the example.

"Like Bruce, I was writing music constantly. Most of the stuff that ended up on my first album was written when I was in Bruce's band. It was written at home and then I would get together with Ernest Carter and rehearse it."

David Sancious also claims that there were never any hard feelings between him and Springsteen.

"In fact it was the other way around. I got an offer from Epic Records to do a solo album. Bruce wasn't directly involved, but he was incredibly supportive. If there was any point where he had an opportunity to say anything about me or my talent, I know for a fact that he had nothing but the most glowing things to say.

"Then after my album was done we got together. I came over to his house in Long Branch and we listened to the whole record. He pointed out a lot of things that he really liked."

Looking back on some of the recording sessions with Springsteen, Sancious says:

"Bruce would direct everyone, 'cause he pretty much knew what he wanted musically. But at the same time he'd recognize that people had ideas and talents, and he was very generous about giving you space to make a contribution.

"For me *The Wild, the Innocent* was a special recording. I did the string arrangement for 'New York City Serenade' and I got to conduct in the studio. That was good fun."

"I remember the sessions were long. There were long days, lots of takes. The atmosphere was dynamic, and Bruce was always appreciative. He could spot a good idea instantly."

When Epic Records offered a contract, David Sancious put together Tone, where he would work with Ernest "Boom" Carter, who had also left the E Street Band, Jersey bass player Gerry Carboy, and a young Patti Scialfa. Tone allowed him to build up his reputation as a virtuoso, and he became one of the most sought after keyboard players.

"I did this body of work with this or that artist. But I really think of it as it's just what I was supposed to do. I was never trying to be clever about anything.

"I guess after doing three or four projects with major artists you've made a name for yourself. But the commitment was not to reach a certain level of success. I've had success, commercially, but there are also certain things I haven't achieved, like having a platinum record or a number one hit on the radio. I've been on a lot of number one hits with other people, but that's not the same as having your own.

"Anyway, the commitment that I made when I was very young was to have a whole life in music. So far that's working out pretty well."

David Sancious did some extensive touring with Sting, Eric Clapton, and Peter Gabriel. He also got a chance to reunite with Bruce Springsteen in 1992, while recording *Human Touch*. He's worked with some of the greats and knows to tell about similarities as well as differences:

"They're different musically, of course. And that's the exciting part for me. It's fun to be able to move back and forth in those worlds.

"But the one thing they do have in common is that they all keep an agenda. Every action of the day is about moving that agenda forward."

Sancious himself is eager about the same things: moving forward, finding new adventures, getting richer through experience.

"I wouldn't wanna be just a guy in the studio who never plays live. There's nothing like being in a band, playing in front

"We would work in the black community of Asbury Park, but we would also cross the tracks and play with the white guys. There were a few others, like Clarence Clemons, doing the same thing."

of a lot of people, and working up a good body of music. Then going on tour and watching the music grow. 'Cause that's what happens. Theoretically it has to get better every time you come around to it."

"Then there was the *So* tour with Peter Gabriel. I got a call from Peter in the summer of 1986, and it became a great combination of the musical talent and the songs. Peter's a nice person to go around world with. He's got a wicked sense of humor.

> ## "Those early years seems a romantic time. I find it hard to remember the negative things that might have happened. It's the good parts that got stuck in my head: the traveling, the laughing, the playing around, all of the long shows."

In this long, successful, career there are a few standouts:

"When I was with Bruce we weren't playing stadiums. It was smaller venues back then. Wherever we played, the place was sold out. I think way back in the really early days there might have been one or two concerts out in the boondocks with small audiences. But nine out of ten places were packed with his fans.

"Those early years seems a romantic time. I find it hard to remember the negative things that might have happened. It's the good parts that got stuck in my head: the traveling, the laughing, the playing around, all of the long shows. You'd come off stage completely soaking wet, just drained. But very happy."

Sting, Clapton, Gabriel?

"I was with Sting for five years, and we toured almost constantly. *The Soul Cages* tour became very special to me, because that's a great body of music from Sting. Also, his father had passed away, and my father was near death. So it was kind of a bonding, we had a lot of conversations about all that. We grew closer.

"I also rate touring with Eric Clapton in 2001 as extremely special, for those same reasons: the combination of musical talent and the songs. I heard B. B. King first, but Eric Clapton is one of the reasons I play the guitar."

These days, Asbury Park won't see much of David Sancious. He got out of town, moved along, and there's not always time to sit around thinking about what used to be.

"I feel that Asbury Park is a symbol for a lot that happened to America. Unfortunately, it's not a unique town in that respect. Asbury had the unfortunate situation of being hit by social changes and economic changes at the same time. You had the malls that destroyed the downtown business. Then you had the race riots, and I guess Asbury never really recovered from all of this.

"Now I'm just glad to hear that they are trying to bring it back. I think the people in that area deserve to live in a more positive environment."

"GUITAR, DRUMS, AND ORGAN ARE GOD"

Vini Lopez

From the early days with Buzzy Lubinsky up until finally recording Steel Mill songs in the 2000s it was always about the same true passion, the same raw energy, and the same undying attitude. "Guitar, drums, and organ are God," says original E Street drummer Vini Lopez.

Vini Lopez is one of the few who were there from the very beginning. He is also one of those who stayed behind, close to an Asbury Park that, while perhaps exuding some faith in the future, is still a bit worse for wear today, a few years into the twenty-first century.

The "Mad Dog" Lopez story begins in 1964. That's when Buzzy Lubinsky, a locally known drummer and DJ who used to play along with the records, introduced Lopez to Bill Chinnock at a dance down in Belmar.

"It's all thanks to Buzzy. I was just a kid, I didn't know anybody.

"Chinnock was putting together the Storytellers and Danny Federici was in that band. Buzzy lent me his drums and they said: 'OK, you've gotta do "Wipe Out."' I said: 'No, I'm not gonna do that.' So I never passed the audition."

Instead, Lubinsky would introduce Lopez to Sonny Kenn.

"Sonny was the first rock star I ever knew. He had the Starfires and Bruce and others would always come to watch us play."

Even before the buzz about the Upstage Club was starting to spread, Sonny & the Starfires had risen to fame in Monmouth County. A fact that turned Vini Lopez into the hottest drummer in the area.

Soon people would find Lopez playing with Ricky DeSarno, singer Tom Wuorio, and high school pal Garry Tallent in the Moment of Truth. He would also join a powerful force known as the Downtown Tangiers Rockin' Rhythm & Blues Band. This act, where Bill Chinnock got his backing from Lopez, Tallent, and Danny Federici, came to dominate the Asbury Park scene in 1966–67.

Vini Lopez is walking down memory lane:

"But in 1967 we broke up Downtown Tangiers, and Federici and I were looking to get some other guys together. Me and Chuck Dillon, I call him my brother, went out one night to check out some guitar players. This was in 1968 as Bruce was playing with his band Earth at this Italian club up in Long Branch. After he'd done his set I said to him: 'Hey, why don't you come down to the Upstage and jam?'"

One month later, Asbury Park had a new guitar hero.

"Me and Danny came there. We saw Margaret Potter at the top of the stairs. There's also Bruce and little Vinnie, that's Vinnie Roslin. So Danny and I jumped in, and the four of us all jammed together. Afterwards we were a band. Maybe not a real band yet, but definitely something that we were looking to do."

We get a solid lesson in history from Vini Lopez: short-lived Child and the significantly more successful Steel Mill were formed when Lopez and Danny Federici pulled in Bruce Springsteen and Vinnie Roslin in the hopes of playing original music.

"It actually started when I met 'Tinker' West, who became our manager. 'Tinker' had a big factory where he made surfboards, and it was possible for us to rehearse there. So 'Tinker' says to me: 'Lopez, if you ever find someone who does original music, come look me up.'"

The question from Lopez that night at the Upstage was: "Do you have any of your own songs?"

Springsteen: "I've got a whole bunch of them."

Lopez: "Good, let's learn 'em."

"Tinker" West booked Steel Mill a few nights a month, and rumor spread across Monmouth County about a new star named Bruce Springsteen.

"People always came to see us. It was almost unbelievable." The secret?

"Steel Mill was blues, rock, jazz, country & western. It just had that edge. We took everything as far as we could, and then we had Federici's B3 organ. Bruce was from the Castiles, Danny played with Chinnock, I played with Sonny Kenn and Little Vinnie had been all over the place with the Motifs. Around here we became like a supergroup, I guess.

"And the response was the same when we started traveling. Especially in Richmond, Virginia. Usually we had Mercy Flight to open for us. It was really amazing down there, but every time we played a song called 'The Wind and the Rain'

got something else. This was a place where musicians from all over Monmouth County met to jam.

"It was a place for guitar slingers, they always used to battle over the throne. And there I was. Big Bobby Williams and I were house drummers, so everyone had to play with us. And everybody made five bucks, no more, no less."

The legendary Dr. Zoom & the Sonic Boom?

"Well, that was a crazy idea, of course. We had two of everything in that band. Two guitarists, two drummers, and even two guys playing Monopoly on stage, Big Danny and Big Tiny, a big, big white guy and a big, big black guy. Danny wore a shirt that said 'pepper,' and Tiny wore one that said 'salt.' We had a ringleader, and we'd recruit from the audience to have them in the vocals section, the Zoom Chorus.

"Everybody made five bucks."

"It just had that edge. We took everything as far as we could, and then we had Federici's B3 organ."

there was a storm. It's true, every time. They're still talking about one gig in this little club called the String Factory. It was no more than the size of a living room and still there were like 400 people crowded up. The place got struck by lightning that night."

By the end of 1970, Springsteen had grown tired of Steel Mill. He brought in horns and girl singers and went from heavy rock to an R & B-inspired sound with the Bruce Springsteen Band.

Vini Lopez remembers:

"That was a whole different thing. People often talk about the Asbury Park sound and this was where it came about.

"We were there long before the Stone Pony. They claim the fame, of course, but they weren't really there. Some people talk about playing the Pony in 1973. Well, in '73 there was no Stone Pony. At that time we were playing the Student Prince."

It was really at the Upstage Club everything began.

"In the mid-'60s, as I was playing with Sonny & the Starfires, they built these Hullabaloo clubs all over the county. Every town had its bands and the bands only played in their home area. We, from Asbury, never went to Freehold. And Freehold bands never came to Asbury.

"When Tom and Margaret Potter opened the Upstage we

After Dr. Zoom and the Bruce Springsteen Band, Springsteen went solo.

"One day Bruce calls and asks if I want to record an album. He'd been signed by John Hammond."

The E Street Band was formally founded later. Springsteen released both *Greetings from Asbury Park, N.J.* and *The Wild, the Innocent & the E Street Shuffle* in 1973.

"Powerful albums. I still play those songs with the B Street Band (a local cover group), and . . . right, we did do 'Spirit in the Night' at Giants."

July 21, 2003. Vini Lopez looks Bruce Springsteen up at Giants Stadium in East Rutherford. He gets the answer he's looking for: It's OK to record the songs from the Steel Mill days, most of them written by Springsteen. Then comes the return question:

"Are you ready to do one tonight?"

Lopez and Springsteen would reunite thirty years after they each went their separate ways. "Mad Dog" Lopez meets the roar of 65,000 Springsteen fans when he sits in for Max Weinberg, playing "Spirit in the Night."

"Cool. Bruce said to me: 'We'll do it like on the album.' So that's what we did and I guess me playing it like that surprised the hell out of him. With Max they play it a whole different way. Bruce actually told me he got that old feel back again.

"That don't mean he misses the old days. I think he looks

back, but I don't think he misses it. We had a lot of fun though. I'll never forget it."

Years along the Jersey Shore, two albums with the band. That's about it. Vini Lopez left E Street in February 1974; *Born to Run* happened a year and a half later. Springsteen was on the way to becoming one of America's biggest rock stars.

"Time just went by. In '75 it had already been a long time since we wished each other good luck. There were a lot of people who thought, and there are a lot of people who still think, that we were enemies. But there were never any hard feelings between Bruce and me.

"I was fired, it's true. Because I was never the sheep. I'm not a follower, I don't get in that line. I would tend to say things 'cause first of all it was me and Danny who invited everybody in. So where are they going with me?"

"It was all about Bruce and not so much the band anymore. I guess I just went off the edge a little."

Regrets, jealousy?

"Regrets? Nah. Jealousy? Nah. . . well, sure. I'd love to have a million dollars. But I'm getting by, I've got it good."

Vini Lopez is asked if he misses the early days. He hesitates slightly, and then says:

"Yes, in certain ways. It's sad to see that kids today don't have the same opportunities as there were at the Upstage. There are clubs where they can play, but it's not a jam situation. I tried to build up something like that at T-Birds, here in Asbury, during the '80s. And it was fun. I didn't get whole bands in, just individual musicians that I would introduce to others. I told them: 'If you want to play, come on in and play. But don't come with your band to rehearse. This is where we jam.'"

Back to the present. Vini Lopez says he moonlights as a disc jockey at a local radio station and that he is working whole-heartedly on Steel Mill, which picks up the old repertoire with the same attitude.

"It started as Boccigalupe & the Bad Boys were doing a gig up in New York. Tony Amato called and asked if I wanted to jam with the band. I didn't want to do 'Johnny B. Goode' all over again, so I asked Tony if they were interested in doing some of my stuff instead. We ended up playing the old Steel Mill songs."

In the first line-up, Vini Lopez allied himself with Asbury legends John Luraschi (bass) and Ricky DeSarno (guitar), plus young keyboardist Eric Safka of Days Awake.

Next time we meet, in autumn of 2005, Lopez has brought in Bernie Brauswetter (guitar) and Bill Kacerek (keyboards) as replacements for DeSarno and Safka.

A few weeks earlier, he'd been able to celebrate the release of *The Dead Sea Chronicles*. Big Danny Gallagher, Richard Blackwell, and saxophonist Tommy Labella were all on the guest list when Lopez's unit covered Springsteen originals like "Going Back to Georgia" and "The Wind and the Rain."

Vini Lopez is proud, and says that he wants to go on tour.

"I want to get out there and play. One of the reasons we're doing Steel Mill again is that the only things left of what we did back then are some crummy recordings. There are bootlegs floating around that don't really do the band justice. Nearly nobody heard a live band do that stuff."

But he isn't interested in a concept tour that rides on the Springsteen wave:

"What was that they did a few years ago? Yeah, they sent a package deal over to Europe and launched it as The Sounds of Asbury Park. Who played? Not the real dudes. Not Sonny Kenn, Bill Chinnock, or me. It was Willie Nile and Joe Grushecky. Of course, they both know Bruce, but one's from New York and the other's from Pittsburgh."

Vini Lopez lets the new Steel Mill stand for what this band once was. If a story's to be told, it should be told in the right way.

So why did you get fired from the E Street Band?

"OK, everything went to hell with Mike Appel. Before Mike was Bruce's manager we shared everything equally within the band. Bruce's cut was no larger than anyone else's. Then Mike shows up and changes everything, without Bruce even knowing what is going on."

"I told him: 'Mike, you are not God. Guitar, drums, and organ are God.'"

Back in the parking lot of the Hawk Radio Station, we have to ask about the nickname: "Mad Dog."

Vini Lopez shows his most crooked smile:

"Everyone had nicknames from the start, and my friends always called me 'Loper.' But onstage I became 'the madman' because of my wild way of playing the drums. Energy has always been my thing, tons of energy.

"When Bruce was going to record his first album he wanted

"I was fired, it's true. Because I was never the sheep. I'm not a follower,
I don't get in that line. I would tend to say things
'cause first of all it was me and Danny who invited everybody in."

us to use the nicknames again. 'Of course,' I said. 'Good,' said Bruce, 'You're Mad Dog.'

"Mad Dog!? Thanks. Thanks a lot."

Lopez's smile widens. "Follow me," he says, and leads us down to the most classic of environments in Asbury Park: the boardwalk.

"They've done a good job here. Put down a whole new boardwalk, so that people don't fall through all the rotten planks and get hurt."

But Lopez doesn't feel unbridled optimism when it comes to the Asbury Partners and their big plans for the revitalization of Asbury Park.

"Asbury never recovered after the riots in 1970. Attempts have been made before, and those who are investing in the city today seem to be in it for real. But how can we get it back to the way it was thirty or forty years ago when the plan is to build beachfront condos?

"They sure have some work to do. The Fastlane was closed after some shootings, so who's gonna buy condos if there's a chance getting shot? Give me break, I ain't walking around down there in the dark. My pop's down here most of the time, in his wheelchair. Always carrying a bat. He knows how to defend himself."

Stone Pony, the Wonder Bar?

"The Wonder Bar, I think, is unfortunately on the chop list.

"The Pony, I don't know. The current owners are the same people taking care of the revival of Asbury Park. I am not saying that they're going to tear down the Stone Pony, but nor do I think that they see anything as sacred.

"Money talks."

FOUR MINUTES, THIRTY SECONDS—ROCK 'N' ROLL HISTORY

Ernest "Boom" Carter

In the beginning of March, while the great Nor'easter is ravaging the East Coast, Ernest Carter is sitting in his backyard, squinting in the sun. The former E Street drummer went Cali in search of a new beginning.

Summer 1970. Racial upheaval, riots. The western parts of Asbury Park are ablaze. In a basement in the neighborhood around Springwood Avenue sits Ernest Carter, age eighteen, doing what he usually does.

Armed police rush in: "We heard a boom! Where did that noise come from? Which of you has a weapon?"

Ernest Carter, now in his mid-fifties, laughs:

"It was me beating the crap out of my drums. Of course, the police heard what they heard and I assume that it might have sounded like a gunshot. I can tell you I got really scared, but my friends all thought the situation was hysterically funny. From that day I was known as 'Boom,' but it was actually Bruce that made it stick with me. And hey, it's not such a bad name for a drummer, is it?"

Vini Lopez became "Mad Dog" . . .

"Ha, ha. You've gotta do a few things to get that name."

Ernest Carter was born in Asbury Park in 1952. He lived on the west side of the tracks, the black side of town.

"Of course I have strong memories of a segregated society. But I also remember my childhood as a very happy time. Asbury Park was a fantastic place, in many ways. Especially for me, since I loved the beach and lived less than half a mile from it.

"The violence came later, around 1969. I was about sixteen or seventeen when it happened. During my high school years it was really bad. The riots were going on, and then, in 1970, the whole town exploded. The National Guard moved in on Springwood, and when people started going over to the east side all the black businesses were burnt down.

"I guess, ever since then nothing ever came back. They changed the name to Lake Avenue for a while, but nowadays it's called Springwood again. When I come back today, since I still have family in Asbury, I can just see that the town never recovered. I've heard people talking about a new beginning and I hope it works out, but . . ."

The music?

"Well, I got into it pretty much through my family. Everybody just had all this music going on. My grandfather was a piano player and my father was, among other things, a drummer back in the day.

"Then he became a photographer, he had his own studio, and he used to work for the *Asbury Park Press*. As a matter of fact he was probably the first black person to cross the tracks. I remember him taking a lot pictures of all the entertainers who used to come to this place in Asbury called the Orchid Lounge."

Ernest Carter talks about his first heroes: Jimmy Smith, Jack McDuff, Jimmy McGriff.

"I was too young to get into the clubs, but my father knew both the musicians and the club owners. I was just blown away by all this jazz, the west part of town was really jumping. Eleven years old I started playing drums, and I got to jam with players like Jack McDuff."

During the later part of the 1960s, the Upstage Club opened on Cookman Avenue. "Boom" Carter hung out with the other kids, but his father never much cared for this club where young musicians experimented with the Doors, Hendrix, and Cream.

"I was underage, and it was a pretty wild place. But Tom Potter, who owned the Upstage, was a photographer, so him and my father were pretty close. Tom was cool, he looked out for us.

"Anyway, my father really didn't dig that scene, and he would come to take me home. Most of the time I'd already snuck out the back door."

What we today call the Asbury Park sound started at late nights at the Upstage Club. But when Bruce Springsteen was touring with Child and Steel Mill, "Boom Carter" was headed someplace else, with a soul band that usually traveled in the South, backing the stars from Stax, Memphis, famous singers like Rufus and Carla Thomas.

A telephone call in February of 1974 changed everything. Ernest Carter picked up the receiver in a small club in Atlanta, Georgia. His best friend from Asbury Park, David Sancious, was on the line asking: "Bruce needs a drummer. Can you make it here?"

The first thought to go through his mind was about getting to go home to Jersey and play with Sancious. Not so much about Bruce Springsteen. Not at the time.

"I had been on tour for a pretty long time. Hadn't heard Bruce since he was playing with a ten piece band, the horns and back up singers. But I never forgot that time at Brookdale College, it was a feeling of: 'Wow, this guy can do both Jimi Hendrix and James Brown!'"

Springsteen had now officially given "Mad Dog" Lopez the axe, effective immediately. But there was a tour schedule to keep, and no one in the band was about to call it off. After three lost nights in Ohio, the replacement was on the way. Springsteen went with David Sancious's suggestion, and "Boom" Carter was hired.

"But that whole thing, playing with a rock band, was new to me. It was very lyrical and kind of over my head. I'd been in R & B and fusion jazz. Listened to a lot of Billy Cobham and wanted to fly around the drums. Now, I was in a different world. It was both fun and confusing.

"My first impression was of how focused Bruce was. He didn't allow any distraction when we were rehearsing. It was all business. The job came first, then it was OK to jam. No bull-shitting around."

Ernest Carter remembers the first rehearsals:

"We were at Garry Tallent's parents' house. I felt rushed. There was so much music to take in, but almost no time. I told Bruce I wasn't really comfortable yet. He said: 'OK, we'll just go with it. You'll manage.'"

Vini Lopez disappeared from E Street after a show in Lexington, Kentucky, on February 12, 1974. "Boom" Carter debuted, practically unrehearsed, in Cookstown, New Jersey, on the twenty-third of the same month.

"The place was completely packed. I was nervous as hell. But I kept Bruce's words in my mind the entire time: 'OK, we'll just go with it.'"

"Boom" passed the test. He was officially inducted into E Street, started to work with *Born to Run* and was out on the road with the band in a little more than half a year's time.

"The first really big gig was Phoenix, Arizona. You could feel all the anticipation out in the air. All the energy there was with Bruce. He just wanted to get going. I sat down behind the drums, amazed and dumbfounded. And didn't really come back to my senses until Bruce started counting in.

"There was always the same energy with Bruce. Always such a strong connection between him and the audience. I remember one night when he broke a guitar string and he started talking to them while he was re-stringing the guitar: 'You know, you have to be more careful with these things. Sometimes they pop.'

"I was just waiting for my chance and then I hit the snare drum at just the right moment. Both Bruce and the audience were convinced that another string had just snapped. He really lost it. Oh, shit I'm in trouble, I thought. But it was OK. Bruce had as much fun as the audience."

A few months on tour. Four minutes, thirty seconds on record. One song. Rock history.

"I might be worth a footnote?"

He's not exactly pretentious. "Born to Run" a footnote?

"Fantastic song, I know. And we really tore with it. We recorded so many versions of 'Born to Run,' but we often ended up back at square one. Bruce worked so hard, he felt that that song could be his big moment. And it probably was.

"I'd been in R & B and fusion jazz. Listened to a lot of Billy Cobham and wanted to fly around the drums. Now, I was in a different world. It was both fun and confusing."

"Mine too."

Ernest Carter says he was "ready to go."

"Yeah, but, wow! This guy was ready to drive. All those fills, all those runs. It was so cool, but the song was also killing me.

"We worked in the studio, went on tour, and then went back to the studio. I could be sitting there for hours until we finally got it right. The next day Mike Appel called: 'Ernest, can you come into the studio?' They wanted to do more takes, but only with the snare. So I thought up a groove.

"It was tough, but we got everything worked out, and when I heard the song on the radio for the first time, I understood why Bruce was so proud."

Strong memories. Great times. But, nonetheless: thanks and goodnight after some 85 shows. The finale with the E Street Band, for David Sancious and Ernest Carter, was played in the Carlton Theatre in Red Bank, New Jersey, on August 14, 1974.

"Yeah, what can I say? David and I. We were young and naive. But nor was there ever any doubt, and never any drama. It just turned out that way. David and I had a history together and we shared a vision that was maybe more jazz than rock 'n' roll.

"For me, David was always more than a friend. He was just as much a hero. So full of talent. When Hendrix, my first hero, messed around and died, David was there."

Ernest Carter returns to fusion jazz and mentions artists like Billy Cobham and Jack DeJohnette.

"David wrote music in the same tradition and we had recorded some demos down in Virginia. Mostly instrumental music. I was really close to this music. It was taking me there, you know.

"All this type of thing was already there, and everything was so obvious for David. Bruce knew this and he respected it. There were never any hard feelings in the E Street Band. It was tight. We took care of each other. And I think that Bruce, who was so focused on his music, gained even greater respect

When he told me: 'Ernest, we're getting out of here!' Well, there had never really been a choice."

But Tone would nonetheless be eaten up by the industry, as the record company said they didn't know how to market the music.

"They wanted to put labels on us. That was pretty hard on David. But we really tried. When they didn't care, regardless, it was like there was no reason to go on. Tone was over."

"Boom" Carter started over in Asbury Park. Billy Hector & the Fairlanes went well, Lance Larson's Lord Gunner Group was moving. But things never took off. At the same time, Bruce Springsteen had become an arena artist, and David Sancious won the respect of the entire world.

"Bruce? I'm just so proud of him. He really worked his ass off. He, just like David, earned all his success. Things just happen as they happen. I also had a few good years with Lance, Billy, and Southside Johnny. I played with Clarence Clemons's

"David was always more than a friend. He was just as much a hero. So full of talent. When Hendrix, my first hero, messed around and died, David was there."

for a guy like David. They both had the same talent, and the same creativity. Bruce knew that people had to make their own choices.

"David's music was so beautiful, but it didn't sound like Bruce's. I remember when we did a studio version of 'Jungleland.' It sounded more like Mahavishnu Orchestra than the E Street Band. I even think there is a take of it on some old bootleg."

It was never a question for Ernest Carter. His friend David was moving on, and the only thing to do was go with him.

"How were we to know where Bruce was heading? Good God, that sort of fame is never possible to predict.

"I have no regrets. But if I had been a few years older and a little less naive . . . I think that we would have been able to do both things, both Bruce's and David's."

On the other hand, the fusion of David Sancious, Ernest Carter, and Jersey bass player Gerry Carboy made Tone into a successful band.

"David's music has always taken me where I wanted to go.

band, the Red Bank Rockers, and I worked for both Todd Rundgren and Paul Butterfield."

Carter says he's had his ups and downs. There have been times when he was not doing so well, when the money wasn't always there. And when Asbury Park started to become a dead end.

"I married Alice, she has two boys. We were a family, and I felt like we needed to get away from Asbury. To start over somewhere else."

California is a long way, but Alice Carter had family there.

"We went back and forth for a while. Lived with friends. Then Alice got a job, she stayed, and I was there alongside her in another eight months. We moved to San Matteo."

California was the start of something new. A different life.

"But the music never stopped. It just started over."

Ernest "Boom" Carter has sat in with Bonnie Raitt and John Lee Hooker. He built his own studio in San Leandro, near Oakland. California became home for Ernest and Alice Carter.

"People bring their demos here. I help them out; as a producer, an engineer, a musician. And then I have my own thing going on. Music I've had in my head for so long but that's never really come out. Because I was always the drummer who backed others, from Bruce and David to Clarence, Billy, and Lance. And it's been more than OK, it's been fantastic. But it's not always been about my own dreams. When I left New Jersey I was like in a dark space, and I just had to get all this stuff out. I had to do my own thing."

A number of the musicians who work alongside "Boom" Carter today aren't aware of his past. Others are.

"You get different reactions. But all I can say myself is: Wow, I'm so proud. And if I ever get the chance again . . ."

"Boom" Carter laughs:

"Look man, I've got another 'Born to Run' in me."

Six or seven months. One song. Four minutes, thirty seconds. Everything that made "Boom" Carter into so much more than just a footnote in rock history.

"The time with Bruce, and 'Born to Run' more than anything. I see everything as a gift from God. It wasn't so many years ago that I found an envelope in the mailbox. There was a check in the envelope. Nothing I had expected or ever even thought of. Some old issue that got worked out, I guess.

"Sometimes, when you think of how everything that happened in the 1970s is over and done with, strange things start to happen. Then you realize you've been a part of something great. That feeling is just fine with me."

Max Weinberg

Hip hop star 50 Cent has left the building with his posse. Conan O'Brien is on his way home. Max Weinberg sits down in the Green Room dressed in a dark suit, striped shirt, and a tie. Dressed for an audience of millions. Dressed for a day at work.

When it comes down to it, Max Weinberg does the same thing as everyone else. Follows a Monday-to-Friday schedule practically the entire year round. He talks about a comfortable, privileged existence. He's never nervous, knowing he can handle the mission.

A cool attitude towards a work day in front of millions of TV viewers. Weinberg is the head of the Max Weinberg 7, the house band that swings night after night as Conan O'Brien makes his entry into the NBC studios at Rockefeller Center.

Once the cameras are off, Max Weinberg notes:

"A wise man once told me: 'Max, don't worry about it. The way it works with TV is that you are never as good or as bad as you think.'

"And that's pretty much how it is. Of course, there are demands to be met, and we work with a lot of different artists. But for me, the TV job feels pretty laid back. There's no way to compare it with Bruce's shows, which are always highly demanding, both physically and mentally. And, you know, I am not that young anymore."

It's no exaggeration to place Max Weinberg among the most famous drummers in the rock arena. Weinberg played on Meatloaf's mega-seller *Bat out of Hell*, he became a permanent member of the E Street Band in 1974, and he has been leading the seven-man orchestra that bears his name since 1993. A band with star quality from top to bottom, the Max Weinberg 7 has virtuosos, entertainers, potent singers, and then there's the guy behind the drums.

"The band was built for TV, and we've been very fortunate to do this every night. It's a full time job that doesn't leave very much time for doing anything but the Conan O'Brien show.

Although we do each year play one night at B. B. King's on 42nd Street.

"That's about it. This is the ideal platform for the Max Weinberg 7."

Not even a second album?

"We did one in I guess 1999, or was it '98? More or less as a record of what we were doing at the time. But I have no plans to make another one."

Stability. Max Weinberg comes back to that: he wants stability. In his younger days he was a drummer for hire, but during the long time apart from the E Street Band, a different angle occurred to him.

"The E Street Band had been my job for many years; it was actually my only real experience touring with a band. I felt very comfortable within the context of the band, but I could never see myself as 'a playing with a lot of sessions guy.' Nor was I interested in going on the road with different bands. Other things had become more important."

Weinberg was born in Newark and moved with his family to Maplewood, then later to South Orange.

"North Jersey had quite a different music scene when I was growing up. Very few original bands, mainly cover bands. But we also had many more places to play than they had in southern or central New Jersey.

"So the groups that I came up with were pretty much show style bands or rock bands that were playing non-original material. It was a little bit different. There was no place to jam, no place like the Upstage Club, and later I had to work pretty hard to rid myself of that reputation."

A few months before Elvis Presley made his classic appearance on the *Ed Sullivan Show*, rock's leading performer was on Milton Berle. Max Weinberg watched the show together with his teenage sisters, who were both Elvis fans.

"I guess I was always bopping around music but I think my first big moment of inspiration was watching Elvis's drummer, D. J. Fontana. The way he played sort of crystalized what I was going to do. After that I was kind of off to the races."

Weinberg's father earned a living as an attorney at law, but was also a gifted violinist. One of his sisters was a talented pianist and singer, and his mother loved the glitter of Broadway. Music and show business were always close to the family.

"In my own naiveté I always thought I was going somewhere. And up until I was twenty or twenty-one it seemed like every level was the natural level to arrive at."

Stax and Motown. The Beatles and the Stones. That's where inspiration came from. Max Weinberg wanted to play songs. Not to jam.

"Towards the end of the 60s it was a bit of a rarity to find someone who actually wanted to stay in the background. I wanted to play melodically, as accompaniment, and because of that I was able to find pretty steady work. I was a drummer for hire.

"Maybe it all went back to D. J. Fontana, but I was also aware of what abilities I had. I never thought I was a very good soloist. This was what I really wanted to do. I liked to play three-minute pop songs. And then, when the jamming and improvisation came in, I was a bit disappointed. I was able to do it, but I didn't really go for it."

A little work came from every direction. Max Weinberg played in a variety of rock bands and was hired for weddings and bar mitzvahs. In 1970, Blackstone, which was mainly composed of

And there it was. A small ad in the *Village Voice*: "Pianist and drummer wanted." Bruce Springsteen had started working on his third album, *Born to Run*, and was now looking to replace David Sancious and Ernest "Boom" Carter.

"Roy Bittan read the ad; I read the ad. But we didn't know each other. I didn't know anyone in the E Street Band. I had heard of Bruce, but had never listened to his music."

In the spring of 1974, Max Weinberg was working with a pick up group and the singer got an opening spot for Springsteen.

"But I got sick during our performance, so I went straight home and never got to see Bruce onstage."

Two pianists who knew Weinberg had already been to Springsteen's auditions. None of them made it, since the job went to Bittan. But word got back to Weinberg: "They're still looking for a drummer."

"I called up and got an audition. I went there without any expectations. The only thing I knew was that the band had a record contract, and that was a good thing."

Max Weinberg was aware of his own qualities: attentiveness, the feeling of always being able to liven up a melody. He didn't show any exaggerated respect. Had never seen anything of the Springsteen cult in Asbury Park.

"I knew the town, of course. I played there for the first time in 1967, at Mrs. Jay's. At that point the place was a go-go bar. Then I knew that things started to happen down there at the end of the 1960s, but that was not just in Asbury. A ton of interesting clubs had opened south of the Raritan Bridge."

His first impression of the band?

"For me, it was all about paying attention. I felt that they'd sort of had it auditioning drummers. There was very little small talk, Bruce got right down to business. We worked for three hours the first night, going through a lot of stuff.

"A wise man once told me: 'Max, don't worry about it.

The way it works with TV is that you are never

as good or as bad as you think.'"

Weinberg's high school buddies, got the chance to record an album for Epic Records. During this period he was also able to sign a contract with the Broadway musical *Godspell*.

"Nothing that ever got anywhere, but I certainly believed that I was going to devote myself, at all costs, to becoming a successful musician."

"Roy wasn't there. It was Bruce, Clarence, Garry, Danny, and me."

Weinberg remembers the rehearsal:

"Bruce would throw out lots of cues, and I was catching. It felt right. There was a chemistry. He liked the fact that I came from New Jersey. Because at that time most people said they came from New York, even if they grew up in Connecticut or New Jersey. But I was living in Jersey, in my parents' house, and I didn't try to hide it.

"We dressed alike, we spoke the same language. Bruce liked that."

Weinberg went out and bought the first two Springsteen albums and within a week there was a call. The second rehearsal went less well, but the job was set. There was no signing, Max Weinberg describes it all as very casual.

"Ten days later we went on tour. And that was fairly interesting, because there were no live tapes to listen to. I had only access to a recording of 'She's the One' in its original form, which sounded really different compared to how we later played it. It had a funky beat that didn't work for me, so I suggested that we put the Bo Diddley-beat to it."

The band did a couple of nights in the studio during October

1974. As Max Weinberg recalls it, one of the songs they worked on was 'A Love So Fine.' Sessions continued through the winter, and in the spring of 1975 an album was recorded.

"The band worked as an ensemble. An old-fashioned rock band built to back up Bruce's songs. I could never be certain of how his music was going to come out. But it was different,

"It was a lot of fun. I mean, it wasn't me all the paparazzis were out to get. My ride was fairly pleasant, and I really enjoyed the larger format. Gigantic stadiums. My attitude was always the bigger the better. The more people the more fun.

"The album, *Born in the U.S.A.*, was also a great boost for me. I felt for the first time that I really hit every song right. I was

"Well, Steve Van Zandt wasn't there, and that never felt right. But it was something more than that. I guess we were moving into a new era."

and I could tell that something very real was happening. In retrospect I guess I knew that we were getting to be a part of something important."

With Weinberg and Bittan in the band, the sound got bigger.

"The E Street Band definitely got a new sound. Roy's piano changed a lot."

Weinberg continues:

"Everything comes from Bruce. From his ideas. Then we all throw in our two cents. The songs for *Born to Run* were very stripped down and then heavily arranged. It was recorded with just bass, drums, and piano. I think that Bruce wrote all those songs on the piano, and for this reason the piano became an essential instrument. Then came the arrangements.

"Bruce's first two albums were not recorded that way. At that point, the whole band was generally in the studio at the same time."

Max Weinberg speaks about the learning curve. He was twenty-four, and new in the band. What happened later, with Springsteen on the cover of *Time* and *Newsweek*, was mostly just a cool thing to see.

"We may have had some recognition, but it would certainly be wrong to say we had any success. Anyway, it wasn't focused on me, and no one was making any money."

There was always respect for the band, though. The critics raved about *Born to Run*, *Darkness on the Edge of Town*, and *The River*. The audience loved the live shows.

"But when it comes down to it, you can't say we really became commercially successful before *Born in the U.S.A.* Then everyone started talking about Bossmania as the Jersey version of Beatlemania. Of course, it was less about the band than Bruce. He almost became larger than life itself, and I think that he saw most of that as a problem."

Weinberg loved to ride the gravy train.

pleased with everything I did on that album. For me this was the end of a ten year growth process, musically speaking."

Even though it continued with the *Tunnel of Love* and Amnesty tours, everyone knew that something had changed. Still, Max Weinberg didn't want to believe that Springsteen was serious when he fired the band.

"It wasn't a surprise. But it was a big shock. I reacted on different levels: horror, and, to be perfectly honest, disgust. I was shocked beyond belief. It was painful."

Nonetheless, Weinberg had seen the split coming.

"I remember the idea was already there when we were rehearsing before the *Tunnel of Love* tour, and Bruce was switching people around on stage. Everyone had had their own personal places, but now he wanted to change things."

Something was different. Max Weinberg says it's hard to pinpoint exactly what it was.

"Well, Steve Van Zandt wasn't there, and that never felt right. But it was something more than that. I guess we were moving into a new era."

In October 1989, band members were forced to face the truth. It was over, and Springsteen was going solo.

"I had felt for a while that something was significantly changing, which is why I was trying to figure out what to do with my own life."

Right after the Amnesty tour Max Weinberg went back to college, with the intention to become a lawyer.

"I was moving on to what I thought was a new career, but in the spring of 1990 I realized that I had made a mistake. I withdrew from law school and just took some time off to think about the future."

Weinberg worked for a while as a talent scout for a record label, but eventually found his way back to drumming.

"One day everything just sort of fell into place. I was walking down the street with my wife and there was Conan O'Brien. He had just gotten the job replacing David Letterman, and I told him I was looking to put together a band. We had several meetings with NBC management, and they liked what I had to say.

"I never told them I had a band. But that I had some good ideas for a band. So I put this group together, overnight, and I didn't tell anybody about the gig we were auditioning for. But you know, we pulled it off. We've now been doing this since August of 1993."

Max Weinberg says that he found his path. NBC became home, and was a generous employer to boot.

"I have to be grateful. When Bruce got in touch with me again and said we should go on tour, I got the OK from NBC. And the same thing happened over and over again. I hope it can continue this way, but I can never take anything for granted. This job is my everyday life."

Touring with the E Street Band is something completely different. Max Weinberg says that the conditions, compared with earlier years, have become much better.

"We can travel with our families. Everyone in the band has

"It's about riding on the bus, it's about talking music. Bands have never been about great musicians, anyway. Even if they don't get along all the time, they're about a common musical orientation. It also comes from individual playing styles and how each other's changed each other."

"In the E Street Band we all have very common musical roots. We know where Bruce's music comes from. Today, when we come together, it sometimes takes us a while to get the right feeling. But we know it's there. Somewhere."

Work in the studio has also changed.

"Even for *The River* we worked most of it out together. With *The Rising* practically every song was much further along as I got to the studio."

Max Weinberg says that recording the song "Born in the U.S.A." counts as one of many highlights. The Amnesty tour also ranks among those special memories that he'll always carry with him.

"Going to countries like Zimbabwe and the Ivory Coast. Experiencing a New Delhi, India, with poverty and wealth right next to another. I think everyone who was on that tour could say that they lived some of the high points of their life. Maybe not musically. The greatest benefit was being able to see the world. And to understand it."

> ## "It's about riding on the bus, it's about talking music. Bands have never been about great musicians, anyway. Even if they don't get along all the time, they're about a common musical orientation."

become more skilled, and there is an all-around higher standard. Before it was so much about energy. I experience the shows being much stronger now, musically speaking. That's something I appreciate.

"Then it's another thing to be put to the challenge every night. Mentally and physically. I'm not twenty-four anymore."

He says that if there's one thing the E Street Band really knows how to do, it's how to play Bruce Springsteen's songs.

"I would also like to point out a show in East Berlin in 1988. One year later the Wall came down, but we got to see what a bleak effect communism had. And we got to see faces that revealed how much that evening meant for thousands of people.

"Bruce often talks about serving the public. Serving the listener, everyone who comes to the show. I share this idea."

THE HOMEWORK GUY

Nils Lofgren

Born in Chicago, Illinois. Brought up in Maryland. Welcomed on E Street, and adopted by the Jersey audience. Nils Lofgren says: "I must have played every bar and every nightclub along the Jersey Shore. I think that makes me an honorary New Jerseyian."

A hotel lobby in Copenhagen, Denmark, May 2006. Nils Lofgren is touring solo. His only companion is called "Boomer," a guitar tech who's also in charge of sound and lighting. Bruce Springsteen has given the E Street Band a break, but it has been a long time since Nils Lofgren had a large record company backing his solo efforts. Taking his own band around the world has become way too expensive.

Lofgren is a bit homesick, but doing well. He finally found the time to record his own album, *Sacred Weapon*, and he feels good about the fact that there's still an audience anxiously awaiting his music.

"It's kind of fun after a year and a half doing *The Rising*. Now, instead of rushing things, I have given myself permission to move slow and to find a balance for my wife and son, my two dogs and two cats. I slowly put together twenty-five new songs, and just eased in to it."

"Eased in to it," he says. This is not just about a new life in the Arizona desert, it's also about the artist finding a new tool for his songwriting.

"I have to thank the E Street Band, because once we got Steven back in the band we had four guitar players. So I started becoming the swing man, learning the pedal steel, dobro, lap steel, and bottleneck.

"I think I'm a good beginner now, thanks to taking lessons from some great musicians. One of them was Mike Auldridge, a very famous dobro player who happens to live in Maryland, where I grew up.

"Then this Jersey guy, Marc Muller, who usually works for Shania Twain, gave some crash course lessons. He understood my problem: five weeks away from the tour, and here I am trying to learn a new instrument. I rented a pedal steel and it turned out to be pretty complicated."

"The good beginner" continues:

"I've played a lot of slide and I've finger picked my whole life. The problem was getting used to the metal. Putting on this metal glove felt terrible. Then I got a few days off and went down to Maryland to see Mike Auldridge for some extensive dobro lessons. I asked Mike: 'Can't I do this without the metal?' He said: 'Nils, you're gonna regret it. 'Cause once you're starting to get good at it, you're not gonna be able to get the sounds you want.' That was good advice.

"Later, I also learned how to play the banjo, and with all these new instruments I surprised myself when I started writing songs for the album. I realized I had all these new sounds to work with. It's neat, after all these years, to be able to do something new."

It's about freedom. A matter of self-esteem and openness.

"You have to give yourself permission. That's one of the things I love about Bruce and the E Streeters. Like myself he's pretty fearless in front of an audience, and that gives you an energy to look for special things. The audience don't care if there are mistakes as long as you're looking for some kind of magic."

Lofgren says he learned all of that before he was twenty. He loves the stage, the audience encounter. Sometimes it's hard to find the patience it takes to work in the studio.

"It's a big challenge making records, but the stage is like home. That's where something very healing happens."

Life on the road?

"Well, to be honest I got tired of traveling twenty-five years ago. It gets harder and harder to say goodbye and leave home."

The name has a Swedish ring to it, after his father. The Mediterranean features are from his Italian mother. But Nils Lofgren was born on the south side of Chicago.

"Every kid in the neighborhood played the accordion. I started when I was five and after learning all the polkas and waltzes I wanted to move on. I had some great classical training."

He was eight when his father got a job in the D.C. area. It was there that Lofgren grew up, got his first guitar, and it wouldn't be long before music started paying the bills.

"That would never had happened if it wasn't for playing the accordion. But yeah, I hit the road at seventeen and just within a few months I wound up in L.A. with David Briggs. Then I followed him to San Francisco and hooked up with Neil Young. Actually, we did a lot of the Grin recordings in San Francisco."

Grin, Lofgren's band, dominated the Maryland club scene. In California, David Briggs would become his producer and mentor.

"David was like a big brother and an amazing source of inspiration. I wrote the song 'Mr. Hardcore' about him way back, because David's been dead a while and I really miss him. Lately, as Neil Young turned sixty, I attended a surprise party

in New York and there were these pictures of David. It was very emotional and I felt I finally had to put the song on record."

Seventeen years old and a professional musician. But still just a young kid, ready to give up everything to live the rock 'n' roll dream.

"Where I came from, everybody loved the Beatles and Hendrix, but people didn't think that's what you'd do for a job. When I ran off to Greenwich Village I wasn't running away from my family, because they were beautiful. I just felt I wasn't a child anymore.

"Guess the whole community thought what I did was terrible. The only kids who dropped out of high school were like the petty criminals who had gotten their girlfriends pregnant and worked at the gas station. So I felt a lot of pressure and I needed to pay my own way."

After no more than eight days in Manhattan, Lofgren fell ill and traveled back to Maryland with his tail between his legs.

"My folks were very supportive. But I didn't want to burden them, so I paid rent and worked really hard. As I got well we took Grin back to New York and then decided that the band needed to get to Los Angeles.

"One night, in D.C., I snuck backstage at this club called the Cellar Door to meet with Neil Young and Crazy Horse. They were kind enough to let me hang out. Neil said he liked my songs and told me to look him up in L.A. He was a great source of encouragement.

"Now, it's been thirty-eight years on the road and that's a little scary. Fortunately, I'm even more excited now about singing in front of an audience. That helps when you're being homesick and still need to pack your bag every morning."

Lofgren says that he fell in love with rock 'n' roll when he was thirteen, playing Beatles songs on his accordion.

"Then, at fifteen, I played the same songs on the guitar. Thanks to the Beatles opening the door I discovered Motown and Stax/Volt, Muddy Waters, and Howlin' Wolf. I loved it all and by the time I was seventeen I started kind of having a style of my own. My writing was inspired by all the '60s bands, and ten years of studying music had given me a great sense of melody. The accordion brought out a maturity.

"Also, I was becoming my own person. I was at this impressionable young age, just crazy trying to be a pro. And I learned so much from David Briggs and Neil Young, working on *After the Goldrush*, *Tonight's the Night*, and the Crazy Horse album with Danny Whitten. They told me: 'Hey, don't ever be afraid to be yourself. Find your own way.'

"I guess I'm still doing that."

In 1975, after four albums with Grin, Lofgren launched a solo career on A&M Records that took off quickly.

"Well, my first albums got a lot of attention. But it was never like your top five heavy rotation. I never got to move from the club scene to 8,000-seat theaters. That's because I never had a hit record. It wasn't like when people get sick of you because the radio is playing your song twenty times a day.

"It's a silly dream, especially since I haven't had a record company for twelve years. But you know, I am a dreamer. I honor playing for 300 or maybe 400 people, but I make records to share."

His first solo record set the music press spinning. *Cry Tough* was the following effort that lived up to expectations. So when it became known that Mick Taylor wanted to leave the Rolling Stones, Nils Lofgren, with the song 'Keith Don't Go,' dedicated to the Glimmer Twin, became a man of many rumors.

"Being a long time fan I did everything I could just to get an audition. I knew that Ronnie Wood was the man for the job, but Ronnie had told me that he was going to stay with Rod Stewart and the Faces.

"Anyway, Ronnie gave me Keith's phone number. I called him up and I must have sounded like some babbling fan, begging him to let me audition. Keith was honest, he told me: 'We want Ronnie but Ronnie won't take the job.' He had heard about me,

"It's not that he fell down. God knows I kept falling down all the time when I was drinking. What I can't understand is how the hell did he get up there?"

The Stones never happened for Lofgren. Instead, in 1983 he did a stadium tour with Neil Young, and one year later Bruce Springsteen called. Lofgren, from Maryland, would be welcomed into a New Jersey brotherhood.

Was it all as simple as that? Were there any complications along the way? Lofgren says that he never gave up his own dreams. It was not a question of exclusive dedication to the music of Bruce Springsteen.

"I love being in great bands, and one thing I know about people like Bruce Springsteen, Neil Young, Sting, and even Ray Charles, is that nobody stays on the road 300 days a year. Everyone has a life and family. So, when you get a chance to play in one of these great bands you know that it's good for your musical soul.

"When Bruce asked me to join, I was thrilled. And since I was used to being the band leader it really was liberating just to be one of the guys. When you're the boss you have to get involved in every little decision. Like stepping in between two roadies getting cranky or being the psychiatrist when the ego of one band member explodes. None of those things have anything to do with music. So yes, it's been good to take a break from all that while playing with Ringo Starr or Bruce."

Steven Van Zandt had left. In stepped Lofgren, already an established solo artist.

"It's not that he fell down. God knows I kept falling down all the time when I was drinking. What I can't understand is how the hell did he get up there?"

he knew that I had this song, 'Keith Don't Go,' and he told me to do the audition. But that never happened, because Ronnie reconsidered. My theory is that Rod said to him: 'OK, Ronnie we have a great thing here. But hey, we're talking about the Rolling Stones. You don't wanna turn that offer down.'"

Nils Lofgren is still a fan, and he kept a close eye on what was going on with the European part of the Stones' 2006 tour, since Keith Richards almost got killed falling out of a palm tree vacationing on the Fiji islands.

"I wasn't looking to replace Steve, just to cover the guitar parts and the singing. Then, it was good when Patti joined the band, because I don't have that high rough voice. I think that Bruce and Steve really have their own sound, it's a bit like Mick and Keith.

"Steve left because he needed to do his own thing. And I guess there was more a feeling of relief when they actually found someone who could do the job. I've been seeing the E Street Band play since the early '70s, and I've been a fan.

"Over the years I've also gotten to know Bruce pretty well and I had met all the others. They always seemed friendly. Bruce knew that I loved his music and I spent two days jamming with the band to find out how it felt. I think they all realized that I wasn't doing this as a favor. The job was, and still is, just as much a favor to me. It's really a beautiful thing."

When the E Street Band reunited, Steve Van Zandt came back.

"That was good, because all I ever wanted to do was to give Bruce a few more tools. Arguably I would say that we are the greatest tool box in rock 'n' roll, and I think that Bruce is the master carpenter."

Springsteen, the live artist, is known for throwing in some curve balls during each and every show. Nils Lofgren is just as known for providing the steadiness in the band.

"Bruce is the leader, but to be in such a great band I have

to feel my contribution should be as important as anyone else's onstage. I can't change what Bruce does. Sometimes he calls me into his dressing room and says: 'Hey, we might do these songs tonight, let the guys know.' It's not always me, though. He might just as well tell Danny or the tour manager. And Roy's a true genius, he remembers everything ever done by the band.

"It's been twenty-two years, but I'm still the newest guy in the band and maybe that's why I keep a big notebook with charts. Also, being one of the main singers it's natural to find Patti and Soozie and say: 'If we're gonna do this, who's gonna sing what?'"

He comes back to the idea of connecting with the audience:

"Onstage I wanna feel like it's my band and with the E Street Band you can't do better. When I was new everyone kept their doors open, so now I try and return the same attitude. I don't ever wanna feel uncertain onstage and if anyone else has that feeling I wanna be there for them. I'm kind of the homework guy."

Nils Lofgren was well prepared when *Born in the U.S.A.* pushed Springsteen into stadium format.

"Well, it was interesting, because I had done the stadium thing with Neil Young in 1983, and already in 1978 or 1979 when I was touring with the Who, the Stranglers, and AC/DC. Bruce asked me about it, but since he's such a great band leader he fell into it pretty quick. There are no short cuts and now it's all very organic and a natural thing."

Almost forty years of being on the road. A long life in rock 'n' roll has taught Nils Lofgren that there is always a price to pay.

"Today, when I walk out on stage it has a more healing potential than ever. The rest of the day is the work. For the first time in my life I have a home I don't like to leave, but I try and think of how lucky I am to have a family to miss while I'm away.

"Me and my wife, Amy, settled down in Scottsdale, Arizona, ten years ago, and since then, leaving home is the hardest part. I get tired as hell, but I love the show. And it's not dangerous work, sometimes it just gets lonely."

He was welcomed on E Street and feels as though he's been adopted by the Jersey audience.

"Starting out with Grin in 1968, I toured the Northeast and I guess I traveled up and down the Jersey Turnpike as much as Bruce did. I spent years doing that and I must have played every bar and every nightclub along the Jersey Shore. I think that makes me an honorary New Jerseyan.

"Actually, Amy is from Jersey. We first met at the Stone Pony twenty-five years ago. At the end of the night I found her on my bus, and we said goodbye on the Asbury Park boardwalk at six AM. in the morning. She was like nineteen then.

"Fifteen years later, playing a bar in Scottsdale, she approached me after the show: 'Hi, remember me?' I said: 'Yeah, you're the one that got away. What happened?' This was at a time when we were both at the end of divorces."

The boardwalk in Asbury Park has been renovated. The Stone Pony is still open. Asbury is looking at a brighter future, but it still has a long way to go. Nils Lofgren says:

"Even by the late '60s, when I was playing with Grin and Bruce was in Steel Mill, Asbury Park was downhill. I guess the heyday was more like the '40s, and maybe the '50s. When I first came to town the place was already a wreck. Kind of a beautiful, haunted boardwalk town with this club that's really just another bar, but with so much history.

"I love playing the Pony. It's like family."

Home is Scottsdale, Arizona, nonetheless. Or Garrett Park, in Montgomery County, Maryland. Nils Lofgren even has his own day here, August 25.

"Yeah, what can I say? That was sweet and embarrassing. They have this summer festival series in a park outside the Strathmore Arts Centre, where local singers used to pay tribute to different artists. Ronnie Newmeyer, who plays bass for me, suggested a Nils Lofgren day and I guess some local politician thought it was a good idea. I didn't even know about it myself until I came home. But it turned out to be a great day, with all these musicians, including my brothers. And the most beautiful thing happened when Bob Berberich, my brother Tom and myself [were] joined by Bob Gordon's son onstage.

"Bob Gordon was the bass player for Grin and a very strong personality in the band. He's dead now, we all miss him, and it never felt right to reunite Grin without Bob. Not until it turned out that his son, like Bob, is a bass player. So on that very occasion we did the first Grin show since the band broke up in 1975."

Nils Lofgren laughs and says:

"I don't know if this is going to become an annual thing; you should never underestimate politicians. But they gave me a plaque or something and in a way it was too bad I had given up drinking, 'cause I could have gotten some good mileage out of this in the local bars."

BLEECKER ST
UMANOV GUITARS 273
MATT UMANOV GUITARS

Soozie Tyrell

In late summer of 2004, Bruce Springsteen made his first political statement. The Vote for Change tour was launched in opposition to the reelection bid of President George W. Bush, and with a few days left until the premiere, the E Street Band regrouped in Convention Hall, Asbury Park. Before rehearsals, Springsteen went around and introduced guest artist John Fogerty. When they got to Soozie Tyrell he said: "John, meet the new inductee."

As we meet, those words have only just sunken in. Soozie Tyrell has been best friends with Patti Scialfa since the late 1970s. She's worked with Bruce Springsteen off and on since 1992, and was on the road with the E Street Band during the entire *Rising* tour of 2002–2003. But this new thing, getting inducted, is a mark of honor that stirs the soul.

It's a tired, but happy, Soozie Tyrell who arrives by taxi where Bleecker meets Cornelia in Greenwich Village, NYC. She is worn out, and openly admits it.

The Vote for Change tour went on for a couple of intensive weeks. A few hours ago, Tyrell wound up rehearsals with Southside Johnny. There are plans for her to do a few acoustic shows in Europe with Southside and Bobby Bandiera.

The day-to-day rhythm is just what Soozie Tyrell needs. But for the moment, coffee seems to be the best cure.

"White Lines," the title track of Soozie Tyrell's first, and to date only, solo album tells the story of her childhood.

"Well, they called us Army brats. Sort of a breed of our own."

The Army sent the family to different bases throughout the U.S. and Asia. Young Soozie caught hold of the wind and followed the white lines along the road.

"That's how we lived until Mom and Dad retired. And then we were left on to the wild blue yonder, the civilian world. But that was the best thing that could have happened."

Tyrell continues:

"Dad wanted to settle down in Florida. I went to high school in Fort Myers, and as much as I loved that town, I knew musically it was a dead end for me. At seventeen I spent the next two summers taking music and art classes at the local college and I was roaming up and down Florida playing with different bands."

At that time, Florida felt like a musical deathtrap. But everything would be different in New York, where Soozie Tyrell came to audition for a band at the age of nineteen.

"I had my ambitions. But coming to New York at nineteen, as they say, the first time out of the fold, was very overwhelming. It takes time to get used to this city, especially when you don't know anyone."

At first she slept on the floor at Songbird Sounds, a studio that was strictly used for rehearsals.

"What was wonderful about living there were the people I met. The band Blondie came there, the Nitty Gritty Dirt Band, David Sanborn. And all these fantastic studio musicians: Hiram Bullock, Steve Jordan, Cliff Carter, Will Lee.

"I didn't quite have the respect for myself back then, the way I do now. But it really was a great place to expand. I played some violin, and did a lot of background singing."

Violin and rock 'n 'roll have never made an obvious marriage, even if Jean-Luc Ponty and Charlie Daniels broke ground in this department long before Soozie Tyrell came onto the scene; long before she was able to help create a more nuanced sound for Springsteen. A sound that had been missing from E Street since the mid-'70s, when Suki Lahav was touring with the band.

"Today my instrument has been given an entirely natural part. Just during the Vote for Change tour alone, there were three big names, Bruce, Dave Matthews, and John Mellencamp, who were using the violin outside of a string ensemble. I think writers outside of country and folk music are catching on to what a beautiful contribution certain violin players can make."

Classically trained? Of course, but there were always other dreams.

"Rock 'n' roll would be my niche, I knew that early on. But I'm just as interested in playing country, Americana, and blues."

Blues?

"Yes, absolutely. Why not? The violin becomes an extension of my voice. It's that way regardless of whether I'm working with my own music or someone else's. I listen to how the songs are written and try to see where that voice belongs. You have to be careful, so that you don't step on a lead singer or stand in someone else's way. The violin can take a lot of space because it's like another lead vocal. You have to find your way."

Bruce Springsteen hears that voice, and understands how to use it. Soozie Tyrell was given a more prominent role over the course of *The Rising* and Vote for Change tours.

"The E Street Band has such a huge sound, so in that type of context I mostly approach my violin as a keyboard. I listen to what Danny Federici does on the B3 organ and what Roy Bittan is doing with his piano. Then I try to paint with big, careful strokes on that canvas. I try not to step on anybody's toes, but instead add something that gives a new dimension to Bruce's sound. I think I've accomplished that."

During the Vote for Change tour Tyrell became a lead figure alongside Springsteen with an unstoppable re-arrangement of "Johnny 99."

"Such a blast! Everyone stands up front and jams with Bruce. The feeling when he just lets me go is transcending. During *The Rising* tour I was given the same chance with different songs practically every night."

Soozie Tyrell traveled the world with the E Street Band and considers the experience invaluable:

"It was a fantastic tour in every way. I have to give a certain amount of credit to John Cooper, whose sound engineering showed that the E Street Band does not just build on a heavy wall of sound. That big wall is there, but John's work makes it possible to define every individual instrument. I almost look upon him like another band member.

"You know, I've had the chance to see Bruce's shows ever since the *Born in the U.S.A.* tour, and I have to say that *The Rising* felt unique. I mean, right in the middle of such a huge sound you can actually hear Steve Van Zandt's mandolin clear as a bell."

At Springsteen's side also appears Nils Lofgren, who Soozie Tyrell greatly admires.

"I can't say enough good things about Nils. A wonderful, caring person who, along with Patti, helped me immensely during *The Rising* tour. He's also the most humble lead guitarist I've ever met. *Rolling Stone* magazine ranked the fifty best guitarists without naming Nils, and that's a huge mistake."

Soozie Tyrell's journey to E Street actually began close to the very spot where we are meeting, on Bleecker Street in Greenwich Village, 1977.

"Towards the end of that summer, I met Patti for the first time. She was performing with Hiram Bullock and Cliff Carter at a small club uptown; I think there must have been eight or ten people in the audience. I really met Patti as a songwriter, and that's how I've always known her. A great songwriter with a lovely and unique voice to boot. When she first joined the E Street Band it was as a background singer but when she

**"We didn't have much money, so during breaks it was onion soup,
tons of bread, and some wine at various bars and cafés."**

released her albums, *Rumble Doll* and then *23rd Street Lull-aby*, everyone knew she had much more to give.

"We performed a tour following the release of *23rd Street Lullaby* and it was so much fun to play her songs live with that band. Especially when we opened for Jackson Browne and Bruce during the Vote for Change tour. Nils was in the band as well as Steve Jordan, Cliff Carter, and a host of wildly talented musicians.

"Bruce showed his appreciation by extending Patti's show at the Meadowlands from a few songs to a full set."

On the streets of Greenwich Village, on the corner of Bleecker and Christopher, Soozie Tyrell, Patti Scialfa, and, later on, Lisa Lowell had their most important scene.

"We didn't have much money, so during breaks it was onion soup, tons of bread, and some wine at various bars and cafés. We met writers, journalists, and other interesting people. We were probably kind of interesting ourselves."

Trickster (Tyrell, Scialfa, Lowell) wrote their own songs and played for an audience where eighty percent of the men were homosexual.

"It was hard to get a date back then. The three of us toget-her formed a very strong sisterhood that garnered respect with the gay audience, but at the same time I think we scared off quite a few of the straight men.

"It's never been easy for women in rock 'n 'roll, and to a certain extent it's still that way. You want to hold on to your femininity, but yet you want to show that you're strong.

"Today, I've reached a point where I don't really care what people say. I know who I am and what I want to do."

Soozie Tyrell starts to tell us about a night, or rather an early morning, when she was walking by a bakery with Scialfa and Lowell.

"Lisa started flirting with the baker, so that Patti and I could grab two baguettes. This was at the same time that Ian Dury was topping the charts with 'Hit Me with your Rhythm Stick,' and we sang that tune while laughing down the street and bopping each other with the bread.

"We came up to City Limits, a nightclub on the corner of Seventh Avenue and Tenth Street. It was four o'clock in the morning, the bar was closing, but we really wanted to get in. One of the owners came to the door and said: 'Sorry girls, we're closed.'

"The three of us started to sing, 'Rock around the Clock' or something, and he finally let us in.

"We became weekend regulars for about three months. First we'd play on the streets, then in the wee hours we'd go to City Limits and get to perform a set on the dance floor after the band on stage had finished. Then we'd promptly pass the fiddle case for gratuities. People were really drunk and never ready to go home so we did very well.

"One night I told the owner that I had a country band, which wasn't altogether true. He booked us, and gave me four weeks to pull the band together. You should know that these were the days when you did four one-hour sets a night so there were a lot of songs we had to learn to fill those sets."

The eight-piece band, Soozie and High in the Saddle, was a local success. Crowds lined up outside City Limits, even in the dead of winter.

Patti Scialfa had already auditioned for the E Street Band. She got to know Springsteen through working with David Sancious, and also Bobby Bandiera who, in the beginning of the 1980s, was the front man in the (second) hottest band in Asbury Park.

"Bobby had Cats on a Smooth Surface and he used to have Patti sing with the band at the Stone Pony. Bruce loved that band and made it into a tradition joining them onstage almost every Sunday. It was then and there that Bruce and Patti be-came friends.

"And, if I remember correctly, Patti actually sang back-ground when Bruce was recording *Born in the U.S.A.* It wasn't anything that ended up on the album, but Bruce called her anyway one day before they were going to start rehearsing for the tour in Philly. He didn't promise anything, but wanted to see what Patti might be able to contribute. She had two or three days to learn his entire catalog, which you know is quite vast."

Soozie Tyrell wished her friend good luck, but also dares to admit that there was a little bit of envy involved.

"It was like destiny, because she always wanted to sing with Bruce. And I'm sure I was a bit envious. Who wouldn't be?"

Tyrell got to know Springsteen herself during the *Born in the U.S.A.* tour, through Scialfa, of course.

"Later, after they had recorded *Tunnel of Love*, we were invited to his place for a type of audition, I guess. Bruce brought out the catalog, this big thick book, and wanted to hear how my violin might sound with his music. I expected that we'd go through two or three songs, but we kept going for what seemed like hours, and he was smiling all the time."

Springsteen's management asked if Tyrell would be interested in joining the *Tunnel of Love* tour.

"For some reason it didn't work out; I'm not quite sure of the details. Bruce brought in a horn section and I was working

with Buster Poindexter at the time. There was a scheduling conflict and I ended up not doing the tour."

Soozie Tyrell was first heard on a Springsteen album in 1992 (backing vocals on *Lucky Town*), and in 1995 she would be given a bigger role as violinist on *The Ghost of Tom Joad*.

Then, in 2004, there was an induction: "When Bruce introduced me to John Fogerty I looked at Patti and said: 'Oh, I wasn't aware of that.'"

And Patti said?

"Me neither."

How'd it feel?

"Oh, my God. I was so happy to finally be asked to tour with *The Rising*, and at that point it was clear that I was an addition, and not a member of the band. But I think the way Bruce's fans embraced me meant a lot. I also imagine that Bruce saw that I actually had something to add, and for that I'm ever grateful."

The E Street connection will open new markets for the solo artist Soozie Tyrell. There will be a follow-up to *White Lines* before long.

"I want to get back in the studio as soon as possible. I hope to record many albums to come. One thing I want to accomplish is a raw-roots-Soozie-Tyrell-belts-'em-out-album; another is to make an instrumental recording. When you've been on the road for such a long time, it's nice to relax with music that doesn't necessarily have lyrics. Sometimes I listen to Celtic music, and I've said to myself: 'Soozie, why don't you make a record like this?'"

But she knows that nothing is obvious in the music industry of the twenty-first century.

"I think I would do very well, especially in Europe, with the right connections. But it's not easy to find backing, or get radio play, given the way the industry looks today. Not once you're over thirty-five. Even Bruce was surprised when *The Rising* went platinum and got so much airplay. He kept saying: 'At my age.'"

"Oh please," I said. "You're Bruce Springsteen!"

ASBU
PRIVATE
PROPERTY
NO TRESPASSING

RY·PARK,

Toby Scott

Backstage at the Wachovia Center in Philadelphia, October 1, 2004. Tonight Bruce Springsteen & the E Street Band are kicking off the Vote for Change tour, with R.E.M. as their opening act. There is a lot of anticipation in the air. In his own little universe of mixing tables, Toby Scott seems calm enough. Almost like it's just another day at the office: "Bruce wants me here tonight to record the concert. I have no idea if that means we're going to be using the material, but he wants me here. So here I am."

He knows the U.S. map well. With a father in the Air Force, Toby Scott grew up in so many different places that he hardly remembers them all.

"For a while we lived in southern California, then in South Carolina, Texas, Nebraska, central California, and later we came back to southern California. So it was there, in Santa Barbara, that I went to high school and college. And it was there that I started to become interested in rock 'n' roll."

There is nothing extraordinary in Toby Scott's path to music. He, like so many others, thought that Elvis Presley was cool. Cool enough for a kid to get a guitar, then temporarily switch to the drums, but soon end up playing the guitar again.

"I was kind of a hippie and I probably looked like a rock musician, because one day in high school a guy came up and asked if I wanted to be in his band."

"Fine. I play guitar," said Scott.

"We've already got a guitarist, but we need a bass player. What do you think?"

Toby Scott bought himself a bass guitar and got the job.

But it wouldn't be long before he came to see other opportunities. First as a manager for various local bands, two of which he actually sent on their way to audition for recording contracts in Los Angeles.

"They got the invitation and went to the studio, but nothing became of it in the end. In one case it was because the singer got stage fright, and in the other there was internal doubt about whether or not they were actually ready. In any case, it was these events that got me interested in recording music."

Toby Scott was friends with Greg Elmore, the drummer in Quicksilver Messenger Service. He got to join the band in the studio, where he also met producers and engineers.

"Then I got my own recording equipment and started working with some people I knew. I became an assistant, and got a sense of what needed to be fixed. Later I learned about producing, but from the very beginning it was only about sharing opinions."

Today Scott is a well-known and respected name in the recording industry. Bob Dylan, Natalie Merchant, the Replacements, Steve Perry, David Sancious, Little Steven, and Steve Cropper are some of the artists who have depended on Scott. Still, it's the decades spent with Bruce Springsteen, more than anything, that established him.

"I've had two different roles: producer and engineer. But with Bruce I have only ever been the engineer, and it has been a calm, comfortable job. We talk, but when you have known someone for that long you also learn how he thinks. The way things work are I just record his songs as I hear them."

Working with Springsteen turned Toby Scott into a fixture on the Jersey Shore music scene. He remembers hitting the bars in Asbury Park, back in the mid '80s, while places like the Fastlane and the Xanadu were still open.

There were also various Jersey rockers who acquired his services.

"I got a call from CBS regarding John Eddie in 1985. They gave me a budget, I was producing all his demos and then they ended up signing him to a different producer.

"Another guy that comes to mind is Joe D'Urso. He's truly amazing the way he plays those little bars in Jersey, and then he goes on tour to England, Ireland, Italy, and Sweden, a couple of times a year. I ran into the guy in Helsinki during *The Rising* tour and I asked what the hell he was doing there?

"Joe said: 'Well, they got me as the after-show act.'"

Toby Scott says that he would gladly take on producing younger artists.

"Because I like working from an instructional perspective. It's great to lend a helping hand where there's talent. There are always things to change, details that give an improved final impression. I think it's about preventing mistakes and helping someone to take the next step.

"There are two kinds of producers. One that turns producing into the entire creative process. The artist wrote the song, he planted the seed. Then the producer comes in and changes everything without the artist's input. That's when the artist just becomes a tool.

"I belong to the other school. The only thing I want to do is give the artist a push in the right direction."

Toby Scott and Bruce Springsteen first met in 1978. Scott was the head engineer in Chuck Plotkin's Los Angeles studio, and at the time Plotkin was busy with Springsteen's follow-up to *Born to Run*.

"Chuck and Bruce were working on *Darkness on the Edge of Town* in New York and when Chuck came back to Los Angeles he wanted me to lend a hand with the final mixing. I didn't know that much about Bruce back then. He had, of course, already had his big breakthrough with *Born to Run*, but Bruce's popularity was still much greater on the East Coast than it was on the West Coast."

Scott thought: "Nice guy, good songs. . . ." But that's where it ended. Life went on; it was business as usual.

Two or three years passed. Chuck Plotkin, who had been mixing *Darkness*, was given the same offer for the recording of *The River*.

"But Chuck had already said to them while working on *Darkness*: 'I am the producer. Not an engineer, not a mixer. I don't want to mix any more albums.' So Chuck recommended me, and Bruce and Jon chose to go with his judgment, since they were not entirely satisfied with the results of earlier mixes.

"I assume that I gave them what they wanted, because when the tour came through Los Angeles a few months later, Chuck asked what I was up to for the next few days. Bruce wanted to record a concert in Phoenix and I ended up working on different shows for the next six months."

After the tour Toby Scott was heading into a project with a French artist. But the same day that the recording was slated to begin, the producer cancelled the entire thing.

And while he was sitting there thinking "now what?" Chuck Plotkin entered the studio. The good news: Bruce Springsteen and Steve Van Zandt are in town to talk about the mixing of *On the Line*, a Gary U.S. Bonds album they had produced.

"I did the job and it turned out that Steve wanted me to mix his first solo album, *Men Without Women*. After a week with Steve there was Bruce on the phone: 'Excuse me, but I would like to start working on my album. Not here in L.A., but in New York.'

"So we moved Steve's project to New York and worked in parallel with what would eventually become *Born in the U.S.A.* After a while it started getting tricky to keep both projects going in one studio. We took Steven's recording to the Hit Factory and worked there six hours a day. At night I was back with Bruce at the Power Station, recording until two in the morning."

The efforts paid off. With *Born in the U.S.A.*, the album and the tour, came success and money.

"Yeah, wow. But I didn't think about it that much. I had already realized that Bruce was really an icon in this industry. From the first album and until *Darkness on the Edge of Town*, he had gotten to enjoy a certain degree of renown. But Bruce was not a big-selling artist until 'Hungry Heart' from *The River* made it to the top of the charts. Then almost nothing happened with *Nebraska* and suddenly everything exploded with *Born in the U.S.A.*"

Toby Scott says that he still treasures the *Nebraska* recordings, and that those songs remain among Springsteen's finest. But he was not present during the recordings, which Springsteen managed together with guitar tech Mike Batlan on a four-channel Teac tape recorder. It might be that Toby Scott had his doubts regarding the Spartan sound profile?

"I'll never forget when Bruce pulled a cassette tape out of his pocket and asked: 'Toby, can we master this?' I just replied honestly: 'Yes, we can.'

"Because the thing is about sticking to a philosophy. It's always about what the artist is trying to communicate. I actually said to Bruce the other day: 'Show me an album someone picks up in a store because of the way it was recorded.' That's not the way it works. You like the song, you like the artist. How the music is put there is kind of irrelevant. Hopefully it's done nicely.

"I've got this little story. A friend of mine asked me: 'What do you think about alternative music?' I said: 'Well, what do you mean alternative?' I got to listen to this radio station for a while and then I answered: 'Now I know what alternative music is. It's the alternative to good music.' 'Cause what I got to hear was terrible. The structure of the songs were so difficult, I couldn't

remember anything five minutes after I'd heard it. There were just too many parts. You could barely hear the vocal, the guitar was all blurry. I would say that this was one single occasion, the one exception, where the engineering part really could do it."

Scott gets back to the philosophy: "I'm there to record the artist. His performance, his viewpoint. It's his concept. With Bruce and others, there have been times when they've said: 'Hey, record this.' And I would go: 'Wow, what am I supposed to do? But OK, let's try it.'

"Because I feel that until we're finished with it and he goes 'OK, this is pretty much the way I wanted it to sound,' I don't know what he may have on his mind. It's not for me to say: 'Oh, you can't sound like this or that.' It was like that with *The Rising*, the way he wanted his voice to sound. He may have something, and I can't always be sure of what that is. He's the artist. I'm the engineer, that you have to consider and keep in mind."

Could it be that simple? Is everything possible?

"I think so. I actually try and pride myself on the fact that seldom if ever have I said: 'No, this can't be done.' I've told Bruce: 'Well, the impossible just takes a little longer.' Because it's really not impossible. It's just gonna take me a while to figure out how to do it.

In Scott's opinion, Springsteen sometimes gets misunderstood:

"He changes from time to time. I don't believe that Bruce is someone like Madonna that the press says reinvents themselves. He has different aspects of his artistic persona, I guess, that not everybody [has] seen. I've seen many different facets of Bruce's songwriting and performing capability, from something as solo and reflective as *Nebraska* and *The Ghost of Tom Joad*, to rock music like *Born in the U.S.A.*, or even some disco sort of stuff like 'Cover Me' and 'Dancing in the Dark.' I've also seen him on the Gary U.S. Bonds record. He is a great R & B writer and singer. You get a little flavor of that on the *Human Touch* record with 'Soul Driver' and some of those songs.

"Another thing that Bruce does pretty well is country & western. I wouldn't say he's a big fan, but there's probably something in the genre that appeals to him for its innocence, simplicity and straightforwardness. We've talked about this, and Bruce often said: 'I sort of liked the sound of the *Tom Joad* band. I wouldn't mind doing something like that again.'"

Over the years the recording business has seen quite a few changes.

"Bruce has gotten used to the changing recording media from tape to Protools. This allows us to do some other things.

"We haven't gone totally techno, we still don't fix anything. When Bruce sings and plays, that's it. There are no readjustments. He's a true artist, he can sing it and play it."

"A few years ago we recorded one song for a Pete Seeger tribute album and he got a fourteen piece band in a room about fifteen feet wide, twenty feet long. Wood floors, furniture. It was a living room, and he wanted to record them while they were all playing acoustic instruments. Wow, gee. We did it and it sounded fine. I'm not gonna tell him: 'This is against my principles.'"

"The thing is," says Scott, "Bruce is a very intelligent and understanding person. He would never ask anything that can't be done. He's not someone that's gonna try and push the envelope just for the sake of pushing the envelope. He doesn't work that way."

We haven't gone totally techno, we still don't fix anything. When Bruce sings and plays, that's it. There are no readjustments. He's a true artist, he can sing it and play it. But the technology allows you to do a little bit more with things and he's slightly aware of it."

"Still, with Bruce, it's mostly first or second takes. He'd say: 'I played it and sang it. That's my performance.' Very infrequently does he retake a vocal. I think he writes songs but he does not practice them. He seems to write out the lyrics and then get an idea of the music. When he comes into the studio and plays the song for the first time, he is indeed playing it for the first time."

GETTING THE VIBE OF IT

Bob Clearmountain

He considers Bryan Adams a close friend. He's worked with the Stones, Simple Minds, the Pretenders, Sheryl Crow, INXS, Robbie Williams. Never-ending story. And when Bruce Springsteen took his final step towards world fame, Bob Clearmountain was part of building a sound almost larger than life.

"*Born in the U.S.A.* was probably one of the easiest records I've ever mixed because it was all pretty much a live band in the studio. There were very few overdubs. They replaced practically nothing. You have to keep in mind that they are a great band."

Bob Clearmountain. A sound pro with his own manager, his own studio, and a mixing table wider than the stage at the Stone Pony. "The guy with the tape recorder," as he was known, is living the good life in Pacific Palisades, California.

"It just came easy to me. Early on I realized I could probably make a living recording music, so that's all I thought about. I never thought it would take me to where I am today. Never. At best I thought I would make enough money to have my own, small apartment in New York."

Bob Clearmountain—producer, mixer, recording engineer—grew up in Connecticut. Towards the end of the 1960s, and in the early 1970s he was a bass player in various local bar bands, without entertaining any rock 'n' roll dreams.

"This was in my mid teens. But when I was about nineteen I stopped doing that, 'cause that's when I started doing this instead."

Clearmountain says that he was always the guy in the band with the tape recorder, the one recording gigs and all the rehearsals.

"And I was the one figuring out the arrangements. So it just seemed obvious that I was supposed to work with recordings.

"The other thing was that I didn't like being onstage. I had a bit of stage fright, never felt comfortable in the spotlight."

Quitting a teen band is a tough call for many young musicians. But it came easily to Clearmountain.

"The last band I was in just had a lot of trouble, and I had always had a hard time keeping bands together. Don't get me wrong, most of my friends are musicians. But it's a different thing when you have to depend on them for your career. Anyway, the guitar player was sleeping with the lead singer's girlfriend. So that was the end of that. And it was too bad, 'cause they were actually pretty good."

The band got as far as recording a demo, and these sessions would make a big impression on Clearmountain.

"We came to a studio in New York, called Media Sound, back in 1972. I got real friendly with the engineer, Michael Delugg, so I kept coming around and finally I was able to talk the studio manager into hiring me. The first time I walked in that studio it was like: Wow, I could live here. I could spend the rest of my life in this place."

Bob Clearmountain chose his path early on. There was nothing else stealing his attention.

"There's a funny little story. My father's cousin was a television writer; he wrote for a game show in New York. When I was about six years old we got a chance to go see it. It was just a game show but I was dying to see a TV show being made. What I was interested in was the camera man and the guy holding the boom mike. It was all about the technical part. You could see it on TV, but I wanted to know how all of that really happened.

"We were in the audience and they needed three kids to

participate in some kind of stupid game. And I'm like: 'No way, I'm here to watch the show.' But my parents held my hand up and sure enough I was picked. They were thinking I was gonna love being on TV, but it was just the worst thing. I was up there with all the lights in my face, and I remember being upset 'cause I never got to see what the camera and sound guys were doing."

Speaking of early musical influences, Clearmountain mentions the Beatles, the Stones, and Traffic. Hendrix was another big thing.

"I also remember listening to *Mad Dogs & Englishmen*, with Joe Cocker and Leon Russell. Those records just sounded like they were having a great time, like there was a party going on in the studio. I wanted to be there.

"I was always into the cleaner sound, like the Beatles' records. I was never really into Jefferson Airplane and records like that, 'cause they were so reverby and washed out. The Beatles were up front and close."

His first proper job came at Media Sound in New York.

Clearmountain was a fast learner in a studio frequented mainly by people recording commercial jingles.

"During the day that studio was based more around movie scores and commercials than records. They used to do most of the music for *Sesame Street*, and this was great for me 'cause I learned how to work really fast. You set up a rhythm section and you gotta have a finished track within two hours. That was good training. Things just had to happen quickly.

"When you're working with a rock band you don't want to get in their way. I'm not one of those guys who'll spend two days getting a bass drum sound. What's more important is getting the vibe of it, getting it spontaneous. Having it fresh."

One of the engineer/producers at Media Sound that he assisted, and later mixed for, was Tony Bongiovi, famous not only for being the cousin of Jon Bon Jovi.

"At night they'd do R & B records. Tony was there recording Kool & the Gang, Ben E. King, Sister Sledge, Gloria Gaynor. Even Stevie Wonder would do a lot of stuff at this place. That was fun 'cause I loved that music; I was a Motown fan.

"They hired me as a delivery boy. But since a couple of guys had just quit, what they needed was an assisting engineer. The first session they put me on was a Duke Ellington recording . . . and I had never met anyone famous until then.

"They actually got me recording real quick. I was assisting on a Kool & the Gang session and the engineer preferred doing jingles, so I got to do the engineering. I actually mixed a couple of their songs, too. Never got any credit, but who cares? Then they came back six months later, and Tony Bongiovi was the engineer. But he got sick, so I ended up engineering two basic tracks. These were the first things I ever recorded from scratch, two songs called 'Funky Stuff' and 'Hollywood Swinging.' Both of them were pretty big hits."

The next move came as Tony Bongiovi established the legendary Power Station.

"Tony had made a lot of money producing Gloria Gaynor, Disco Star Wars and other disco stuff. He was opening his own place and he wanted me to work there as the chief recording engineer. I said: 'Well, if I can help design it and try to attract rock clients.' That was okay with him. So we built it and I had quite a bit of input.

"Tony's just insane but he knows a lot of stuff about making hit records. Unfortunately, he's not as good a businessman."

Some of the best-selling artists would stop by. Bob Clearmountain has a hard time remembering all the names.

"The studio had Blondie, Mark Knopfler and Dire Straits, the Stones, Roxy Music, Huey Lewis, Chic, plus a bunch of punk bands. I also did a good portion of the Bryan Adams records there."

It was at the Power Station that Clearmountain first encountered Bruce Springsteen.

"I was really into the whole punk rock thing. Tony and I were co-producing a band called Tuff Darts and they were friends with Ian Hunter from Mott the Hoople. Ian came down to help out and we hit it off pretty well. Shortly after that he was doing his own album, *You're Never Alone with a Schizophrenic*, and he hired the E Street Band as his backup."

"They were used to the Record Plant, which was like recording in a dead closet where it was hard to really get a big rock sound. The Power Station was open and quite live, with a huge sound. So the guys loved it and told Bruce to check us out. He was about to start working on *The River*, and in two days we recorded and mixed a song called 'Roulette,' which never was on that album."

"At the time I had other commitments, and that's why I couldn't continue these recordings. So I suggested to Bruce that he should work with Neil Dorfsman, who is a brilliant engineer.

"Later, when they did *Born in the U.S.A.*, Neil would record about half of the songs, and Toby Scott did the other half. Then we ended up mixing it at the Power Station."

Bob Clearmountain says he wasn't all that familiar with Springsteen. He'd heard, and loved, the song "Born to Run," but never listened to the albums. Clearmountain had grown up with the sound of the Beatles and his head was still into British rock 'n' roll, pop and R & B.

"But I got to see Bruce a couple of times and thought he was a brilliant performer. That's when some of the songs really got me. Especially 'The River.' I always kind of get choked up when I hear that song. It reminds me of things that happened when I was a kid."

There was a vision shared; artist and studio crew agreed on a big sound.

"In my opinion they should be big. Bruce thought that as well. In fact, he thought it more than anyone else. He kept pushing me to make the drums bigger and bigger. In the end I thought it got to be a little bit heavy-handed on a couple of the songs, but it was the right thing to do because he wanted it to be bigger than life."

Bob Clearmountain is not about to change the media image of Springsteen.

"Bruce is just the nicest guy: respectful, honest, cares about the music. He's also extremely focused, always trying to get a certain picture across. It's not really about him so much as the characters he's portraying in his songs.

"In almost every Springsteen song there's a character, and you kind of have to understand who that character is and what his or her circumstances are. You have to understand the conflict. A lot of pop music just hasn't that deep meaning. But with artists like Bruce it's a very deep thing and it's such a great experience learning to respect that in the mix."

"The job," he says, "is not about telling artists what to do.

"To this day, I've had the philosophy that I never really go into a project with my own idea of how it should be done. I ask the artist and the producer what they feel are the significant elements, then I try to get into their heads. It's their music, not mine. It should be a reflection of what they want. I just try to pull the best things out of it, and go for the stuff that they feel [is] important, then perhaps suggest things they hadn't thought of, with their perspective in mind."

Clearmountain keeps a low profile, and doesn't mind that his efforts seldom get much attention in the media.

"I don't really care that much. Of course, it's nice to get some credit once in a while, but to me the exciting part is actually making the records. I just love recording music. That's why I got into the business in the first place.

"In fact, I've been much more comfortable doing this. It's a lot more stable than being a musician. I'm not depending on a bunch of other guys; it's all up to me."

All the years in the music industry have made it clear to him that fame doesn't come easily.

"Sometimes I feel bad for people in the spotlight. They're constantly hounded by fans and photographers. They rarely have any privacy.

"Not only that. There are so few rock stars that maintain. They're there for a couple of years, then what happens? Where did they go? Their label moves on to someone younger and more MTV-ready. It's kind of depressing. I wouldn't trade what I'm doing for anything."

Bruce Springsteen is an artist who went through some changes. Bob Clearmountain feels that Springsteen is becoming more intimate in his performing, more personal as a songwriter.

"It's a lot smaller these days. He doesn't go for the big stadium thing so much anymore. He's done these acoustic tours. It's just him and it's very intimate."

Clearmountain says that Springsteen is an artist who likes to get involved.

"I'll play a mix for him, and there are times when he's looking for a different approach. Then we'll talk about it and get on the right track.

"I think it was the *Lucky Town* album. They had been working on the record for a long time. Roy Bittan was co-producing and he really liked a lot of reverb. All the rough mixes were just soaking with reverb, so they were used to hearing the songs that way. To me it just didn't sound right. Bruce is the kind of singer you want to have up front, almost in your face. I want to see his face, hear every breath. So when I took a completely different approach, they had a lot of trouble getting their heads around what I was doing. They told me what they wanted. I did that, they listened to it and finally said that they kind of liked what I had from the start better."

There's always work in progress, always something new to experience.

"I learn something exciting every time. Even if it's music that I don't like very much, things that I wouldn't buy. It's a different type of appreciation from when you sit down and listen to a record. I believe you're using a different part of the brain. When I'm working on something I can listen to the same song over and over again all day. But I have trouble listening to the same song twice through if I'm just putting a record on."

Clearmountain is just as interested in dealing with seasoned, experienced artists and musicians as being up against the raw energy of bands recording their first album.

"Sometimes I prefer working with less experienced musicians. It's nice to have a young, energetic band, but it's also amazing when you have incredible musicians. They're two completely different experiences. The unexperienced bands sometimes don't play that well, but there's a rawness in the fact that they might not totally know what they're doing, they're just going for it. If they're really bad, then it can be a problem."

"If you're the producer there's more to say, but when I'm mixing that's already been done. I might make a comment or two."

"Betty was living in Marina Del Rey. She said to check out the west side, and I never really realized that it could be such a completely different thing. I was doing lots of work here anyway so I got an apartment over here and eventually we got this place.

"Nowadays I do most of my work here, at home. Occasionally I'll go to Vancouver to work with Bryan Adams in his recording place, or do live gigs like the Rolling Stones movie I'm working on at the moment. It was recorded and filmed at the Beacon Theater in New York. It's nice to get out once in a while."

He's also just recently built a new tracking room in Santa Monica, in the same building as his wife's company, Apogee Electronics.

"He kept pushing me to make the drums bigger and bigger. In the end I thought it got to be a little bit heavy-handed on a couple of the songs, but it was the right thing to do because he wanted it to be bigger than life."

Being one of the most sought-after in his profession, Bob Clearmountain chose to go independent. He has a manager who takes care of the rough sorting. The great thing about the job is to be able to pick and choose.

"It all became sort of inevitable. I was on staff at Power Station getting a salary, and clients were booking me specifically. They wanted to hire me separately from the studio. So I got a manager and just felt weird about taking a salary from the studio and also getting paid individually. It was like getting paid twice for the same thing.

"Then I started traveling: Sydney, San Francisco, London, L.A. Before 1992, I used to come out here to work with Bruce. They put me in some hotel and I just hated being on Sunset Strip. It seemed to be a horrible life. Why would anybody want live in this place?"

But after meeting his wife, Betty, Bob Clearmountain finally learned to appreciate L.A.

"It's a private studio. I'm not really booking it out; it's mainly just for my own projects and for Apogee to be able to do real-world testing."

The location of his mixing room is somewhat remote, the surroundings are magnificent, and the climate the best imaginable. The contrast with a stark Manhattan, where the cold months can mean pure physical exhaustion, is complete.

Way back, in the late 1960s, Bob Clearmountain started out on the East coast. But growing up he was never heavily into the so-called sounds of Asbury Park. That's why he finds it hard to characterize what defines the Jersey Shore music scene:

"I guess that Southside Johnny's early albums gives you a pretty good idea of what it was about. Then again, there's just no denying what a huge impact Bruce has had on just about everything that ever came out of New Jersey, or anywhere else for that matter."

"THERE'S NO FINER BAND IN THIS LAND AROUND"

Kid Leo

Those were the years before everything was programmed to the most minute, researched detail. Before commercial powers took over. The Golden Years. The golden age of rock 'n' roll. "Records were my instrument. Records. Nothing else. I grew up with Alan Freed, Mad Daddy, and Johnny Holliday, and I slept with a transistor radio under my pillow. Today the DJ is a different animal, one who'd rather become the next Howard Stern than know anything about the records he plays."

Lawrence J. Travagliante. Long Italian name. Not easy to pronounce. Impossible as a stage name. Lawrence became Leo. Kid Leo. Kid, after the greats of the boxing ring. Heroes like Jack "Kid Blackie" Dempsey.

Kid Leo is one of the last of his kind. The last DJ.

"There was once a time when every disc jockey could make a difference because of what they played. Today, I doubt there's even one radio station in America that might possibly influence the course of rock 'n' roll.

"The corporatization of radio has changed the landscape dramatically. Radio stations are no longer actively involved with the process of breaking a record. They actually perceive music as somewhat of a 'necessary evil.' Back in the day, when I broke a record the rest of the country's DJs would perk up their ears."

He's the voice from Cleveland. A DJ who made it through the transition in the 1960s from the streamlined format of non-stop Top 40 to a broader, more intrepid range of underground bands and progressive music.

"We wanted to discover new bands. To be the first to play what was yet to happen. We wanted to get to know the artists and expose their talents, their contributions to our culture."

Kid Leo started out at a college radio station. Later, as doors opened, he got his foot in. WMMS was playing the songs that got kids to turn up the volume. Kid Leo would soon become the most important radio voice in the Midwest. And he liked the sound of the E Street Band.

"Some songs from the first album, *Greetings from Asbury Park, N.J.*, stood out. But what crystallized the essence of Bruce Springsteen was seeing him onstage. That was where the songs took on an entirely different life.

"Then came *The Wild, the Innocent & the E Street Shuffle*. It became my *West Side Story*. A rock 'n' roll play with characters I knew. People from the street, my people."

And, later, *Born to Run*.

"Bruce held on to the innocence and the romance. At the same time, the music communicates frustration and a constant longing to escape. *Born to Run* was the essence of everything I loved about rock 'n' roll."

From the release of *Greetings* until *Born to Run*, Springsteen had been a regional artist well known and highly respected in the Tri-State area. But the rest of the U.S., and the rest of the world, hadn't yet gotten the message.

Mike Appel, Springsteen's manager, wanted to spread the word. For the artist's sake, and for his own. Kid Leo remembers:

"Bruce's first two albums sold poorly. Columbia wasn't that far away from dropping him. At the same time, Jon Landau was becoming an ever more important person in Bruce's life and career. So, Mike Appel did what he could to save the con-

"There were three of us, and today I am the only one left. God bless their souls."

tract with Columbia and maintain his own position as manager."

Kid Leo became their means. Kid Leo in Cleveland, Scott Muni in New York City, and Ed Sciaky in Philadelphia. Mike Appel hand-picked three DJs.

"There were three of us, and today I am the only one left. God bless their souls."

Leo, Muni, and Sciaky each got their own letter. A letter in which Mike Appel described his artist as something extraordinary. As the biggest thing since "Rock Around the Clock." And he included a tape of "Born to Run."

"One song, just "Born to Run." And this was in October of 1974, almost a full year before Columbia released the album."

Kid Leo already liked Springsteen. But "Born to Run" gave him something else, something even bigger.

"It had everything. The Phil Spector wall of sound, the attitude of a garage band, characters so fully drawn that I not only knew everyone of them but I also hung around with them."

"So I decided to make 'Born to Run' the WMMS anthem every weekend. By Thanksgiving our listeners had crowned it 'record of the year' in Cleveland."

Springsteen came to town in February 1975. The album was almost finished, and he wanted to try out his songs on a Midwestern audience.

"'Jungleland,' 'Backsteets,' 'She's the One' . . . the audience was enraptured. The band received multiple standing ovations. Then Bruce launched into 'Born to Run.' The entire auditorium stood and shouted out every single lyric. They knew the words by heart, there was not a soul in the crowd who didn't know and love that song.

"Bruce was a little taken aback by all of this and after the show he wanted to know why the audience knew 'Born to Run' backwards and forwards. Someone told him: 'This DJ, Kid Leo has been playing the song as the weekend anthem since October.'

"That's how we met. He wanted me brought backstage. I can't say we became close friends, but there has always been a mutual respect. From that day on he allowed me to MC every show he played in Cleveland until I left for New York in 1989."

Kid Leo was one of the chosen. And he is unique in Springsteenland as a presenter. This fact alone makes him the only person who has ever been MC for a concert with Bruce Springsteen & the E Street Band.

"That's what they tell me. And I guess that speaks well for me. It means Bruce liked my way of working and I'm most proud of that fact. He appreciated my passion."

During the *Tunnel of Love* tour in 1988, Kid Leo entered the stadium in a carnival suit with a pink jacket. Ten years earlier he had started the show at the Agora with the classic lines: "Ladies and gentlemen. The main event: Round for round, pound for pound. There's no finer band in this land around . . . Bruce Springsteen & the E Street Band!"

"That was on the advance tour for *Darkness on the Edge of Town*, before the album was out. They had three radio broadcasts. One in New York, at the Bottom Line. One in L.A., at the Roxy. And then there was Cleveland, at the Agora, to take care of the Midwest."

Three weeks later, the E Street Band opened up the arena tour, their first in front of audiences nearing 20,000 people. The scene was set at the Coliseum outside Cleveland, and Kid Leo knew the stakes. He wanted to sound just like a ring announcer at a Heavyweight Championship Fight and so he opened: "Ladies and Gentlemen. The Main Event. Round for round . . ."

People are going nuts. The excitement knows no boundaries. Enter: Bruce Springsteen, laughing, talking in front of the crowd:

"What's the matter Leo? Can't you think of nothing new?"

In fall of 2005, Kid Leo is sitting in a skyscraper where Sirius Radio is based. He came to New York, some sixteen years ago, to work for Columbia Records. But this is where Little Steven Van Zandt broadcasts "Underground Garage," with Kid Leo as operations manager and DJ.

His love for the job remains. Despite all the changes, despite the fact that he is no longer broadcasting live. Despite the fact that young DJs know everything about Howard Stern and nothing about Alan Freed.

Kid Leo says that Asbury Park has to fight for the Stone Pony. In the same way that New York, through Little Steven, fought for CBGB.

"I've had my fair share of magical moments at the Pony. My fondest memory is the night of the national radio broadcast that I hosted at the club. It involved the launch of Southside Johnny & the Asbury Jukes's debut album. This took place over Memorial Day weekend in 1976. It seemed the entire East Coast roster of rock royalty was there that night.

"To debate the Stone Pony's place in rock 'n' roll history is something for critics to do. Those that were there know what the venue meant. I wouldn't say that the Stone Pony is a more important rock club than, let's say, CBGB was by any stretch of the imagination. However, the Stone Pony's survival means more to the existence and renaissance of Asbury Park, N.J. than CBGB meant, or any one institution could ever mean, to New York City. Small towns like Asbury Park should see their civic leaders bend over backwards to save any establishment that has vast historical importance to any element of culture, commerce, or creativity."

Born to Run was a long time ago. But Springsteen is still out there. Is there a chance that the world might ever again see a rock star of the same quality?

Kid Leo hopes so. And he believes so.

"Today the spotlight is on pop, not rock. But there is a wealth of garage rock talent out there. However, it is a hard row to hoe if you want to make it as a rock 'n' roll star. Unfortunately everything today seems to be more about celebrity rather than music.

"With Bruce it's exactly the opposite. Whether it's on stage or on record, the music creates the celebrity and celebrations.

"I think Bruce is the only artist I can truly say this about: He has never been afraid to grow up on his records. Bruce's concerns on *Born to Run* were those of a twenty-five year old. He addressed different situations on *Born in the U.S.A.* when he was thirty-five. When *Tunnel of Love* came out it addressed the very personal problems he was experiencing at the time.

"That's how you measure an artist: by integrity and maturity."

"Small towns like Asbury Park should see their civic leaders bend over backwards to save any establishment that has vast historical importance to any element of culture, commerce, or creativity."

Southside Johnny Lyon and Bobby Bandiera

On the cover of the Asbury Jukes's 1976 debut album, Bruce Springsteen recalls his first meeting with this weird, insulting guy called Southside Johnny. Point taken. But Springsteen's also on to something when saying that Johnny Lyon probably was the only local kid capable of delivering straight R & B five sets a night.

It's also a well known fact that there are times when Johnny Lyon brings his Jukes to phenomenal heights. When he's the head of the world's best bar band. On evenings such as this.

The difference is that we're not hanging out in a bar on the Jersey Shore. We're leaning against a man-made rock face in the monstrous Mohegan Sun casino in Uncasville, Connecticut. The Jukes, tonight with Mark Pender and Richie Rosenberg on horns, are heading towards a huge finale. Taking it all back to where it started, playing 'I Don't Want to Go Home.'

A few hours earlier, backstage: Southside Johnny Lyon and his lead guitar player, Bobby Bandiera, are expecting company. Lyon raises his voice: "Come on in, what are you waiting for?" Bandiera reaches out his hand, says hi and wonders: "Could I have some lutfisk? I would like some gravlax."

It's not the first time Lyon and Bandiera are entertaining Swedes. Through the years the Asbury Jukes have been a veritable touring machine, playing in Malmo, Stockholm, and Gothenburg. Not to mention smaller cities like Lulea and Jonkoping.

"Malmo," Bandiera shouts. "Do you remember, John? Nude models backstage. And they got to see our underwear."

It's that type of evening. Lyon and Bandiera start shooting the breeze while the tape is rolling. So we try to find something to focus on. We ask Johnny Lyon to take us on a journey back in time. He says: "Of course, if I only could we'd go back to 1922."

Then Lyon gets back to the topic and tells us that Ocean Grove, Asbury Park's small neighbor, is the town he grew up in.

"I still live there for part of the year. You see, I'm still growing up."

Johnny Lyon starts talking about a house he owns. A house on the beach, with no heat.

"Can't stay there in the winter time. It's below freezing inside."

Bobby Bandiera:

"We gotta get him some animals. Any kind of furry animals."

Finally, though, Southside Johnny Lyon can't help taking this from the beginning.

"The Asbury Park music scene? Yeah, I started hanging out with different musicians around 1962–63, I guess. I became friends with a drummer whose name was Doug Wayne. Doug came from north Jersey and he was a troubled soul. But he played with Sonny Kenn, who was number one at that time."

Vini Lopez would replace Doug Wayne on the drums, while Johnny Lyon sang and played harmonica. Sometimes he even played bass.

"We performed in Hullabaloo clubs and other places where kids hung out. But in the middle of the 1960s, Sonny got tired of playing Chuck Berry covers. He wanted to do more blues, so he started the Sonny Kenn Blues Band instead."

Lyon continues up to the year 1968, at which point Tom and Margaret Potter had just opened the Upstage Club on Cookman Avenue in Asbury Park.

"That's where all the musicians hung out. Bruce, Steve, Garry. And everyone played together because we all knew the same material. There were no formal bands, everyone improvised. And

while, and when he came home at night it would take like an hour before he could finally open up his hands."

Lyon and Van Zandt believed in something better. A rock 'n' roll band that had blues and soul.

"I knew I wanted to have someone on horns, but I wasn't sure how we could arrange it. Steve was always much more aggressive, so he took the lead. We started by hiring a saxophone player who was a few years older than us. An Italian. He hated our guts and refused to speak to us.

"'You don't have a goddamn clue what you're doing,' was the only thing he said."

Southside Johnny Lyon got his horns without the angry Italian. When the first album was about to be recorded, Lyon and Van Zandt brought in a horn section from Philadelphia. It sounded alright, and the Asbury Jukes had finally gotten their own sound.

The hype that followed was connected to Bruce Springsteen's 1975 breakthrough. This all happened less than a year after Springsteen released *Born to Run*, and Southside Johnny, along with his Jukes, got launched nationwide, and internationally, as the next Asbury Park sensation.

"Well, we got to record an album. A few white guys fooling around with black R & B! Unthinkable."

The band still had no recording contract. But, to everyone's general excitement, *I Don't Want To Go Home*, with Steven Van Zandt as producer, found its way into stores.

"And so we got to make another record (*This Time It's For Real*). Then I understood even less, as if that was possible."

Johnny Lyon explains that when he played the songs for the record label execs, he could see on their faces that it was not going anywhere.

"But they gave us a break, and then they had us go on tour."

Lyon loved every minute of it. He was able to go on tour. If only for a short while, he got out of New Jersey.

"I fought hard to be sensational every night. Because I really didn't want to go back home again."

sometimes there'd be someone who succeeded in convincing different club owners to book us. We made 100 dollars a night at best, and that's everyone put together."

Sonny Kenn was still the star. His band had been the best of all the cover bands that were working the Shore. But everything started to change with the Upstage. Kenn turned towards the blues, and more and more people wanted to start writing their own material.

Johnny Lyon became the singer in the Blackberry Booze Band.

"Paul Dickler played guitar, Dave Meyers was on bass. And then we had Kenny Cutler on drums. After a while I kind of took over the band and fired the guys who started it."

Not very nice, was it?

"Not nice, but true. And I kept the drummer."

The Blackberry Booze Band was the first step on the way to forming Southside Johnny & the Asbury Jukes. But without Steve Van Zandt, Johnny Lyon probably never would have started the long journey that he's still on.

"Steve was working the jackhammer out on the Turnpike. He made a lot more money than the rest of us, but for a guitar player it was ridiculous. Steve lived with me and my wife for a

He was driven by something that Bruce Springsteen was always known for as well: the will to go farther, to get to some-

"We started by hiring a saxophone player who was a few years older than us.
An Italian. He hated our guts and refused to speak to us."

"I fought hard to be sensational every night.

Because I really didn't want to go back home again."

thing better. Not to be just one musician in the crowd, not just to belong to some average band from Asbury Park.

"We really wanted to get out," says Johnny Lyon.

"A Jersey thing," confirms Bobby Bandiera.

They talk about their love for the Garden State. But also the constant feeling of being from a place that was the butt of jokes made elsewhere in the country.

"The people playing in bands from New York were cool," says Lyon. "They were almost foreign. We came from Asbury Park, New Jersey."

Some thirty years later, Southside Johnny realizes that he's made it farther than most. He has never topped the charts, and he most likely never will. But he is still out on the road with his band, and the audience is right alongside him.

Bobby Bandiera has been with Johnny Lyon since 1986. Bandiera came in as a replacement for lead guitarist Billy Rush, but was already a driven front man, who had been burning up the Jersey Shore since his teenage years, himself.

"Billy called one night when I was laying at home with the flu. He asked if I wanted the job. I knew that I wasn't the man for it, but I said yes . . . of course. And I've never been quite right since."

The boss clears his throat:

"I've got an ulcer, and its name is Bobby."

Bandiera recalls that he first started to make decent money in music as a teenager.

"Top 40 bands were popular. My father was always borrowing money from me; it wasn't the other way around."

In the beginning of the 1980s you would find Bobby Bandiera up front in Cats on a Smooth Surface (Bandiera, Glen Burtnik, Fran Smith, Jr., Ray Andersen, and special guests), which even today is considered to have been the Stone Pony's ultimate house band.

"Cats. Damn good band," says Johnny Lyon.

Bandiera himself takes a more diplomatic approach:

"Fairly good, for being a cover band. We had a few songwriters who came and went, but it never took off."

Why not?

"Asbury already had Bruce and Johnny. We didn't want to be like them. But we didn't know how we should be. The only thing certain was that we wanted to create a more rock-oriented sound."

Bandiera says that he was often in the audience at the Stone Pony when Southside Johnny was onstage.

"I always used to think: I wish I was a part of that."

Lyon: "He's lying!"

Bandiera: "No, it's true. In any case I remember that I thought so one night when I had gone down to Asbury from Orange in the company of Jack Daniels."

"I think Steve was playing with Johnny. That was around the time when Steve was in the middle of moving over from the Jukes to the E Street Band, and I remember that the audience loved him. He had a certain style. Steve really added something. And then I came along. Cool."

Johnny Lyon laughs and says:

"Bobby still gets paid, exactly what he got paid in 1986."

When Bobby Bandiera took the job another member of Cats was also invited to become a Juke, but he had started a family, and declined the offer.

"I'd also started a family," says Bandiera. "The difference is that I was dying to get out."

"That's the problem you find with a lot of musicians from Asbury Park," says Johnny Lyon. "We've always had tons of talent in town, but very few who wanted to go the distance. For me it was the exact opposite. I wanted to see Paris."

Bandiera: "And Jonkoping, Lulea, Lund."

Apart from being a long-time Juke, Bobby Bandiera has often shared the stage with Bruce Springsteen, and even toured with Bon Jovi. On the side he fronts his own band, as well as the popular Jersey Shore Rock-n-Soul Revue. Bandiera says that along the Shore there are always opportunities for anyone who's good at this game, willing to work and able to think for themselves.

"Bobby's always playing," says Lyon.

"Yeah, but I also have four ex-wives to support. So there's a lot of child support and alimony . . . just kidding."

Lyon: "Damn, that was my line. Get your own."

**"We've always had tons of talent in town, but very few who wanted
to go the distance. For me it was the exact opposite. I wanted to see Paris."**

Bandiera plays because that's just what he does. There are still clubs that will pay 5,000 dollars to any given cover band, but Bandiera's band is not one of the crowd. He wants to write his own songs and earn respect that way.

"Then you also have to be willing to pay the consequences," says Lyon. "When we started with the Jukes, this was just before the first album, most cover bands were making more money than us. It's sad that all these clubs don't want to give real talent an honest chance just because people would rather pay for something they already recognize. McDonald's sells."

About the Asbury Park sound, the one that's such a legend, Johnny Lyon says:

"There's no such thing. It never existed. I was listening to R & B, Steve loved the Yardbirds, Bruce was doing his own thing. We played everything you can imagine together, sometimes we even played country with Albany Al Tellone."

But the common denominator is obvious nonetheless: The energy. Springsteen, Lyon, Bandiera, and Jon Bon Jovi all work themselves half to death onstage.

"So much came from guys like Bruce, Steve, and Garry," says Johnny Lyon. "Steve was already unbelievably focused when he was only fourteen or fifteen years old. He and Bruce paved the way. So I thought: 'Fuck it, I can do that!'"

"It's partly that we love what we're doing. But deep down there's something else too. The fact that we knew from the very beginning that music was the only way out. The only way to avoid working in a factory."

Bobby Bandiera:

"You see it in people who have made a name for themselves over the years, guys like John and Bruce. They've always had focus, and that's not something that has changed with age. It's the same thing with Jon Bon Jovi."

Johnny Lyon:

"Jon has a great rock 'n' roll spirit. I have always admired him, I just can't stand looking at him. He's a little too ugly."

Bandiera: "What? He's better looking than some women I know."

Lyon: "Jon is better looking than all the women you know."

The tape runs out. Johnny Lyon poses somewhat unwillingly for a last picture, and Bobby Bandiera gets the last question:

"Is it true that you're the one who came up with all the nicknames?"

"Yeah, it was me. Absolutely. You should know that Richie Rosenberg isn't 'LaBamba', and Mark Pender isn't 'the Love Man'. Not at all."

Some secrets are best kept, but one can't keep from asking:

"What does Bobby Bandiera go by?"

"The only thing I ever get to hear is 'asshole.'"

Mark Pender and Richie Rosenberg

Nowadays Max Weinberg is boss, with NBC paying the salary. But sometimes they long to get out. To go on tour and make certain that just about everybody in the crew feels a little bit insecure. Welcome to happy hour with Mark Pender and Richie Rosenberg.

It's Saturday night. At the Stone Pony in Asbury Park we're having a party for Richie Rosenberg. His band, LaBamba's Big Band, has just turned twenty, and among those here to congratulate are Southside Johnny, Bobby Bandiera, and Glen Burtnik.

"LaBamba" himself gets the party going, but the one who really steals the show is the guy on the trumpet. Mark Pender steps up, and those who don't already know who "the Love Man" is have just found themselves a new hero. Because Pender doesn't just hit the high notes on the trumpet.

Like "LaBamba," "the Love Man" is a singer who can hold his own with the best of them. Southside Johnny Lyon, dressed for the occasion in a white shirt, knows that duels with Richie Rosenberg and Mark Pender have a highly uncertain outcome.

Next time around it's Tuesday afternoon. An ordinary day on the job for Rosenberg and Pender. Now the scene is the NBC building right in the heart of Manhattan. It's a weekday with Conan O'Brien and the Max Weinberg 7 on late night television.

Guess who's stealing the show? Yep, the guy with the trumpet, as he demonstrates a lung capacity that would put a deep-sea diver to shame.

"Ah," says Pender, once the cameras are off. "I know it seems difficult, I even thought it was impossible myself. But it's just a question of technique and training."

Then Pender and Rosenberg hop in a taxi that takes them down to a hotel where 33rd Street meets Seventh Avenue. They come with us in the elevator, fourteen floors up, and into a room of dubious tourist class. We assume that Pender and Rosenberg have seen worse, but nowadays these guys are used to travel-ing in style. With the Max Weinberg 7 or LaBamba's Hubcaps. Sometimes with Southside Johnny, sometimes with Bruce Springsteen. Mark Pender also keeps his own band going on the side.

They've been playing together since 1981, when Rosenberg first brought Pender to a Diana Ross session and then introduced him to Southside Johnny.

"Like it or not," says Pender, putting his arm around the boss, "he's stuck with me now."

Richie Rosenberg is indeed the boss, at least when it comes to LaBamba's Hubcaps or LaBamba's Big Band.

"Ah, you know. I like to pass it around. We have fun together," says Rosenberg.

He's got his hat on. One wonders if Richie Rosenberg ever takes that hat off? The hat, the suit, and the trombone are his signature. Rosenberg and Pender are class players, always ready to have a good time.

Mark Pender seems boyishly delighted as he gets to tell his favorite story from 1988, when he, Richie Rosenberg, Mike Spengler, Mario Cruz, and Eddie Manion were the Miami Horns. The horn section that brought soul to Bruce Springsteen & the E Street Band.

"The lipstick. Yeah, this was before one of our vocal numbers. We used to leave the stage to get the wireless mikes and then come back out again, to dance and sing with Bruce.

"Now, Patti's down there, putting lipstick on. She offers to put some on me and Richie. OK, why not? And now we're ready to get back onstage.

"There's me, 'LaBamba' and Bruce in between. He had this thing where he used to grab us and pull us close, and this time as he's looking at me I got this red lipstick on and I give him a little . . . Then he goes over to 'LaBamba' who does the same bit. Bruce drops the lyric. He certainly wasn't expecting that.

"He never actually said too much about it, and we never tried it again."

Mark Pender is originally a jazz player from Kansas City. He came to northern New Jersey and New York at the age of twenty-two.

"I came out here with soul/jazz organist Charles Irwin because his band had a record deal on Columbia. We recorded the album and then Columbia decided they weren't gonna use the tracks. I guess they got some good musicians to do it instead."

Pender didn't get too discouraged, though, and decided to stick around.

"Well, I was told it was OK to leave the band, and then we had this big party where the guys said to me: 'Hey, knock 'em dead.'"

"I couldn't go home after that."

He says that New York offers all the opportunities. The recordings, the touring, the live gigs, and the parties.

place to hang. I had heard about Bruce playing down there, but I wasn't really familiar with his, or let alone Johnny's, music. I thought basically it was all a folk act."

"Anyway, as I got to the Pony they were all there for the audition."

Pender: "Johnny, Bruce, Steve? They were all there? Wow, was the earth set on fire?"

Rosenberg: "Nah, we were just going through the songs for the second Jukes album, *This Time It's For Real*. Johnny and Steven were getting the rehearsals together."

Southside Johnny would be following up his debut album (*I Don't Want To Go Home*). The Asbury Jukes were launched just after Springsteen's monumental breakthrough with *Born to Run*, and Steve Van Zandt was the obvious link between the Jukes and the E Street Band.

Mark Pender says:

"Steven's fingerprint in the whole thing is pretty heavy."

Richie Rosenberg continues:

"Steven arranged and wrote many songs for the early albums. I don't want to take anything away from Johnny and it wouldn't be right to say that Steven was the man behind it

"Johnny, Bruce, Steve? They were all there? Wow, was the earth set on fire?"

"There are so many people from different cultures. It's just a magnetic place."

Richie Rosenberg, for his part, became one of the major Asbury heroes early on, starting out with Southside Johnny in 1976.

"I got a call about the gig while I was in another band. They had this audition at the Pony. I guess they were trying to see what a trombone would sound like with all the material. They had used one on the first record, but now they wanted to find out what it would be like to have a steady trombone in the lineup. I was the only person at the audition."

Pender: "Just you and Johnny? That must have been scary."

Rosenberg: "I mean I was the only trombone player there. And it was all kind of confusing, because I really wasn't familiar with the Asbury Jukes. Didn't even know who was Johnny, who was Steven, or who was Bruce."

At the time Riche Rosenberg was living in Philadelphia, and Bruce Springsteen had started making a name for himself with some legendary shows at a venue in Bryn Mawr called the Main Point.

"They had a lot of jazz, and folk music, too. It was a great

all, but he definitely played a big part. I just think the combination of those guys created something very special.

"Steven actually managed the band back then, and he was a strong force to deal with. He wouldn't take no for an answer from promoters or nightclub owners. I feel that the Jukes are where they are today, still able to move themselves around, thanks to Steven. It wouldn't have happened without him."

Mark Pender:

"But Johnny sure kept it going good. He could have slowed down. Throughout the '80s I just wondered how he kept going? He recorded great music, but never once had a hit."

Pender also recognizes that the success, and the songwriting, of Bruce Springsteen was a necessary, and major, influence on the Jukes.

"There are songs that Bruce never recorded because he gave them to Johnny. Great Jukes songs like 'Hearts of Stone' and 'The Fever.'"

The Asbury Jukes quickly earned the reputation of being the world's best bar band, a rep that still lives on to this day.

"And it's true. Even when we're not there," says Mark Pender.

The way things turned out, Pender and Rosenberg will be missing as the Jukes go on tour overseas. The job at NBC with the Max Weinberg 7 demands their attendance year-round.

"I think we're lucky to be in this situation where you find time for the kids. On the other hand," says Pender, "there's really nothing like the friendship that comes with traveling."

Richie Rosenberg sighs slightly:

"Yeah. Guys play together differently when they're travel-ing together too. It was fun back then. Nothing was ever hard to deal with."

Rosenberg is laughing as he continues:

"We started out with an old school bus. Then there was this huge Silver Eagle. I'm not sure if Steven or the record company bought it, but Steven designed the inside. It had Steven all over it. All the curtains were Hawaiian."

They've had good times on the road, even though band members would be missing every now and then:

"Yeah," says Pender, "we did leave a couple of guys behind, right? Once Eddie Manion was asleep while the rest of us got off the bus. We came back thinking he was still asleep, which he wasn't. Eddie had gone for a little walk, and we took off without him."

just hanging out there with him and Toby (Scott). It's tense but it's also laid back. He doesn't have all these people there, he's not entertaining. It's just a few guys hanging out, recording music. It's a really cool atmosphere."

Rosenberg: "I especially remember this one session. We

"Johnny sure kept it going good. He could have slowed down.
Throughout the '80s I just wondered how he kept going?
He recorded great music, but never once had a hit."

Rosenberg: "Well, at least we were going east, back to Asbury."

Spending decades working with both Southside Johnny and Bruce Springsteen, Mark Pender and Richie Rosenberg can compare.

"Johnny's shows," says Pender, "are mostly clubs and theaters. Bruce's shows are all large now. But the funny thing is that they are both incredibly dynamic front men, and still really different personalities. Bruce is this one man dynamo. You see him up onstage and you can't keep your eyes off him. Johnny, on the other hand, has that looseness. There have been times when we've seen Johnny and Bruce together, and Johnny is killing everybody."

"We did these shows where Johnny, Bruce, Jon Bon Jovi, and Steven were all onstage. Boy, I tell you: You gotta keep your eyes on Johnny."

Rosenberg fills it in:

"There's always been a deep respect from Bruce towards Johnny."

The Tunnel of Love tour?

Pender: "I think it worked pretty darn good, and for us it was just sad to see the whole thing end. It lasted just under a year, and it was amazing. Europe, in particular. In the U.S. we had done venues somewhere between 20,000 and 40,000 seats, and in Europe there are like 80,000 to 100,000 people at the shows. I had never played in front of anything like that. And it was never hard connecting. The fans were all so along."

Rosenberg: "There are no disbelievers in those crowds."

Springsteen in the studio?

"It's just great that he involves us in different situations," says Rosenberg.

Pender agrees as he goes on:

"We get to his house and it seems almost secluded. You're

had been in the city, working with Joe Pesci, who was doing this Italian character, Vincent LaGuardia. It was hilarious. Later we drove to Bruce's house."

Pender: "Yeah, yeah. But let's get to the best part of that day. It was out on the ranch, we were on a break. Bruce had this 1930s motorcycle with a sidecar, 'LaBamba' gets in and they go for a quick spin. When you look at these two guys, with the helmets on . . . Man, there's actually a photo."

Rosenberg: "It's a very private photo."

Richie Rosenberg started his own thing in 1984, and it somehow happened that the Hubcaps grew to become LaBamba's Big Band.

"We started playing the Pony Wednesday nights. Glen Burtnik was on bass, Bobby Bandiera on guitar, Kevin Kavanaugh on keys, Eddie Manion on sax. We did a lot of soul tunes and rock tunes. I'd say it was about time. Richie had never really fronted a band and he's just a loveable band leader. The Hubcaps turned out to be such a good party band," says Pender.

But it also stayed on the party level. Richie Rosenberg tries to explain why the Hubcaps never was a band with recording or international touring ambitions:

"Throughout times we did some original material, but there was never really anything that we would record. It was basically a cover band."

Pender: "I'd say it was definitely original. And I think we should have gone to Europe. But you always see the missed opportunities. Then again we were pretty busy over here and the guys had started families.

"I think we were all happy to see it take form like it did. Richie did try to take us on tour in the U.S., but logistically it's terrible to get to Europe. It would cost a fortune just to fly everybody over."

Rosenberg: "It's a lot easier to go to Cleveland."

Pender: "Yeah, we had a hell of time in Cleveland, didn't we?"

Being a virtuoso, Mark Pender finally also decided he should get a little band of his own. The Mark Pender Band is becoming a frequent attraction in Manhattan, and Pender hopes to spread the word:

"Several years ago, a few years after 'LaBamba' started doing the Hubcaps, I was playing around north Jersey and every now and then I'd catch up a good steam. Then it was time to go off on tour again, and that's when the band would break up. Anyway, I've been trying to write songs for so long. The band is a vehicle for me to get up front and sing and do my own material. I just hope that it keeps growing."

With the exception of a short period when Mark Pender was touring with Robert Cray, Rosenberg and Pender have been together. E Street drummer Max Weinberg fixed the reunion while putting together the Max Weinberg 7. Richie Rosenberg says that there was no audition to be in the band. Weinberg just made some calls, picking out the crew.

When this was done, the MW7 was up against twenty-five different bands in the audition for *Late Night with Conan O'Brien*, and they blew the competition away.

"We knew Conan's producer, who had also been the road manager for Diana Ross. I guess that wasn't a bad thing," says Rosenberg, who felt a lot more confident than Pender:

"Yeah well, I've never done that many auditions, but the ones I did never worked out very well."

Rosenberg: "I was a lucky bastard then. The only audition I didn't make was Joe Jackson. He called me back the next day and said: 'Man, you did a really nice job. Thanks for coming out, and if we're gonna take on a trombone, which I decided not to, it would have been you.'"

On Max Weinberg, the band leader, Rosenberg says:

"We've known him for a long time, and we share history. It all ends up good."

Pender: "Max has his way. He does good. But I think he would like to be Bruce. Hell, I would like to be Bruce."

Rosenberg: "Who wouldn't?"

"And what girl wouldn't like to be Patti?"

So, what's up with all the nicknames, including E Streeters as well as Jukes? While laughing Richie Rosenberg says:

"Well, Mark tends to want to give the audience his love."

Pender's reply is less about making fun than showing admiration:

"I think that 'LaBamba' does the same thing. He gives a whole lot of love to people. There's nobody else that I know who'll get onstage, no matter what circumstance, and not pretend. You feel you know this guy when you see him up there. That's the great thing we've had playing together. We come to play, and not to be drugged by the whole situation."

Rosenberg, looking slightly embarrassed, gets back to the true nickname story:

"For me, it didn't come until I went to the Pony. Everybody down there [has] nicknames. Bobby Bandiera is the official nicknamer."

Pender: "Maybe we shouldn't. Bobby's usually a bit rude."

Rosenberg: "True. Anyway, nicknames seems the first order of business down there. Gary Anderson, a roadie with the Jukes who passed away some years ago, came up with mine. We were in the back of the Pony, drinking like crazy. Suddenly Gary yells out: 'LaBamba!' Bruce happened to be there and did this give me an 'L . . .'"

Pender: "Richie really is 'LaBamba.' I've been 'the Love Man' since Stevens band, the Disciples of Soul, was on tour. We were staying at this hotel and I had just gotten my first walkman. I brought some Marvin Gaye along, and there I was in my room, with the headphones on, singing like crazy. Apparently Steven had been knocking on my door for about twenty minutes straight. There was no answer, but he'd heard me singing all these love songs. So at night, onstage, he goes: 'Oh, on trumpet we have "the Loooove Man"!'

"I thought it would drop. You know it can be hard to explain when you're having a relationship with someone who keeps asking: 'How come they call you "the Love Man"?'

"No answer works."

"You know it can be hard to explain when you're having a relationship with someone who keeps asking: 'How come they call you "the Love Man"?'"

SHADES OF BLUE

Lisa Lowell

Lisa Lowell is talking about years gone by. About being one of the colors on someone else's palette. Her friends, Patti Scialfa and Soozie Tyrell, broke out of anonymity. In the middle of her life, Lisa Lowell says: "I was a late bloomer, but it's my turn now."

Scialfa became Mrs. Springsteen, and Tyrell worked her way into becoming a touring member of the E Street Band. But their band, Trickster, which used to wreak havoc along the streets of Greenwich Village, was always a three-person act and finally, after twenty-five years of songwriting, Lisa Lowell is ready to take a step forward.

"It took a long time to find my voice, and to process what my message was. I've had bands, I've played my music live over the years. But I needed to get to a certain point before I could put out a body of work that made sense."

Lisa Lowell says that the music industry doesn't scare her any more. She's in talks with Gaff Music, and her debut album is in the works. But everything takes time.

"My relationship with this industry is complicated. I've seen a lot of true artists give up too much of themselves for the sake of some A & R guy who couldn't even find middle C. It's about money. Money before art.

"That's why," continues Lowell, "I am glad I'm doing it now, at a certain level of maturity. Hopefully the years have given me a bit of wisdom about how to approach my record."

Lisa Lowell speaks of herself as a team player. There was a time when she wasn't "great with pressure." A time when she enjoyed being a part of a group, just helping to support somebody else's vision.

This is the voice that gives a particular blue shade to the music of Southside Johnny & the Asbury Jukes, David Johansen, Garland Jeffreys, Patti Scialfa, and Bruce Springsteen.

"It's been great fun. And also satisfying, because you get your performing out. But at the same time there has always been a longing to carve out my own niche. That's why it was inspiring when Patti and Soozie recorded their albums."

Regarding what will be her first solo album, Lowell says:

"There'll be some rockers. But I also think we've lost a tradition of strong melodies: the Carole King stuff, Brill Building. Even Laura Nyro. She was a genius and so ahead of her time.

"That's why I want to write that type of song for people of my own age. I'm going for the art, not for the industry. I think Garland may do a guest spot on my record. And who knows, I might be able to drag Patti and Soozie in. My working title for the album is *Beautiful Behavior*."

Mr. Springsteen?

"I don't want to exploit that poor, dear soul. He's got kids to take care of, and eighty million plane rides to do. If he'd offer, I don't think I would turn him down."

Scialfa, Tyrell, Lowell: Trickster. A somewhat legendary circus on the streets of Greenwich Village.

"You've doubtlessly heard dozens of crazy stories."

Lisa Lowell describes a three-headed female beast. Three wills, each on their own path, but having come together. Three women against a then extremely sexist, male-dominated world of music. A group on a mission to fight the status quo.

"All those clubs in the West Village. They got our tapes, 'lost' them, and then asked for new ones. So instead of playing on their stages we would block their doors by standing in front of the club. We had a huge audience on the streets."

Bleecker Street, Greenwich Village. Its own swirling universe

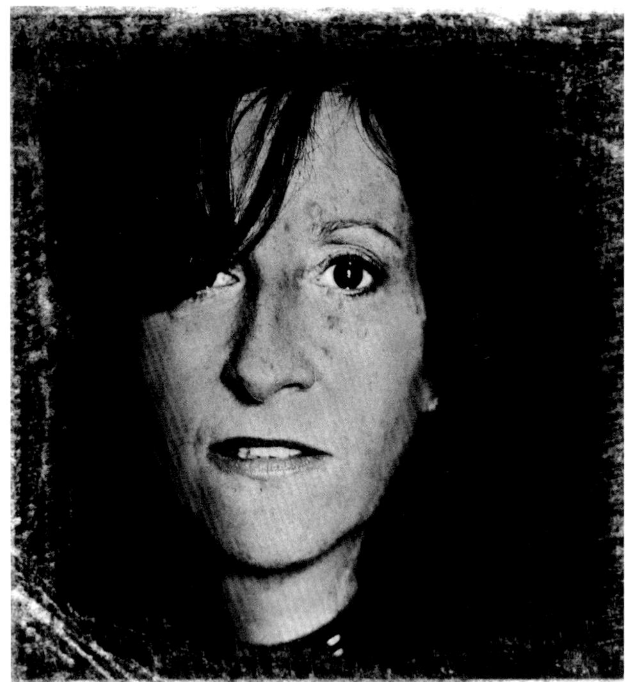

in the gigantic cosmos known as New York City. Lisa Lowell went there towards the end of the 1970s, after shedding her doubts about her own ability as a singer.

"I grew up in Long Branch, New Jersey. A scenic little seaside enclave. Dad was a brilliant jazz drummer who used to play with Benny Goodman and Artie Shaw. Mom was, and still is, a killer singer. I'd say she's a local jazz hero. Both of them were powerful sources of inspiration."

There was music all over. Everywhere. And it was contagious.

"There I was, a skinny little girl in tight jeans and high heels who wanted to sound like James Brown. In those days that never worked."

"One day some of my friends came into this practice room, pulled me out and said: 'Lisa, you're always out here flirting. You have a terrible tone on your saxophone. We want you to sing with us this summer. You're really not a sax player.'

"A great moment for me. It was an acknowledgment."

Back from Boston, she put together her own jazz band. But the local music scene felt a bit limited.

"I remember driving up and down the Shore feeling real antsy about being local. I was afraid I would disappear if I didn't find the way out of Jersey."

"Then I met this brilliant drummer named Howie Wyeth, the late, great, who made me realize that it could be fun and lucrative to be a backup singer. I just knew I had to get out, it was move out or die."

Lisa Lowell was off to New York, with the cat and the conga drums. She got a job as a waitress at the United Nations, of all places, and moved in with a film editor down in Soho.

Patti Scialfa, who grew up in Deal, just minutes from Long Branch, was already a part of her circle of friends. The reunion came in Greenwich Village.

"Patti already had songs that just blew me away. And she had writer's confidence. Definitely more confidence than me and Soozie, where the writing was concerned. I loved her for that. There weren't that many women who would dare to make their way in the rock 'n' roll industry."

"Damn, in some ways, that's still the way it is. This is one of the last bastions of a sexist world."

Lisa Lowell talks for a while about how Trickster conquered Greenwich Village. How they set their own stage on the streets.

"They got our tapes, 'lost' them, and then asked for new ones. So instead of playing on their stages we would block their doors by standing in front of the club. We had a huge audience on the streets."

She laughs and continues:

"I got the jazz bug, but I was too chicken when it came to singing. So I started playing saxophone instead, and went off to study at the New England Conservatory of Music. That was where everything changed. Because after a few drinks at a party I would get the nerve to sing.

"There we were: three skinny, hippie-looking chicks from the 'burbs who dressed really eccentric, put on red lipstick on the corner, drank cheap wine, smoked cigars, and played for anyone who wanted to listen. Then we sat in the Lion's Head, a bar in the Village, and counted the money. Like three old trolls.

"We were living the bohemian life. It was wild. It was great."

Off the streets, Scialfa, Lowell and Tyrell toured with Southside Johnny Lyon. Lisa Lowell had known Lyon since she was fourteen. She loved the band, and was convinced that the tour with the Asbury Jukes would let her live her rock 'n' roll dreams for all eternity.

"Of course, it was something that could never end. You got on that bus and you didn't have a care in the world. It was what we were going to do for the rest of our lives. A few months later we were dropped off in Times Square and it was all emptiness. I was like a puppet without strings, almost like I'd lost my family.

"Then we went on. We were riding a roller coaster for two years."

On tour with the Jukes, the Trickster attitude was still

there. Lowell says that Southside Johnny tried to play father figure. He was the boss who told his Jukes to leave the girls alone.

"But we didn't stay away from anybody. We did what we pleased. No one could tell us what we could and couldn't do. I actually think we scared Southside a little bit."

Lisa Lowell says that Southside Johnny has always been an amazing singer.

"I've known John for such a long time. He's a highly intelli-gent man, underrated as a singer, and is perhaps cast in much too big a shadow from the greater world view.

"The comparison between Johnny and Bruce just makes no sense. They both come from around here, from the same musical gene pool. But conceptually they are quite different, in spite of what they have in common."

When Southside Johnny couldn't take the backup trio to Europe, Lisa Lowell left. She went to Berlin, Germany, to write songs, and when she came back there was work with David

"The air is thinner up there. There's an adrenalin aspect to it, and there's a feeling of being an astronaut adapting to a completely different environment."

Johansen or, as he was more often known, Buster Poindexter.

"Soozie was sort of David's sidekick. I was more in the background, dressed in some type of acrobat costume. David had a hit with 'Hot, Hot, Hot,' and it kept the entire band, the Banshees of Blue, alive for twelve years. Amazing what one hit can do."

Patti Scialfa had gotten into the E Street Band. Tyrell and Lowell were also to join the inner circle.

"The first time I saw Patti with Bruce at the Meadowlands I was weeping uncontrollably. I felt like a runner up in a beauty contest. But that was okay. We were so proud of Patti, so happy for her.

"We used to hang out backstage and would be there while they were doing her hair. I'm sorry to say we didn't enjoy that on the Southside tour. God, the best we ever got back then was a couple of cheeseburgers. I guess it seems a little immature in retrospect, but at the time, when Patti joined the E Street Band, in spite of her talent, it felt like she had gotten very lucky in the rock 'n' roll lottery."

Springsteen's music had always been close to Lisa Lowell. Working with him, singing backup on several albums and finally going on tour with the Seeger Sessions Band, became a remarkable experience.

"Everything is so simple in the studio. Bruce knows exactly what he wants. He's very commanding, but in a quiet way. Does everything in one or two takes. He might ask you to sing like an angel, or gospelly, or a drunk cowboy. It's still OK. He's so confident it rubs off on everyone else."

But there are two sides to every coin. Lisa Lowell says that if she had been in Patti Scialfa's shoes, someone would have had to call a shrink pretty quick.

"The air is thinner up there. There's an adrenalin aspect to it, and there's a feeling of being an astronaut adapting to a completely different environment.

"Then, suddenly, it's all over. You go back to being a civilian again. That's when you remember you've been there by association. It wasn't your gig. You were just a color on someone else's palette. Someone who needed Lisa's blue dusky sound.

"Being a sideman isn't always easy, you are always having to juggle gigs, dealing with inconsistent monies and hope that your cronies will show some loyalty when the work comes in. Being good isn't all there is to it; there are so many great musicians, but we aren't all rock stars.

"People can be very misinformed. They might see me and think: 'Wow, Lisa sings with Bruce, she must live in a huge house.' Well maybe I do!" She laughs.

"These jobs come and go. That's how it is for most people, and there are so many good musicians. It's just amazing how much talent there is. I never think I'm better than others. I just think I have a certain thing, and if someone wants that certain thing they'll call me.

"I suppose I've been lucky. This career is definitely nothing I ever could have plotted. The things I've done were not through savvy politics. It was all through sheer passion. You've got to follow your heart, and hope it doesn't break."

Lisa Lowell says it's a wild ride and you've got to stay "wild, willing, and hopeful" to do what you want to do, for as long as possible.

"Sometimes people come up to me in New York and say: 'Hey Lisa, how's it going? Are you still singing?'

"What do you say to that? I'm not dead yet. And I even look fairly good, don't I? Did someone get me a job at McDonald's that I don't know about?"

"IT'S NOT JUST NOTES AND RHYTHMS"

Alan Chez

As the show is taping David Letterman says to his band leader, Paul Shaffer: "The new trumpet player sounds good."

Shaffer replies: "Doesn't he? His name is Alan Chez."

Letterman: "Did he get the gig or not?"

Shaffer: "I'm waiting to hear from you, Dave."

Letterman: "He stays."

Alan Chez believes that everything happens for a reason, and, as things turned out, the trumpet player from Jersey City would end up in New York City. He jammed in clubs all over Manhattan, met Paul Shaffer, and went on tour, at first with the World's Most Dangerous Band, later with Robert Cray and Tower of Power.

Chez always traveled with the Jersey attitude.

"Let's play. Let's break a sweat. Let's give the audience as much as it can take, and then a little more. When I was in California with Cray there was always talk about what songs would be saved for the encore. The others in the band would usually choose between two or three pieces.

"I would say: Let's do 'em all! If you're sweating, I'm sweating. For me there were no limits. That might be because I don't drink, I'm always fresh as a daisy. Or maybe it's that Bruce Springsteen three hour concert."

The address is Fifty-third and Broadway. We choose a backstage entry, since the fans are lingering right around the corner, hoping to get a glimpse of David Letterman or some of his guests.

Alan Chez receives us in the band's dressing room. He's munching on snacks and is in a great mood after another day on the job. Another day in front of millions of television viewers in 49 different countries. The Late Show is *the* late-night show, Letterman is *the* late-night host, and the CBS Orchestra is definitely among the most swinging house bands.

It's no wonder that "Chezman," as he's called, loves this job.

"I've been with Paul and Dave for nine years, now. And I swear, no two days are alike."

It was after his tour with Robert Cray in 1995 that Chez got back in touch with his old friend Paul Shaffer.

"I didn't want to go on the road anymore. So I called Paul and said: Hey, if you want to hire a trumpet player full time, I'll stay home."

"Okay, we'll see if anything turns up," replied Shaffer.

One month later it was time for the sweeps period, when the ratings of television programs determine their future. Chez did three weeks with the CBS Orchestra. It was "thanks and hey, great having you here."

Then one day in the studio, Letterman, in his usual way starts shooting the breeze with Shaffer, and in front of an audience of millions, Alan Chez finds out that he's got the job.

"After the show they called from CBS and asked if they could speak to my lawyer. I tried to play it cool, but what the hell. I'm a Jersey rat. I play in the clubs, I don't have a lawyer. Couldn't even find one in the yellow pages."

Chez's father called himself Chet Peters and sang country & western in Jersey City with his wife "Trixie" on backup

That's John Bongiovi, also known as Jon Bon Jovi.

"This was the late 1970s; I couldn't have been more than fifteen years old. No one in the band was older than fifteen. Jon was the lead singer, we had David Rashbaum (David Bryan of Bon Jovi) on keyboards. Me and David went to school together; we also played in the same high school band. David was actually a trumpet player. He played first and I played third trumpet.

"It's funny 'cause Atlantic City Expressway were really terrible when we started off. We did these local Battle of the Bands and we always lost. Even to country & western bands."

Still, here and there, people would listen. And, sometimes, they even liked the band.

"I remember one time when the owner of the Fastlane came by and said: 'Well, we don't like the winning band, but we like you guys. Would you like to come and play in the club?'

"The cool thing was that we ended up not just playing there. We became the house band."

vocals. Alan's two older brothers, Michael and Peter, completed the Cheznovitz family.

"They both played trumpet, so for me there was no other way. What kid doesn't want to be like his older brothers?"

Sometimes, when there was a party with no parents around, they'd wake him up.

"My brothers would be drinking with their friends, and they were supposed to be like the baby sitters. Well, they'd wake me up in the middle of the night and tell me to get my horn out and play. If I messed up they'd beat me up.

"Kind of strange, don't you think? Anyway, now it's paying off. Now, look who's doing good, ha, ha, ha."

The family moved to Edison, N.J., where Alan's father, the country singer, had started the town's drum corps. Alan, as a young boy, grew up with the band. He became one of the soloists, always ready to push the limits.

"Nervous? Never. It was a pure adrenalin kick."

Rock 'n' roll would deliver an even greater kick when the Fastlane in Asbury Park became home to the Atlantic City Expressway.

"It started in Sayreville, at Jon's place."

During these years the Fastlane was a runner up to the Stone Pony, the second hottest club on the local music scene. This was the house where John Bongiovi, David Rashbaum, and Alan Cheznovitz honed their crafts.

"Well, we started off as a Springsteen and Southside Johnny cover band. We got better and better, and after some time the guys from the Jukes would come down to see us and be blown away. We had three trumpets and one saxophone player. It was just balls to the wall. Damn, Jon sounded so good."

Alan Chez talks about Wednesday nights at the Fastlane. About being a teenager and the supporting act for Edgar Winter, Southside Johnny, and others.

"It didn't matter who we warmed up for. Atlantic City Expressway always got the main dressing room. Yeah, it's true."

That was made clear for the stars who came to Asbury Park. Worse than the fact that Winter or Johnny Lyon had to change in the warm up area was the fact that the alcohol commissioner could strike without warning.

"None of us were old enough to even be in the club. So when the red light was switched on, the quickest way out was through the main dressing room, which was right by an alleyway."

"Let's play. Let's break a sweat. Let's give the audience as much as it can take, and then a little more. "

"Deep down I think Jon always wanted to be like them. I actually think that more than anything he would have wanted to do the same thing as Southside, with the horns."

Atlantic City Expressway built up a reputation as the next big thing from Asbury Park. But, while still teenagers, the way to the top was not the simplest thing in the world. As a seventeen year-old, Alan Chez was given the offer to tour with Southside Johnny & the Asbury Jukes. "School first," said Mama Cheznovitz. "Alright Mama," said Alan.

"We'd be out late and drinking beer even though we weren't of age yet. Then we'd show up to school dead tired. David (Rashbaum/Bryan) and I went to the same high school in Edison, and we'll always have fond memories of the school band director."

Alan Chez talks about one exhausted Thursday morning when he was called into the teacher's office. The band director, Andy DiNiccola, who had been playing the night before with Atlantic City Expressway's opening act, cut straight to the point:

"Alan, you guys sounded real good last night. What time did you get home?"

"Like four in the morning."

"Alright, take the couch in my office. I'll wake you up before your next English class."

"I'm sure he did same for David. He was just a great guy to have for a band director."

The Atlantic City Expressway toured up and down the Jersey Shore for a number of years.

"What happened? Well, we were still a cover band and there was not much else to do. I quit, and Jon quit to be a heavy rocker. He put together John Bongiovi & the Wild Ones and played a type of thrash metal. Music that had nothing to do with Asbury Park or even Bon Jovi."

Still, friends would remain friends. Chez was in the horn section for Bon Jovi's warm up tour for 38 Special. He was also on the road with the *Slippery When Wet* tour. Through the years, there have been a number of studio sessions.

"Jon likes the horns. But I don't think he's ever used our recordings on any albums. It always got to the point when the manager said no horns. I guess he thought that heavy metal and horns didn't go together. Which turned out to be not true since Bruce Fairbairn, who produced *Slippery When Wet*, is a

trumpet player. He's done a damn good job, both with Bon Jovi and Aerosmith."

Alan Chez remembers one Bon Jovi night at Madison Square Garden in particular.

"Bruce Kapler, the saxophonist, and I were waiting in the wings. The crowd got jumping and the floor started to move. My heart was pounding. Hard.

"Jon is a friend of mine. I love working with him, and if he had not had a heavy metal career on the way I think he might have chosen some other path. We grew up with Bruce and Southside. Deep down I think Jon always wanted to be like them. I actually think that more than anything he would have wanted to do the same thing as Southside, with the horns."

Some eight years with Atlantic City Expressway, several years with Richie Rosenberg's Hubcaps. Tours with Dave Edmunds, Robert Cray, Tower of Power, Midnight Thunder, Joe Bonnano and the Hitmen, The Finns, Benny and the Spydrs, and the World's Most Dangerous Band.

"We've been doing the Hall of Fame with Paul Shaffer since the '80s. Actually, I have a fairly interesting week ahead of me. Look at the schedule: Hall of Fame induction for U2, the Pretenders, and Percy Sledge at the Waldorf Astoria. Then back to *The Late Show* to play with Al Green and the Four Tops."

Alan Chez always feels respect, and he's never uneasy.

"This is what I do. It's what I've been doing since I was fifteen. You're where you have to be, and you do your job. Letterman gives us ten weeks off every year. I'm cool for three days; after that my wife wants to kill me."

He gets back to his days in Edison, growing up:

"I don't know if it's the water in New Jersey. But I do know we're not like everyone else. Music has always been the way out. I share Bruce's point of view, that the music can always show you something better. Think about it: What feels best after a fight with your boss, your friends or your wife? Exactly. Music is the escape, it takes you someplace else. It's like a drug.

"Damn, every time I hear 'Hearts of Stone' or 'I Don't Want to Go Home' it all comes back to me. Man, I'm sixteen again. I can smell, and taste, and remember where I was. Even what girl was waiting backstage."

Alan Chez stayed in New Jersey. No one in Manhattan can understand it, but the fifty-six miles one way from Newton, NJ, to the job in the city is what Alan Chez needs to clear his head.

"My wife Cat and I, we've got six wonderful kids at home. Five girls and a son: Meika, Marie, Michelle, Jessica, Morgan, and Travis.

"But that time in the car has to be just mine. This is when I'm reminded of those rides down the Garden State Parkway. It's just me and the music I love: Beaver Brown, Bruce, Southside."

The contract with CBS goes on.

"Can't complain. I've been working with Paul for a good many years now, and I am still the youngest in the band. But I can never sit down and say: OK, I've had enough. That's not how it works.

"I guess I'm the only halfway successful horn player from Jersey who hasn't actually been a member of Southside's band. I've played with them lots of times, but I've never been a member. I came to New York because I wanted more. And I never want to stop playing. I'm always after something new. I can't say what, but this is not where it ends. I see things that haven't been done yet. I hear them in my head.

"Maybe it's that I'm looking for the way back to the music we grew up with. Bruce got pretty close with *The Rising*, and Southside is still playing. But still, it's not the same anymore. Not like the early Bruce or the early Southside. It doesn't have the soul to it."

Alan Chez says it again:

"It's a Jersey thing and there is definitely a Jersey sound. Seattle, for instance, had their time with Nirvana. But it's different with Jersey. We have something that's timeless. It's not just notes and rhythms. It's not white, it's not black. It's soul, rock 'n' roll, R & B. And it all fits together."

SCHOOL OF ROCK

Glen Burtnik

He declined the offer from Bon Jovi, but accepted when there was a call from Styx. Years later, back home in New Jersey, Glen Burtnik would finally make it to the top, composing a love duet for Patty Smyth and Don Henley.

Jack Black is the star of the movie, but the real School of Rock has a different master.

"I bet most musicians always wanted to be on the radio, working as DJs," says Glen Burtnik.

He welcomes us to the Hawk Radio Station in Ocean, New Jersey, just outside Asbury Park. This is where Glen Burtnik moonlights. His shows are taped on Thursdays and broadcast on Sunday mornings.

Target audience?

"Obviously, you want to reach young people. This is a classic rock station. I talk about the history of rock music. I'll play a song and then try to explain where the influences come from.

"I might talk about who wrote it, who played it, or even the instruments used on the particular recording. I think it's almost educational.

"In my experience, young people are interested, but they know far too little about music history."

Glen Burtnik says that his son Beau, who fronts his own band, the Dibs, and also plays bass with his dad, inspired him to take the radio job.

"Beau pointed out that whenever he'd ask me about a song I'll give him this big history lesson. I'd talk about the song, who wrote it, and at what time it was recorded. This band used to be that band, and so on

"So when I was invited to do a radio show I thought: 'OK, we'll do a School of Rock!'"

Glen Burtnik was born and raised in Irvington, New Jersey. In the '60s, as the Beatles happened, he fell in love with music and started making up his own songs.

"I know, you were looking for something more original. But it's just the truth. From the moment I saw them on Ed Sullivan, the Beatles changed everything. That was the trip. I wonder if I [would have] been a musician without the British invasion."

But Burtnik also wanted to dig deeper. He was moving on, getting into folk music, guided by the work of Bob Dylan and Pete Seeger.

"I had the guitar, and as soon as I learned how to play it I was writing more and more songs.

"After that, I guess things never really changed. I have always been a songwriter."

The Beatles were still there, nonetheless, and Burtnik made a u-turn. After a few years playing the local nightclub scene, he went to an audition for a show where the producers were looking to find sound- and look-alikes.

"The show was called *Beatlemania*. I auditioned and I got the part playing Paul McCartney.

"That went on for a while. Then I started working with Jan Hammer and spent some time in L.A., playing with a few different bands."

We're at the end of the 1970s, as Glen Burtnik makes his move back to New Jersey. Still working his way up when Jon Bon Jovi comes along with the offer.

"Jon and Richie Sambora went down to the Stone Pony one night. They had just signed a recording deal and Jon was looking for a second guitarist/keyboard player."

The offer went to Glen Burtnik, who said no thanks.

"Yeah. Ain't it funny?"

He knows that accepting the offer that night probably would have made a big difference. Moneywise as well as musically.

Still, you turned them down?

"Well, at the time I was busy with other things. Like playing with Bobby Bandiera in Cats on a Smooth Surface. That was a great gig, and those were great times.

"I guess everybody knows that Bruce Springsteen would come down to the Stone Pony almost every Sunday night to jam with us. The place was packed. Mostly, I'd say we were just a bar band playing old cover songs. But we played them well. That's why Springsteen would hang around, having fun."

Cats on a Smooth Surface was known as the local heroes, the house band rockin' the Pony, while Springsteen had already made it big, nationwide as well as internationally.

"This was like the early '80s, but to me Bruce was already

pretty big. *Born in the U.S.A.* sure pushed him to another level, but there were already albums like *Born to Run* that made him important. So I'm not that surprised about the way things turned out. He's obviously a very good songwriter."

Burtnik talks about his time with Styx without seeming entirely convincing.

"Well, it's obvious that I had realized what kind of career I could have had with Bon Jovi. I had also had some time

"Well, it's obvious that I had realized what kind of career I could have had with Bon Jovi. I had also had some time to think about what I wanted to do and maybe I wasn't meant be a solo artist."

Springsteen took off, Bon Jovi took off. And Glen Burtnik became one of the LaBamba Hubcaps, as Asbury Jukes trombone player Richie Rosenberg put together the next Stone Pony house band.

"At first I was the bass player. Then Bobby Bandiera left and I switched to the guitar. I also became the singer."

Still, there was always a part of Glen Burtnik that wanted to pursue a solo career, and come the mid 1980s that's what happened. A & M Records got hold of a demo. "Here Comes Sally" had the potential, and Burtnik was signed. After *Talking in Code* (1986) came *Heroes and Zeroes* (1987). Things started to happen, and Glen Burtnik was making a name for himself in North America as well as Europe.

"Well, maybe I was. But then one of my managers threatened somebody at the record label and that led to this legal problem where I couldn't go anywhere else. They weren't gonna release any records of mine until we had straightened all that legal stuff out."

The company philosophy had changed, and Glen Burtnik was hung out to dry.

"Yeah, and that's when Styx called."

The heavier rocking band Styx, formed in Chicago in 1969, was looking to replace guitarist Tommy Shaw, who went on the road with Damn Yankees. Glen Burtnik, who had once snubbed Bon Jovi, decided not to turn a second offer down.

"I was married, we had kids. Money started to become more important. At that point I also had enough material for an album to follow up *Heroes and Zeroes*, so in the end it turned out that Styx recorded some of those songs instead."

Edge of the Century, with five Burtnik originals including the single "Love is the Ritual" and the title track, was released in 1990.

"It was an interesting gig. It was good."

to think about what I wanted to do and maybe I wasn't meant be a solo artist. At least that's how it felt after having all these legal problems. Maybe I should just take a job when offered. I had decided not to pass on the next opportunity."

Glen Burtnik toured with Styx from 1989 until 1994, and then, in 1999, he was called back.

"In the interim Tommy Shaw was back with Styx, and I made my solo albums, *Palookaville* and *Retrospectable*."

Burtnik was back to recording his own stuff, partly thanks to one big song.

The year was 1992 as Glen Burtnik sat down with former Scandal singer Patty Smyth. They came up with this ballad titled "Sometimes Love Just Ain't Enough." The song was recorded as a duet with Smyth and Eagles star Don Henley, and this time Glen Burtnik was topping the charts.

Thinking back, he smiles and says:

"A number one hit. It made me money; I was getting a lot of respect. There were lots of offers. Everybody wanted to work with me, they wanted to have my songs. Suddenly, all my work seemed to have a bigger value."

Burtnik is not talking about revenge, but:

"Well, it was a whole new situation. My solo albums really never sold enough, and here was a song that was all over the place. So through that I met John Waite and a lot of different 1980s rockers."

Nonetheless, in 1999 he was back in Styx.

"I thought I was done touring but they offered me a job replacing the bass player. I took it, and I stayed with the band until 2003. By then I just had to leave."

Glen Burtnik says he couldn't take it anymore. Styx was

always on the road, always touring, and that wasn't the life Burtnik was looking for.

"So now I am back home, writing again and recording albums."

In 2004 *Welcome to Hollywood*, a thematic song cycle of snapshots from Glen Burtnik's life in American pop culture, was released.

"*Palookaville* was kind of calm down. It was a less rock album. This time I came back from the big rock show with Styx and I was in the mood to write songs that were a little more rock, a little more aggressive."

Burtnik says he always has to change things around.

"That's just the way it is. If I don't change, I'll burn out."

Glen Burtnik's time at the Stone Pony, with Cats on a Smooth Surface and LaBamba's Hubcaps, places him right alongside some of the greatest from the Asbury scene. He is often mentioned in the same context where Bruce Springsteen, Jon Bon Jovi, and Southside Johnny are among the most obvious names.

This makes him proud:

"I am glad for Bruce's sake, and for Jon's. They are both great songwriters, both full of energy. And most important: they're sincere. Bruce and Jon both write straight from the heart. That's what I try to do. That's what I believe in. I really can't do it any other way.

"Bruce, Jon, Johnny. They all set great examples, as performers and songwriters. But that doesn't mean that they have been my greatest influences."

Way back, in the 1960s, it all started with the British invasion. The Beatles. Glen Burtnik still loves that music and he loves to talk rock 'n' roll history. But when it comes to Asbury Park and the Jersey Shore, he'd rather look to the future. The music scene in Asbury Park, according to Burtnik, is still in the course of development. There's more to all this than nostalgic trips with Springsteen, Southside Johnny, Bon Jovi, or Glen Burtnik

"Asbury Park is a cool place; there are traditions here. But everything changes. Maybe we will never see a new Bruce Springsteen arise. On the other hand, that's not the end of things. Music goes on. It will never end. Not in a place like Asbury Park."

John Eddie

In the middle of the 1980s, Born in the U.S.A. served as the model. The record companies were looking for the next Springsteen and they found John Eddie. Twenty years later: John Eddie knows that his big breakthrough is never going to come, and he knows that old labels are hard to get rid of. "Without Bruce I don't think I would have had a career in music. But he casts a long shadow."

John Eddie wanted to be a priest, because priests got noticed in church every Sunday. But he would choose another path, because Grandma loved Elvis, and his three older sisters were into Motown, the Beatles, and the Rolling Stones.

The kid was headed into his teenage years. He'd moved from Richmond, Virginia, to southern New Jersey, and he had just discovered David Bowie.

"I was a fan, almost like a groupie. When Bowie was in Philadelphia to record *Young Americans,* me and some friends would hang out outside the studio."

And it was from listening to Davd Bowie, that John Eddie heard mention of Bruce Springsteen for the first time.

"There were a couple of older guys outside the studio, saying that Bowie might be recording a song by this Jersey singer named Springsteen. The song was called 'It's Hard to Be a Saint in the City.'

"A few days later I got sick, and when my sister went to the shopping center I asked her to buy me a new record. Either some old stuff by Alice Cooper or an album by that guy Springsteen. She came home with *Greetings from Asbury Park, N.J.*"

And?

"At first I didn't get it. I was a kid, and I thought it sounded just like Van Morrison. But by the end of the weekend Bruce was better than anything I had ever heard before. I was starting to understand what he was trying to communicate. It wasn't so hard to see why someone like David Bowie wanted to record one of his songs."

John Eddie, who at that time would be playing guitar in various teenage bands, had found a new hero.

"And then I got to see him live. I was actually on the way to a Bowie concert, but my friend's sister had gotten hold of some tickets to Bruce's show at a nearby college. The tickets were only two dollars."

John Eddie talks about meeting this theatrical artist.

"Theatric yes, but dressed in blue jeans and a t-shirt. Bruce was something completely different from Bowie. He was definitely for real."

"I can do that," John Eddie thought to himself.

"But never in the same way as Bruce. He wrote songs that were nine minutes long, and I had already learned to love pure pop. I was listening to the Raspberries and Nick Lowe. So the ambition was to start writing like Bruce, but still the songs wouldn't last any longer than three minutes.

"The problem was that Bruce himself had started doing the same thing. And he did it so much better than everyone else."

Bruce Springsteen's career exploded in 1984 with *Born in the U.S.A.* The record companies began feverishly searching for the next Bruce to make money off of.

CBS signed John Eddie. His debut album contained classic blue-collar rock. Max Weinberg was sitting in, playing drums, Nils Lofgren made a guest appearance. There were rave reviews in Europe, while reception in the U.S.A. was mixed.

"*Rolling Stone* magazine put the album to death. It wasn't so much about the music, instead I got the feeling that it was something personal. They stated, for example, that I had fired my band, which I had not done."

John Eddie shrugs his shoulders.

"My own thoughts on the album are that it turned out OK, but there are several songs that I never play anymore. Haven't done so since I turned forty-five. A song like 'Jungle Boy' was written when I was eighteen or nineteen. It's a matter of credibility."

He knows that CBS wanted the next Springsteen.

"But I was never the one they were looking for. I used to say that I was an E Street Wham. Then I grew up, became old and bitter."

John Eddie is laughing. He might have gotten a bit seasoned, but this guy's really not that old. Don't know about that bitterness either. He's just walking down memory lane, laughing about his days as a rock star.

Then he takes us back to a time when he used to read every article written about Bruce Springsteen. A time when John Eddie and his friends would romanticize the myths and legends of Asbury Park and then hitchhike there on weekends.

"Asbury Park was no more than an hour away from my hometown, but it still felt like such a big deal to go there. Palace Amusements, all the clubs. The Stone Pony. The Fast-

"Cool. He was one of eleven or twelve people in the audience."

That happened again on a number of occasions.

"We still run into each other every once in a while," says John Eddie, "but not as often as we used to."

The industry decided to put a label on John Eddie, and they wanted to stick to it. But everything that happened with the second album, *The Hard Cold Truth*, turned into another, less fortunate, story.

It started when John Eddie went to Los Angeles to work with Dwight Yoakam's producer, Pete Anderson. They wanted to do a rock 'n' roll album with country influences.

"When CBS found out about it they sent my manager, Tommy Mottola, to L.A. to convince me that this was not what they were looking for."

Instead, John Eddie flew to Minneapolis to start over with Larry Crane from John Mellencamp's band.

"That sounded OK to me. Mellencamp had, after all, done a number of good things."

In the end, there were three different producers involved. John Eddie says that he didn't stand up for himself, and that the results were "schizophrenic."

"I am still proud of some of the songs. But drum machines

"Asbury Park was no more than an hour away from my hometown,
but it still felt like such a big deal to go there.
Palace Amusements, all the clubs."

lane. We were sitting there staring, saying 'Wow, did you see those guys? They're with the Jukes' as soon as members of the Asbury Jukes horn section would walk by."

John Eddie was a fan. At the time he identified and compared himself with the rock 'n' roll tourists from Europe and Japan. The ones who still make their New Jersey pilgrimage.

And he still admires Springsteen:

"Bruce the person, above all else. His humbleness. Bruce knows exactly when he can help a band by jumping up onstage to jam. In the same way he knows when it's best to let things stand as they are. He's never been out to steal the spotlight."

Bruce Springsteen jumped up for John Eddie the first time at Clarence Clemons's club, Big Man's West, in Red Bank.

are never a good thing."

The album never made any charts, the contract was turned over to Elektra, and John Eddie chose to start over with Neil Young's producer, David Briggs. An album was recorded, but never released. He shows a crooked smile as he tells a tale about the classic battle between record company and artist.

"They spent 400,000 dollars on that record, but refused to put it out. I wasn't allowed to tear up the contract, either, so I ended up in a trial that lasted three and a half years. Pretty clichéd, right?"

John Eddie says that he doesn't really like to talk about those days. Because by the time the recording sessions were over, one of his closest friends was killed.

He bows down, eyes on the floor, and says:

"I sank deep. I just didn't care any more. I would do any kind of gig, almost without getting paid. I'd play just to get by.

"Anyone who'd offer me seventy-five dollars to sing for his dog's birthday party got himself a deal."

But there was a way back, with a little help from loyal fans.

"I was playing a shitty little gig on a snowy Thursday night. There were just a few people in the audience, but this one guy comes up to me and asks when am I going to put out something new. I told him I didn't have a label or any money to make a new record. He tells me he'll pay for it. I figured he was drunk and he probably was, but he turned out to be a guardian angel. Because believe it or not, he actually came through for me and got me back in the studio."

Happily Never After was released on an independent label.

"An unbelievable story, I know. But that was what gave me the inspiration I really needed, and I had gotten back to writing

songs just for acoustic guitar. Every song could stand on its own, and I couldn't care less what others thought about it."

John Eddie felt free and creative. And for some reason he, once more, had gotten the attention of the industry.

That's why, in 2003, the Lost Highway label released the commercial comeback *Who the Hell is John Eddie?*, an album recorded in Memphis under the guidance of the legendary Jim Dickinson.

"This one's my favorite. The album isn't country, but it has twang. It speaks for me, it tells who I am today. And it has actually sold better than anything else I've recorded."

Who the Hell is John Eddie? took him out on the road again. John Eddie has opened for John Hiatt, Los Lonely Boys, and Lisa Marie Presley. With the songs from this album he won his old audience back, and found a new one along the road.

**"They spent 400,000 dollars on that record, but refused to put it out.
I wasn't allowed to tear up the contract, either, so I ended up
in a trial that lasted three and a half years."**

John Eddie seems to be a happy man. He was given a second chance, and being skilled enough to grab that opportunity makes him proud.

We're backstage, at this club in Philadelphia owned by radio station XPN World. Tonight's supporting act, country rocker Terri Hendrix, is out there in front of the audience. John Eddie is anxious to get ready.

"Never played here before," he says. "Don't know what to expect."

Half an hour later he goes on stage. The house is packed.

"Fancy," says John Eddie to the audience. "What kind of place is this, anyway?"

Then he sings "Play Some Skynyrd," the song that captures the atmosphere in a redneck bar where only cover bands ever bother to play. He works his way to the final line of the chorus: *Who the hell is . . . ?*

The audience sings along. Fancy place, maybe. But right here, right now, in Philadelphia, everyone knows who John Eddie is.

The Stone Pony

STAGE ENTRANCE

HISTORY WRITTEN ON THE SIDEWALK

Lee Mrowicki

Time-worn by salt spray from the sea, much of what has been now begins to pale. Crumbles apart. But certain things remain. Lee Mrowicki reads: "Hey Brucie! . . . Sugar Miami Steve."

Outside the Stone Pony there is history written in cement, composed by heroes such as Sugar Miami Steve Van Zandt. Today, the sidewalk, like the club, gives the impression of being past its prime. But perhaps it's like Lee Mrowicki says:

"A lot has changed in Asbury Park. But there are things in this town that will never disappear. In some remarkable way, Asbury has lived its own life independent of the world outside. And that's how it will always be, as long as Donald Trump doesn't show up to buy it all, including the Stone Pony."

A few generations along the Jersey Shore have virtually made the Stone Pony and Lee Mrowicki synonymous with one another. He was a DJ during the golden years and well beyond them. He saw Asbury Park's rise and experienced the beginning of the town's decay. Mrowicki has been there on the long journey of the white pony.

Lee Mrowicki says that it is hard for him to talk about all the things from the past. Playing the Pony was what he did for thirty years, and reminiscing can be very emotional.

"Sure, it happens that I wish I could go back. We always had a cool attitude at the Pony. Everybody knew that Bruce would come here to play with someone, or just to have a beer or two with his friends. The locals were used to meeting Bruce, and they learned to respect his privacy. There were always people looking at him, but it was very rare that anyone had to step in. Most of those who passed through the doors knew the rules: Bruce is here. OK, leave him be. It was totally uncool to bother him, and anyone who couldn't follow the rules would soon find themselves in the street.

"I've had so many great moments here. But you usually don't appreciate that type of thing while it's taking place. It's just something you think about a long time after it happened."

Lee Mrowicki was twelve years old when his family moved from Jersey City to Asbury's neighboring town, Neptune.

"Jersey City was a multicultural place. It's close to Hoboken, and there is a scene that fostered a lot of well known artists. Sinatra, of course. But he was not the only one. I grew up with bands that played on the street corners, and I listened to black R & B bands on the radio. Then came the Beatles."

Mrowicki learned to play the guitar. And he still plays, even though it has been a long time since he was part of any band.

Looking back, he remembers that the kids in Neptune never hung out with the kids from Asbury Park. There was a clear rivalry between the schools.

"My impression was that nobody appeared to live in Asbury. You went there to go shopping or just to enjoy yourself. Maybe to listen to some music. The well known areas were downtown and at the beachfront. We didn't know much about the rich neighborhoods in Deal, which was to the north, along Ocean

"In some remarkable way, Asbury has lived its own life independent of the world outside. And that's how it will always be, as long as Donald Trump doesn't show up to buy it all, including the Stone Pony."

"One sound? I don't know, but I guess that my definition in that case would be a band where the singer has a raspy voice and where there's a saxophone player."

Avenue. And we didn't know the streets west of the railroad tracks; Springwood Avenue and other places where the black population had their homes."

In 1966, when Lee Mrowicki came to town, Asbury Park was, more than anything, a shopping Mecca.

"It's true that a lot changed after the upheaval of 1970, but the fact is that there was still life along the boardwalk. Asbury Park continued to be a vacation spot, at least until the middle of the 1970s."

The music scene was nothing new. It didn't start with Bruce Springsteen, even less with the Stone Pony. Lee Mrowicki knows that Glenn Miller played in Convention Hall and that people came to Asbury Park for music much earlier.

"What happened in the end of the 1960s had a lot to do with the Beatles. Every high school had its bands, and each band had its own Beatles imitation. But Asbury Park was not unique in that respect. There were tons of places to play along the Shore."

The Upstage Club changed that scene. When Tom and Margaret Potter opened the joint on Cookman Avenue, Lee Mrowicki was fifteen and living in Ocean Grove, a town that, according to Mrowicki, had "liberal interpretations of drug policy."

The Upstage became home to Mrowicki and his peers. Those who weren't old enough for the nightclubs, but who had grown tired of high school bands playing Top 40 gigs.

"The school dances were important anyway. A lot of things started there, when Buzzy Lubinsky was DJ. Buzzy spun records and played drums to all the songs himself. Then he brought in Vini Lopez. Vini became Buzzy's protégé and they started playing both soul and R & B.

"I met Vini at the dances, in 1968 I believe. He was four years older than me and it wasn't often that younger guys got to talk with the older ones. But I got along fine with Vini, and now we've been friends for almost forty years."

Vini Lopez brought attitude to the Upstage. Lee Mrowicki says that psychedelia had begun to take root, and that the Upstage was the place where music did not follow the norms. White kids listened to, and played, black music—soul and R & B.

Mrowicki also met Bruce Springsteen at the Upstage. He felt a sense of respect, and recognized that Springsteen was a unique songwriter.

"I grew up with Bruce's music and can relate to everything that he talks about. Before *Greetings from Asbury Park* came out, I got to hear demo versions of the songs. When *The Rising* was recorded I was also given a chance to listen prior to its release. I guess that when you get close enough to an artist, the relationship grows deeper. It's no longer about being a fan."

But *The Rising* was an album that reached deep into the heart and soul of Lee Mrowicki.

"It was shortly after 9/11. I was on the way home, playing the album on the car stereo, and I just burst out in tears. We were in a period of great fear. I knew people who died in the attacks. And here was an artist who did something I had never experienced before. Bruce talked about people who died and were let into heaven. He told the story in a way that was unbelievably powerful. I have never, not before and not since, heard any other singer, songwriter, journalist, or writer grasp the subject with such emotional strength."

Lee Mrowicki says that he's always felt connected to Springsteen's music. He witnessed greatness early on; he was close to all this when Springsteen turned Asbury Park into an international trademark. But Mrowicki, with thirty years at the Stone Pony, doesn't want to equate the artist with what has been called the Asbury Park sound.

"We always had different influences. Southside Johnny & the Asbury Jukes played at the club three nights a week: Tuesdays, Thursdays, and Sundays. On Mondays the Pony was open for country rock, and Wednesdays were about heavy metal. One sound? I don't know, but I guess that my definition in that case would be a band where the singer has a raspy voice and where there's a saxophone player. We've had bands like that, but we also had a ton of others."

The local scene went through a number of changes. The record labels that first came to Asbury to find the next Bruce Springsteen soon wanted to have something else. Lee Mrowicki says that for many Asbury artists, it was the kiss of death to be associated with Springsteen.

"Everyone and everything was compared with him. Take a

guy like George Theiss. George really had all the potential in the world, but he never got that lucky. You have to remember that Bruce recorded three albums before he had any success. After that he continued to develop."

When it comes to the future of music in Asbury Park, Lee Mrowicki says:

"Nowadays it's become so much harder to make a profit. Everything used to be cheaper, not just the bands. Today, for example, we're talking astronomical figures just for insurance. It's not uncommon for people who fall and get hurt to sue the clubs."

"Maybe," continues Mrowicki, "everything would have been different if a record company had thrown in a million dollars. But that never happened, and while Bruce took the elevator to the top, Johnny got stuck on the third floor."

Lee Mrowicki says he has a lot to be proud of. He has a life of music to remember and he's found a way of showing how much this has meant to him.

Mrowicki spends countless hours doing volunteer work based in music. Daytime you'll find him at the Freehold Music

"I think that was the first time that people outside Asbury really cared about the Stone Pony and our local music scene. That was when Asbury started being referred to as America's Liverpool."

Nobody knows if Asbury Park will ever get back to what it used to be. Like when Southside Johnny & the Asbury Jukes went national before the release of their debut album. Back then, in 1976, Lee Mrowicki was working in promotion.

"It was cool, because the management at a large station in New York tried to get Bruce involved. But Bruce didn't sign contracts. So the local station, WJLK, got the chance to do the broadcast, despite the fact that we really didn't even have the equipment necessary.

"Bruce showed, of course. That was nothing strange to the people of Asbury Park. We knew that he used to play with the Jukes."

Springsteen came out for the show. As did Ronnie Spector, Lee Dorsey, and assorted E Streeters. The Stone Pony event attracted DJs, record labels, and the media. The broadcast was nationwide, with millions of people listening.

"I think that was the first time that people outside Asbury really cared about the Stone Pony and our local music scene. That was when Asbury started being referred to as America's Liverpool."

Southside Johnny got a proud launch. The path was marked out for the Jukes, but Johnny Lyon's crew never made it to the top.

"There were different reasons. The Jukes were ahead of their time and Johnny wasn't Bruce. He wasn't the James Dean type. The band recorded albums but never got enough radio play. They had a following in Jersey, Philly, and Boston. But in Chicago or Austin, Texas there were not many people listening.

Center, but he's also well known as one of the founders of Jersey Artists for Mankind, which, among other things, released the single "We Got the Love."

"I'm never going to be a millionaire, but I have earned a nice living within the music industry, and it just feels good to do something meaningful. It's a matter of using one's talents in the right way, in charity and education.

"There is power in music. It's about big feelings; happiness and sorrow. Music stirs the soul; it touches your heart and your brain."

Lee Mrowicki talks about a major moment, perhaps one of his greatest.

"We were organizing a Christmas party for a handicapped children's benefit. During the break, between various performances, a young guy got onstage and sang 'Silent Night.' It was clear that he suffered from Down's syndrome, but his heart was into the song. Everybody applauded him and then thought nothing more of it.

"Half an hour later a woman came up to me and said, 'Thank you. That was my son who was singing. He has been shut within himself and not said a word in over two years. Tonight he sang, and then went straight over to his friends to join their conversation.'"

Mrowicki says that he broke down in tears.

"I cried, everyone cried. With a Catholic upbringing, maybe I should start believing in miracles? But all I know is that there is great power in music."

HOME COOKING
PEP

Bob Benjamin

Sometimes music can mean something big. Sometimes music can do beautiful things. Sometimes rock 'n' roll can bring life. This is what Bob Benjamin believes in. This is what his friends believe in. And every year, in the fall, they all see the proof.

A hell of a disease, Parkinson's. As we meet, Bob Benjamin has been fighting it every day for the last decade. He says that life is OK. There are good days and bad days. But life is always OK.

This particular day his opponent is playing mean. Bob Benjamin walks bent forward, hobbling slightly, towards the car. Then he starts to jog, and he's just about to lose balance before managing to grab on to a post. He comes to a stop, takes a breather, laughs, and says:

"I used to play hockey, so I can usually manage a fall. If I run then I can only fall forward, with the hope that my arms will break the fall. When I walk slowly there is a greater risk of falling backwards and hitting my head."

The doctors made the diagnosis in 1995. At the time Bob Benjamin had just gotten the job as manager for Pittsburgh's Joe Grushecky. He was at his office, printing out the lyrics to *American Babylon*, the Grushecky album produced by Bruce Springsteen.

"My elbows hurt. But as a former athlete I just thought the pain was some complication from playing hockey."

Then the pain started showing up a little too often. Benjamin visited doctors, but got no answer. Not until a neurologist conducted a thorough exam.

"It was almost a relief to get a diagnosis. Now the illness had a name and I knew what I had to do to fight it."

Benjamin says that the medications usually keep the worst symptoms at bay for three or four hours. But to some extent, the condition does as it pleases. It's up and down. Some days are worse than others. He's learned to be cautious.

"I've stopped commuting to New York, and sometimes I can't drive a car. But tonight I'm thinking about going down to Asbury Park. John Eddie is playing the Stone Pony."

Bob Benjamin shows determination. The fight is still on, and he has resolved to win.

"They say Parkinson's makes people depressed, but that's not been my experience. Maybe I'm the one who is the great pretender, since I am happy."

"Light of Day" is a song written by Bruce Springsteen. Light of Day is also an expression that brings hope to Americans with Parkinson's. It might not be cause to believe in miracles, but it's at least enough to get people believing in the healing power of music. Because the Light of Day concerts in Asbury Park and Sayreville don't just bring together some of the East Coast's most renowned rock artists; Willie Nile, Joe Grushecky, Garland Jeffreys, Gary U.S. Bonds, "LaBamba" Rosenberg, Jesse Malin, and, of course, Bruce Springsteen. The major goal is to collect money for Parkinson's research.

It started on a small scale, with a birthday party at the end of the 1990s, and Bob Benjamin remembers how that party brought in a few thousand dollars. In 2004, after three nights at the Stone Pony, he was able to donate $120,000 to research: the profit from admissions and some more or less appealing rock artifacts sold at auction. Max Weinberg's drumsticks, Nils Lofgren's guitar.

But the largest attraction was called Bruce.

After the premiere at the Stone Pony in 2000, Light of Day moved to Sea Bright's Tradewinds, which later closed its doors. Then, in 2003, it was back to the Pony. Still with Joe

Grushecky as the official headliner. Never with Springsteen on the poster.

"The fans count on Bruce. I can only hope, and up to this point he has been amazingly generous. The next step is for me to get up the nerve to ask him if he might be able to commit in advance. It would mean unbelievably much."

That promise never came for fall of 2005. For the first time, Light of Day was held without Springsteen, who was out on the final leg of his *Devils & Dust* tour. But Bob Benjamin got things the way he wanted anyway. Light of Day had grown. The three-night event was premiered at the Stone Pony and the two remaining shows were held at the significantly larger Starland Ballroom in Sayreville. In addition, Benjamin had taken the show on the road, to the House of Blues in Los Angeles and even all the way to Italy.

The fans got Pete Yorn and Jesse Malin, Southside Johnny and "LaBamba," Soozie Tyrell and Gary U.S. Bonds, Willie Nile and Joe Grushecky, and much more to boot. But, for 2005, they got no Springsteen.

"I want Light of Day to grow even more, and I need Bruce for that. We'll see what happens in the future, if I dare to ask."

Question asked or not, on December 2, 2006, Springsteen was back onstage for the cause. First he would join Philly-based rockers Marah and just after midnight the Starland Ballroom was rewarded with an hour-long set with Springsteen and long time pal Grushecky.

Joe Grushecky's career was on the way to taking off in the middle of the 1990s. His friendship with Bruce Springsteen first resulted in his recording a few songs written by Springsteen. Their collaboration soon developed into production of a full-scale album, and finally, Springsteen toured as a guitarist in Grushecky's band. The album was hyped, but sales never lived up to expectations. Grushecky was soon back as an independent artist, and his manager, Bob Benjamin, holds no fantasies of anything changing:

"This job has its moments, it really does. But the market is tough for artists like Joe."

Bob Benjamin grew up in New Rochelle, twenty miles north of New York City. He became interested in music in high school and the first album he bought was Don McLean's *American Pie.*

"I was only sixteen when Bruce played at the Bottom Line in New York, and the minimum age to get in was eighteen. But my friend had an older brother who was there to tell me about it. So I bought *Born to Run*, for $2.99. I was sold immediately and I got both *Greetings* and *The Wild, the Innocent* a few days later."

Springsteen had something Benjamin had never heard before. The lyrics were the first thing to capture him.

"It was definitely the words that made Bruce unique. Even more unique than Dylan."

In 1976, he discovered another Jersey hero, and when

"They say Parkinson's makes people depressed, but that's not been my experience. Maybe I'm the one who is the great pretender, since I am happy."

Bob Benjamin runs a management agency in Highland Park, with Joe Grushecky as its most established artist. Other clients include Dawne Allynne, Boccigalupe & the Bad Boys, and Joe D'Urso. Benjamin also owns a record label, which he runs on the side.

"Well, Schoolhouse Records is at least a label, and I have a distribution network for releases. But all the records are financed by the artists themselves."

Neither Grushecky, Allynne, nor Boccigalupe (Tony Amato) can live on their music alone, which makes Benjamin even less likely to grow rich off their careers.

"Joe D'Urso is the only one for whom music is a full-time thing. But Joe has to work hard, he is always out on tour."

Southside Johnny took the Jukes to Buffalo in October of the same year, Benjamin elbowed his way to the edge of the stage.

"I was hooked. These guys from Jersey, Bruce and Johnny. No New York bands had what they had. Energy, passion. The Jukes played with hats and sunglasses. They were so cool. You wanted to be like them."

A few months passed before Springsteen came to town. In February of 1977, the tour bus was braving the season's worst snowstorm. Bob Benjamin's journey with the E Street Band had begun, and the first real payoff came in Toronto some weeks later.

"I went up and got an autograph. I'd never met any rock stars before, but this guy seemed nice."

**"I want Light of Day to grow even more, and I need Bruce for that.
We'll see what happens in the future, if I dare to ask."**

It was spring of 1978 and Bob Benjamin was still in college. *Darkness on the Edge of Town* was released, and Benjamin wrote an article on Springsteen for *Thunder Road Magazine*. In May he went to the next concert, hung out by the stage, and talked a bit with members of the E Street Band.

"They asked if I wanted to meet Bruce, so I went backstage. I knocked on the door to his dressing room. Bruce opened and said: 'Hi, come on in.' Then he wondered what the fans thought of the show. The next day we had breakfast together, Bruce, me, and Garry Tallent. I started talking about a song, a bootleg version of 'Rendezvous.' But Garry warned me: 'Don't say anything, you'll make him angry.'

"I remember that Bruce had to borrow money to pay for breakfast."

A few blocks away was the theater where the band would be playing that night. Benjamin asked if he could be there during sound check, but the answer was no.

"So I stayed there, outside, until the sound guys let me in. I hid in the balcony and from there I taped Bruce's entire sound check. He doesn't know anything about that."

His friendship with Springsteen started there.

"I was a fan. I'm still a fan, and I'm glad to be able to help out when Bruce needs me. He called during the work on the *Tracks* box set. 'Hey, bootleg man,' he said. Because sometimes I know more about Bruce's songs than he knows himself. I've collected his material since the end of the 1970s. A song like 'Iceman,' for example, he had completely forgotten about. How can you forget a song like that? It's fantastic. "

In 1980, the same year that *The River* was released, Bob Benjamin took his college exams. Willie Nile, whom Benjamin knew from school, released his first album. Benjamin did an interview, and the article was published in Buffalo. A dedicated rock 'n' roll fan was on the way to becoming part of the music industry.

Bob Benjamin moved to New York, worked in a record store, and started commuting between Manhattan and Asbury Park.

"An hour and a half one-way. No problem. The bars stayed open until three in the morning."

At the end of the 1980s, Benjamin got a job as a sound scanner for *Billboard*. He traded New York for New Brunswick, N.J., and stayed with *Billboard* for three years. Then came the promotion assignments, first for John Prine and then for the New York label, Razor & Tie.

"We sold 300,000 copies of John's *The Missing Years*. Amazing when you consider that he released the album on his own label."

Then, halfway into the 1990s, the next opportunity arrived when Barbara Carr, from Springsteen's management, suggested Benjamin as a new manager for Joe Grushecky. That was about the same time the disease appeared.

Some ten years later Bob Benjamin says that certain days are better than others, but that life is always OK. He's fighting hard, and expects to win. The Light of Day concerts to follow will bring in even more money, the compilation album *Light of Day* (which pays tribute to the songwriter Bruce Springsteen) is going into its second edition at press. It has sold 25,000 copies to date. Profits from concerts and albums are donated to research on Parkinson's disease, cancer, and ALS.

Springsteen's "Light of Day" has become a symbol for the true power of music. It has shown that rock 'n' roll can make a difference. Bob Benjamin says that he likes the song, that it inspires him. But "Bootleg Man" actually has other favorites: "Badlands," "Darkness on the Edge of Town," "Promised Land."

That's what he wants to hear in future Light of Day shows.

Because the fans are counting on Springsteen to be there, and Bob Benjamin hopes that's how it will turn out.

He can even imagine asking: "Hey, Bruce. Will we see you at shows to come?"

Tony Pallagrosi

In the mid-1970s, Tony Pallagrosi would be rocking the Shore with the Asbury Jukes. Later he became the founder of the Stone Pony house band, the Shots. These days you'll find Pallagrosi on Jernee Mill Road in Sayreville, central New Jersey, running one of North America's top ten concert nightclubs.

Tables are set at the Starland Ballroom. Tony Pallagrosi is expecting 500 guests for the most intimate 2005 Light of Day Concert.

Last night the house was packed as Joe Grushecky brought in the Houserockers, along with Garland Jeffreys, Willie Nile, Jesse Malin, and Pete Yorn. Tonight, Grushecky, Malin, and Yorn are back for the finale, but this time around playing their songs acoustic. Light of Day, part three, is hosted by Gordon Brown's Writers in the Raw. Tony Pallagrosi, co-owner of the venue, is sitting upstairs in his office, enjoying a pleasant evening that's bringing in good money for a good cause.

Pallagrosi tells us how he and Jerry Bakal bought the Starland Ballroom in September of 2003 and opened the place three months later.

"Today we are the leading concert nightclub in New Jersey. As a matter of fact we're among the top ten venues in North America, in terms of ticket sales. According to *Pollstar* magazine, the Starland Ballroom was number nine in 2004, and after the first half year of 2005 we were fifth."

Checking the calendar you will find heavy rock bands, such as Skid Row, Quiet Riot, and W.A.S.P., among the top acts.

"Yeah, we get a lot of heavy rock, 'cause that's where music's at for the most part on this level. There are many bands touring, playing that kind of music, that can do 1,000 to 2,500 seats and that's what we look for."

Heavy metal in the 2000s. But that's not where Tony Pallagrosi started out. Pallagrosi, a former trumpet player for the Asbury Jukes, the Shots, and Cold Blast & Steel, says that the first music he really loved was jazz.

"But I wasn't good enough to be an outstanding jazz musi-

cian, not by any stretch of the imagination. So I developed an interest, naturally, in R & B. I learned to love the way the horns were produced on Stax/Volt records. I always had a deep feeling for the way Wayne Jackson sounded and playing like him was a lot easier than trying to copy Miles Davis, Clifford Brown, or Dizzy Gillespie. And by doing so, that's where I ended up."

Tony Pallagrosi grew up about twenty miles south of Asbury Park, in a beach town called Lavallette. But as a kid he was always going to Asbury, because there was a big shopping district and his mother enjoyed spending money at Steinbach's department store on Cookman Avenue. Pallagrosi is remembering ice cream soda and skating lessons.

"Asbury Park was really beautiful in those days."

A couple of years later rock 'n' roll came to town, with Tony Pallagrosi among the kids seeing the Rolling Stones at Convention Hall.

"This was back in 1965. Seeing the Stones was my first professional musical experience. I was a big fan, of course, but I can't say that this was the show that really affected me. That came a little later, when I was in Convention Hall to see Ten Years After. The band opening was Mott the Hoople, and I remember the curtain rising. My first view of Ian Hunter: the sunglasses, the top hat, that big white gown. He was pounding out the riff to 'All the Way from Memphis.' I was mesmerized by that, and the next day I ran out and bought my own pair of sunglasses. I've been wearing them ever since."

In the early 1970s Tony Pallagrosi had gotten to know saxophone player Eddie Manion. They were working the dance clubs together with a band called Amusement. Come 1973, the band fell apart, Manion joined the navy, and Pallagrosi went back to college.

"About two and half years later I had heard that Eddie was back, so I went to see him at his family's house in Lakewood. They told me he had come home but was out for the moment. I said: 'Well, tell him I've got another band for him to join.'"

Manion and Pallagrosi got back together, rehearsing a couple of months with a band in Toms River.

"It was just horrible. Eddie said: 'We shouldn't be doing this. Let's go down to the Stone Pony because a friend of mine, Vini Lopez, who used to play with Bruce, is now playing with the Shakes there. Maybe he'll know if there's any job to find.'

"That night Vini walks over and before Eddie says anything Vini goes: 'A friend of mine, this guy Southside Johnny, is looking for a baritone sax and a trumpet player.' Vini said he'd get us an audition, and that was it."

The Asbury Jukes were already together. The debut album was recorded, but had not been released. As Pallagrosi and Manion got their audition, Johnny Lyon was still playing the local club scene.

"As we see Johnny at the Pony he tells that we're hired and just as he turns to walk away he says: 'And by the way, we have an album coming out.'

"I had come out of college, and I just wanted to take a semester off. So I said to Eddie: 'Holy shit, I thought I was gonna do this for six months, but this is like a real thing. I don't know if I really want to do this.' Then Eddie goes: 'If you fuck this up I'm gonna kill you.'"

Tony Pallagrosi stayed with the Jukes for a couple of years. The band was drawing attention, things were starting to happen. Nonetheless, he chose to leave.

"If you wanna know the truth I didn't think I was good enough, and that made me feel uncomfortable. It was like I hadn't really paid any dues to be here. I wasn't looking for it, and it just kind of fell in my lap. I left because I was in a negative space."

He says there were no regrets. It was time to do something different. For a while Pallagrosi tried bartending, but six months later he was back in the game, forming his own band.

This was the Shots, and the glory days of the Stone Pony.

"Yeah, I would say so. The Pony was open seven days a week; drinking age was eighteen. The place was rockin'."

Tony Pallagrosi recruited his players among a circle of friends. Billy Hector came in from North Jersey, there were long-time pals David Nunez, Steve Rava, and Michael McCabe. He would also hook up with locally famed singer Donnie Bertelson.

"Donnie, I would say he was as good as Peter Wolf. He danced as well, and he sang his balls off. A soulful guy. He just had problems."

At this time Asbury Park would see bands such as the Shots, the Shakes, and the Cahoots. Tony Pallagrosi says the Shots outplayed them all.

"I think we were the best band around, 'cause we could play stuff that others couldn't."

Still, that record deal never came.

"Well, a couple of guys in the band, myself included, wanted to write, but then drugs played a big part. I was as much to blame as anyone else, as far as getting high and crazy. Donnie and I would sing a set, just like Pete Townshend and Roger Daltrey, then we'd go into the dressing room and beat the shit out of each other.

"Donnie was very emotional. I would call songs that I knew would tear him up. It was bad, just bad."

Neither the Shots nor Donnie Bertelson would find the road to success. A few years back, Bertelson was killed in a fire.

"Donnie was a beautiful soul, but kind of lost. He found it, he was a great R & B singer. He just never embraced it."

Picking up the pieces from bands such as the Shots and the Cahoots, Tony Pallagrosi would start over in Cold Blast & Steel, primarily a cover band with Lance Larson singing. And as Larson left to do his own thing with Lord Gunner Group, Cold Blast & Steel was over.

"I said to Eddie: 'Holy shit, I thought I was gonna do this for six months, but this is like a real thing. I don't know if I really want to do this.' Then Eddie goes: 'If you fuck this up I'm gonna kill you.'"

Instead, Pallagrosi joined an all-star band from Virginia, doing "the whole Boston to Richmond thing."

"That lasted three years, and I met some great players, including Robbin Thompson, who used to sing with Springsteen in Steel Mill. It was interesting to be part of the beach music scene 'cause all that was huge in the Southeast. It wasn't like the Beach Boys. This beach music came from Little Willie John and bands such as the Catalinas. They sold millions of records in that area, but crossing into Delaware nobody knew what it was about."

It was regional, though. Not local, like the Asbury Park scene.

"Not at all. They had radio stations, record stores, labels. Asbury bands had none of that. It was a Jersey Shore thing. The Shots would have 500 people on a Thursday night at the Stone Pony, but you take us and put us in the Tradewinds then

"I had booked Fatima Mansions, and as the opening act we had some kids from Pennsylvania called Live. They were like seventeen years old, but I'll never forget standing with my back to the stage as Ed Kowalczyk started to sing.

"Holy shit! Who was this guy, with this huge voice? That was cool."

Pallagrosi ran Legend Productions for a number of years. Then he heard about Jerry Bakal, who had a company called Swing Street. Bakal was doing jazz shows, but all of sudden he signed Chris Isaak and sold out the Count Basie Theatre in Red Bank.

"I got pissed off. I thought I should meet this guy, and I dogged him for six months. He was the general manager of

"Donnie, I would say he was as good as Peter Wolf. He danced as well, and he sang his balls off. A soulful guy. He just had problems."

we wouldn't do that. Same thing with the Jukes, initially. Until they got signed they wouldn't do tremendously outside of the Pony. It was really centered and unique in that tiny area. Everybody seemed to wanna check it out there. The Stone Pony was like a totem pole. It seemed much more powerful to pray there."

Tony Pallagrosi got out of the business for a while, and later he would turn to managing nightclubs, such as the legendary Fastlane, and Club Xanadu at 911 Kingsley Street, the house that was once home to the Student Prince.

On May 26, 1984, Club Xanadu became world famous as Bruce Springsteen jumped onstage with local act Bystander for the first public performance of "Dancing in the Dark."

"I had a great time doing that and I got to run the place with Diamond Dallas Page, who became a world-famous wrestler and who is one of my best friends to this day."

In the early 1990s, Pallagrosi was persuaded to start his own business.

"Well, one day this girl shows up at my house. She had incorporated a name, she even brought a little logo, and she told me: 'You have an account, now why don't you do something.'"

This is how Legend Productions was founded. Tony Pallagrosi can't recall the first few bookings, but there is one little gig at the Brighton Bar in Long Branch that easily comes to mind:

Convention Hall and they had done a whole bunch of shows that tanked. Finally, we got together and I told him that I could have saved him an awful lot of money. We shook hands and have been together ever since."

Pallagrosi and Bakal founded Concerts East and handled bookings for all the leading venues along the Jersey Shore and beyond.

"But nowadays we really focus on the Starland Ballroom. We used to have an agreement with the city of Asbury Park. Then they sold Convention Hall and the Paramount to the Asbury Partners. We still promote shows there, but we've also taken many shows out of there and put them in here. It's very run down, and quite frankly it sounds like hell."

Tony Pallagrosi admits that Convention Hall is a romantic, legendary venue.

"But like anything else when you're around it all the time and really have to deal with it, it just declines. As a producer of shows you try to have some consideration for the audience. You don't want to give people crappy sound or bad environment. That was one reason for me to find my own place. I want to run it like it should be run. Couldn't do that at Convention Hall or the Stone Pony. And pretty much the way the Asbury Partners were dealing with Convention Hall they made it increasingly difficult for us to make money there.

"They almost forced us to find our own venue. I thank them."

> **"Then they sold Convention Hall and the Paramount to the Asbury Partners. We still promote shows there, but we've also taken many shows out of there and put them in here. It's very run down, and quite frankly it sounds like hell."**

He claims that the decline of Asbury Park started years, in fact decades, prior to the 1970s riots.

"What you have to understand is that Asbury Park was known for a lot more than just the music scene. First of all, it was a shopping destination. In the 1930s, '40s, and '50s, downtown was huge. People came to shop at Steinbach's. This was before the malls started to become the epicenter of shopping.

"Asbury Park was also the closest functional beach to New York City. But as the Parkway was built in the '40s there were like twenty or thirty beach towns further south less crowded, cheaper, and more available.

"Over time the Parkway, the moving of shopping districts from downtown to the malls, the drinking age at the bars, the riots . . . all of these things each played a part in the decline of Asbury Park."

Tony Pallagrosi says that he enjoys talking about things that used to be. But he'd rather live in the moment and look into the future. He thinks that the building of high-priced condos by the oceanfront will attract people in their fifties looking for vacation homes, or maybe a permanent place to live. They won't be coming to town because of rock 'n' roll.

"I don't see a Jersey Shore music scene. That's all gone. There's a New Jersey music scene, but certainly not in the tradition of Asbury Park. Bruce Springsteen translated, but the other stuff from Asbury never really did that. Bruce doesn't play the way the other bands were playing. The rest of us were blue-eyed soul bands, and occasionally we got a college gig 'cause some kid on the college board liked us. But none of that is around. Southside is around, but he never had any hit singles. The fact that there are still plenty of places in this country that want to see Johnny is just a credit to his talent and enthusiasm."

ON THE ROAD TO FREEHOLD

Going west from Asbury Park. Route 66 becomes 33 and we stop at a diner, this fabulous little train car. At this very spot John Sayles directed a scene for *Baby It's You*. This is also where the cover shot for Bon Jovi's *Crossroads* was taken.

Let's grab a tuna fish sandwich with fries and it'll hold us for the rest of the day. Sometimes breakfast is all you need, as long as your first stop is a diner where friendliness itself offers refills of coffee before you're even seated.

This is dinerland, New Jersey, on the road to Freehold. And one wonders if Springsteen eats here every now and then? The friendliness itself deserves it.

What we already know is that he did park his car a couple of miles farther west, to pay the Valentino family a little visit. This was back in the early '70s and he even sings about it on the *Greetings from Asbury Park, N.J.* track "The Angel."

Hubcap Farm is an incredible little business. They've got hubcaps everywhere you look. Buick, Dodge, and Chevy, of course. But nowadays, the Valentinos have had to give in and sell a little Japanese plastic as well.

This is a place that says a lot about today's Freehold and just as much about the Freehold Bruce Springsteen grew up in. The differences between now and then are big. Bigger than the difference between a Dodge and a Subaru.

The Freehold we got to know in "My Hometown" was part of the 1960s. When the textile factory closed, and the gap between whites and blacks grew wider and wider. Back then there was no place for kids with long hair playing rock 'n' roll.

In the early 2000s, Freehold is known to be the hippest town in western Monmouth County. People are moving in, despite the fact that there is no longer any employer equivalent to the Rug Mill. But people want to live in Freehold for other reasons. The town's turned into a nice place to be. A place to live, even if everyday life might entail commuting to the office in Manhattan.

Traces of Bruce Springsteen are not overly evident. In fact, it's the other way around. Yeah, you're likely to see the truck he bought for the fire department driving around with *Born to Run* written on it, but it's also a well-known fact that Freehold believes it best to toast its famous son by respecting his private life. Not by putting up statues.

The town's closest thing to a monument is Vinyard Park, a little spot to stop and rest, inaugurated a few years ago. It's where some duplex houses once stood. Tex and Marion Vinyard lived in one of those houses, and it was in their living room that the Castiles and other teen bands found their haven.

The first house Springsteen lived in, on Randolph Street, is gone. The other two, on Institute and South, are still standing.

And during tours, new generations of Freehold residents, who might have grown up listening to Eminem or 50 Cent, can look on in disbelief when busloads of people from different parts of the world are guided by Springsteen acquaintances who just spin the same old yarns that have already been told from the stage a thousand times.

Springsteen's fully aware of this. So the idea that he might show up around Institute or South Street on occasions like these is pretty far-fetched.

It's said that he spends most of his time out on the ranch, but he can also be seen in town every so often. Maybe because there are still a few old friends around, or simply because he likes to take the family for pizza at Federici's.

Next door there's Main Street Music, the local record dealer, and you'd probably expect Springsteen to be among the regulars? Well, the guy behind the counter doesn't look too happy while telling that the rock 'n' roll icon never once set foot in the store.

PLEASE
BEEP
YES WE'RE
OPEN

VINYARD
PARK

THE BASS PLAYER WHO STAYED BEHIND

Michael Wilson

The hippest town in western Monmouth County has the hippest mayor. "I never had enough talent as a musician, so this is how things turned out instead," says Mayor Michael Wilson.

As of 2005, it had been twenty years since Michael Wilson was first elected mayor of Freehold Borough. He'll set a new record for longevity in the office within the course of his current term.

"The old record was exactly twenty years, 1920–1940. Funny," says Michael Wilson, "in politics you take it one year at a time. I was not counting on being re-elected.

"I guess I must be doing something right. Otherwise they would have kicked me out a long time ago."

Wilson doesn't seem to approach his position with a great deal of formality. He meets us in a short-sleeved shirt, khakis, and sandals. No socks. Cool guy. And friendly.

The mayor is sitting pretty when the pictures are taken.

Michael Wilson belongs to the 1950s crowd, but he represents the new Freehold. The successful and hopeful Freehold. A small Jersey town that seems to have few things in common with the Freehold Bruce Springsteen depicts in his songs, such as "My Hometown," which talks about the depression that took place when the textile factory closed and made half the town jobless. Or "In Freehold," where the intolerance of a "redneck town" is the subject.

"That was then, this is now," says Michael Wilson. "It's hard to compare. But Bruce wrote those songs based on his own experiences. And I have to give him credit. I saw Freehold in the same way Bruce did, during the 1960s."

"The textile factory closed, and people lost their jobs. The stores closed. We had racial tension and riots. Freehold was a depressed town."

Michael Wilson talks about tough times in a tough city, with a strictly conservative, blue-collar mentality.

"Bruce noticed those things. He was an outsider, with his long hair. Street people as many would say."

"Different," says Wilson of Bruce Springsteen. "Special."

"Nobody knew what was going on in that head of his. Except for Bruce himself. He was a loner who transformed when he got up onstage. A little bit like Dr. Jekyll and Mr. Hyde.

"But Bruce probably just wanted to have a little fun. We used to hitchhike to the beach together, every summer. And my clearest image of Bruce from that time was that he was always making people laugh."

Bruce Springsteen had talent. Most people saw that. Michael Wilson was a close witness to it all. And like Springsteen he dreamed his own rock 'n' roll future.

"But I was never really talented enough. So this is how it turned out. I became mayor instead."

Wilson says he got his start as a bassist and singer in a band called the Legends. Tex Vinyard, manager for the Castiles, with Springsteen and George Theiss, also lent the Legends a helping hand. And one night, when Wilson's gang played at the Freehold YMCA, Vinyard showed up together with Springsteen.

"I was playing bass without having my amp turned on. Bruce was the only one who noticed and he pointed it out to the others during a break: 'It'd probably be better for your bassist to turn his amp on.'"

The mayor laughs.

"That was the end of my bass playing days; I never got over

it. But seriously: Bruce did me a huge favor. He got me to realize that it was better if I just stuck with singing."

Tex Vinyard had his priorities clear. The Castiles came first, the Legends were the baby band.

Springsteen Street. Just a little inscription in stone, with Bruce Springsteen as one of many other names, outside the Hall of Records. And then there's that yellow fire engine. It says *Born to Run* on the driver's cab, the donor being, you guessed it.

"I guess I must be doing something right.
Otherwise they would have kicked me out a long time ago."

Michael Wilson describes a turbulent time when dances and Hullabaloo clubs kept kids off the streets. What Springsteen sang about—that the way out was through music—was a reality for many young people in 1960s Freehold.

"And then we had Tex Vinyard and Marion, his wife. Marion was a saint. Tex was . . . interesting. He had a big heart.

"The thing was that since Tex and Marion had no children of their own, they opened their home up to us. All the bands used to hang there. The Castiles practiced in their dining room almost every day of the week."

The breakup came after high school. Bands split up, teenagers making their way into adult life. Many, including Bruce Springsteen, left Freehold. Others, like Michael Wilson, stayed behind and started to work on a comprehensive improvement plan. More and more people started to flow into a much nicer place, with beautiful Victorian houses and a friendly downtown environment.

But when the textile factory shut its doors, the social structure changed entirely. Freehold started to become a city without a dominant workplace.

Michael Wilson explains that the Nestle coffee plant is today Freehold's leading employer, but he also says that there is really no core business in the area.

"People do a little of everything. Some work here, downtown. Others commute to New York.

"The main thing is that we got the town back on its feet again. If Red Bank is considered the hippest town in the eastern part of Monmouth County, Freehold can be considered its counterpart in the western parts."

Hip and blossoming. But low-profile all the same.

The most striking thing when you drive down the streets of Bruce Springsteen's hometown is the fact that he's not there. Freehold, with its 12,000 inhabitants, has no Graceland. No monuments or statues. Not even a street sign that says Bruce

Freehold holds a unique position in American pop culture, but no one seems particularly interested in turning the rock 'n' roll myth into business.

"Street signs," says Michael Wilson, "would just get stolen by tourists. So it's not a very good idea."

The truth is that Bruce Springsteen is not actually as far removed as it might seem. He lives on a ranch, a few miles from here. And you can see him sometimes in Federici's pizzeria, together with his family or a few old friends. Freehold residents speak of Bruce sightings, but they don't bother the homecomer.

"We're proud of Bruce. That's why we also respect his private life. There have been proposals for statues, but we decided against it. And Bruce actually thanked us in his song 'In Freehold.' He thanked us for not embarrassing him.

"Bruce moved out of town. But he's still around, and he's no monument."

Springsteen has only sung that song, 'In Freehold,' in public on a few separate occasions. The premiere was in 1996 as part of a charity concert at his old school, St. Rose of Lima. One of the verses holds a story about his buddy Mike, now mayor of Freehold. Springsteen's remembering the days when they all used to have a lot more hair.

Michael Wilson laughs and says:

"I didn't exactly understand what he said. At first I thought he was only referring to me. So I caught up with him afterwards and asked: 'What do you mean? He used to . . .'"

"But I'd heard him wrong. Bruce reassured me: 'No, no. I sang when WE used to . . .'"

"On a later occasion, at the Continental Airlines Arena, he dedicated the song to me. It was a nice feeling."

In 2004, Springsteen got into politics for the first time. He promoted Vote for Change and toured in opposition to Bush.

"Bruce had never talked about politics in public before. But deep down I always knew that he was a Democrat. I think most people knew that," says Wilson, who sees Springsteen a little now and then. That's how it's been since 1988.

"That's when Bruce came back home for Tex Vinyard's funeral. It was probably the first time in twenty years that we spoke with one another. The first time since high school.

"We live in different worlds, Bruce and I. But we share a common past, and I see him as trying to be as much of a participant in the affairs of the town as he can."

That's why Wilson, Springsteen, and George Theiss were also speakers at the inauguration of Vinyard Park. A little oasis in town located where Tex and Marion Vinyard's house once stood.

"He was busy recording *The Rising* down in Georgia, but took time out to come back here. Bruce said that the inauguration of Vinyard Park was something that he absolutely did not want to miss. He was there for Marion's sake."

Now we're standing at the very spot. Michael Wilson leans against the sign: Vinyard Park. Across the street stand the renovated remains of what used to be the Rug Mill.

On the record that made Bruce Springsteen one of the biggest names in rock 'n' roll he tells about the textile factory closing down, and young men facing the fact that jobs won't be coming back to their hometown.

Michael Wilson, the bass player who ended up being the mayor, wonders:

"No one here, not even Bruce himself, could have guessed that he would one day make rock history. You can't predict that type of thing. But you can see talent, and Bruce had talent."

We shake hands with the mayor. He says: "It's great that you came here, to Freehold. Please come back. I have to run now, I have a dentist appointment I've got to get to."

The mayor goes off. In his short-sleeved shirt, khakis, and sandals.

"Bruce moved out of town. But he's still around, and he's no monument."

George Theiss

There's an obscure little song written by Bruce Springsteen. You won't find it on any album, and you'd be among the chosen few if you've ever heard it performed onstage. It's a song about being the outsider in a blue-collar town, and earning the first few bucks with a teen band. That band, the Castiles, was started by George Theiss.

It's August of 1968, and they're standing onstage together. George Theiss on vocals. Bruce Springsteen on guitar. After some three years, it will all be over. Theiss and Springsteen will have drifted apart. The inevitable breakup of the Castiles is just a fact.

"We started to grow up, and had different ideas. That's just how it happened," says George Theiss.

He still lives in Freehold, works as a carpenter, and leads a low-key family life. But George Theiss has never given up his music.

"I've got a little studio downstairs. I can spend hours, days in there, with coffee and cigarettes. I'm just pushing notes around. It drives my wife crazy, and sometimes it does the same to me."

George Theiss laughs. He's picky, too picky. And he knows it. But Theiss could never settle for being mediocre. He could never stand to be just another rocker in the crowd. Just playing for fun would never be enough.

"I've thrown out so much stuff over the years. And as soon as you're done with one song, you can be sure that the radio will be playing something that sounds almost exactly the same a few weeks later."

Theiss says that "of course he has a few decent recordings, but they've never been good enough."

One that he's missing is the first, and only, single with the Castiles. Two original songs, "That's What You Get" and "Baby I," were recorded in Bricktown, New Jersey in May, 1966. George Theiss guesses that there must not be any more than five or six copies in circulation.

"I've never seen them, but I'm sure there's one at Bruce's house."

The Castiles were good, among the best bands in the Freehold area, according to those who remember. George Theiss was fourteen, going on fifteen, and when he started the band he had already made a name for himself.

"My first band was called the Five Diamonds. We performed in long raincoats and cowboy boots. Then I continued with the Sierras, who tried to go up against Vinnie Roslin's band, the Motifs."

The Castiles?

"Well, we weren't so different from the others. Influences came from the British invasion; the Beatles, the Stones, the Who. I was no big Elvis fan, at least not before 1968, when he did his *Comeback Special*."

The band was formed in 1965.

"Bart Haynes, our drummer, lived in a duplex house. One night when we were jamming there, Tex Vinyard came over. Tex was Bart's neighbor, he liked what we were up to, and offered to help the band. Tex and his wife Marion didn't have any children of their own, so they took us in, and let us rehearse in their house."

Haynes (drums), Theiss (guitar/vocals), Paul Popkin (guitar/vocals) and Frank Marziotti (bass) were the original lineup. But Tex Vinyard wanted to have a third guitarist, and that's where Bruce Springsteen came in.

"We'd been playing together for about a year when Bruce came along."

The Castiles now had two front men. Theiss was the lead singer, Springsteen the lead guitarist.

"We had our designated slots, and you couldn't cross those lines for a while."

Did Springsteen's sound improve the band?

"I can't say. Everything took a natural course. We developed different ideas."

The Castiles appeared around New Jersey and did a series of gigs at the Café Wha in New York. There was even talk about the band doing some extensive touring.

George Theiss is remembering the Castiles in the midst of change. The first change came when Bart Haynes was drafted and later killed in Vietnam. Then Frank Marziotti, who was a few years older than the others, chose to leave.

In came Curt Fluhr (bass), Vinny Maniello (drums), and Bob Alfano (organ).

The Castiles were hot. Girls loved the long-haired boys from Freehold.

"That's probably why we thought so highly of ourselves."

But it just turned out that way. Things had come to an end.

"It was not so much that Bruce and I drifted apart. It also had to do with Tex. You have to remember how young we were when everything started. Of course we always did what Tex told us to. He liked that, and he liked the attention he got when things started to happen with the band. But as we got older we also started to have our own views on things."

George Theiss would never underestimate the importance that Tex and Marion Vinyard had during the early years in Freehold, and it bothers him that things with Tex became a bit icy.

"It didn't have anything to do with the Castiles. Much later, Warner Brothers got in touch, and they were interested in my new band. I met them without Tex knowing about it, and when he found out he went wild. I tried to explain to him, tried

lot of really great things over the years. On the other hand, I was surprised when his first album came out. I remember hearing a song by the Allman Brothers around the same time and thinking: OK, this must be Bruce."

"Because Bruce was more into playing guitar. I thought he would more or less follow the same musical path as Jeff Beck or Eric Clapton. Instead he sort of moved in with Dylan."

George Theiss had gotten close himself a few times. But there were always things that got in the way, like when the Asbury Park favorites, the Cahoots, were on the way into the studio.

"The Cahoots, right. We were . . . I never really knew where we stood. Tony Amato did a lot of managing, and all the business stuff. He took a lot of the abuse for us.

"I was probably the most even. I think most of the guys would say: 'At least George is kind of normal.'"

While still laughing, Theiss continues:

"But in any case; Tony was the one who took care of the contacts with various record labels, and I didn't really know what to think when he would tell us how we were doing. He would say a few paragraphs, and you'd have to scan through those paragraphs. Tony's a good friend, now just as then, but like I said: I never really knew what was going on with the record companies."

That's why it was George Theiss, the singer and the songwriter, who put the brakes on when Tony Amato would present different possibilities.

"We knew Bruce and were friends with a lot of the people that were working for him. Tony probably used this a lot when he was talking with record companies. I guess there [was]

"We started to grow up, and had different ideas.

That's just how it happened."

to apologize. But I don't think Tex ever forgave me. It pains me to think about it, now that he's gone."

Bruce Springsteen? Theiss sees him now and then, such as when they both attended the inauguration ceremony for Vinyard Park.

Regarding his childhood friend's enormous success, Theiss says:

"I don't know, I guess things just happen. Bruce has done a

some interest in the band. But how serious was it? I still don't know how it all turned out."

Theiss has no doubt in his mind when he says:

"The Cahoots were good. But we weren't ready. We never would have lasted."

Why not?

"Take Mike Scialfa, Patti's brother, for example. We never knew if Mike would show up to play or not. It was always:

'Where's Mike?' That's how Tony eventually got into the band. He was doing sound for us and just worked his way into playing keyboards.

"Then we had John Oser on vocals and harmonica. John was really good, but he was from Toms River. I was from Freehold and the Asbury area guys had no problem with Freehold, but Toms River . . . John Luraschi, Tommy LaBella, Steve Schreager, and Tony Amato often ended up having disputes of various kinds with John Oser. Nothing serious, just bullshit, but nonetheless."

The Cahoots would never amount to anything outside New Jersey, and George Theiss chose to start over. He put together the George Theiss Band, with Amato, Schreager, and a few others at his side. But in later years, playing would become a bit more sporadic. Now and then, when Amato is not busy with Boccigalupe & the Bad Boys, Theiss tries to book a date. In the fall of 2004, he says that the last gig was at a benefit for Vini Lopez, who had recently lost his wife.

"I hadn't played with the guys for two years but it felt good. I still like to play. Part of me just wants to have a good time, that's the part that makes me think: of course, of course, we're just having fun. But then the other side, the cautious side, takes over.

"That's why I always end up tearing my songs apart. Redoing them, over and over again. The guys in the band would go: 'Come on, let's just play the song.' And I would say: 'I don't wanna just play the song, I'm tired of just playing the song. It's boring.'"

George Theiss says that he would like to make another fresh start. Maybe find some musicians who want to learn something new without being in a rush.

"Some new rhythms, some new instruments. Whatever. Otherwise everything will turn out like it did before. You end up playing the same old songs. And making the same mistakes. I'm sick of all that. Just hate it."

Such pickiness got in his way more than once.

"Yeah, probably. But I really tried. I went to all the big labels, and got rejection letters from them all.

"It wasn't the best timing, either. For example, I went to Columbia when Journey was really big and was told: 'We're doing Journey now.'

"I knew that I wasn't going to run out and do something like Journey. I mean, by the time I got back from the studio they would want me to do something else."

Now George Theiss says that he doesn't need a label.

"If I had been persistent enough, they would have come around sooner or later. I'm sure of it. But then I would rather turn to a friend who is a successful producer. This guy, from the early Columbia days, has worked with Vanilla Fudge, Bob Marley, and a ton of other artists. His policy with me was always: 'When you have something, come on in and we'll record it.'

"We actually did record a number of things with him after the Castiles. But we were kids, just wasting time. I wasn't going to listen to anyone. He already had experience and know-how back then, but we thought we were so cool ourselves. That gunslinger attitude."

George Theiss sometimes has his regrets:

"Yeah, I wish I had listened. Now I can be thankful that he's still in touch. Because the musicians he's offered me are so good that I'm about ready to carry their equipment. These guys are never seen out anywhere, they just want to play. And they sound fantastic."

Maybe George Theiss will end up finishing a recording he can be satisfied with.

"I'd like to play, and I know that I can. Age is not a problem, if I could just get off my butt and find the right people to work with. The problem is that I get a little stuck. It's been like that my whole life. There was always something that got screwed up.

"So what I'm looking to do is just one good album. Something that would really make me proud. That's what my dreams are about."

STOP

INSTITUTE   ST

39½

HAPPY

MOTORING

MEN

Pete Yorn

A longing to get out of New Jersey. Then the escape from heavy winter snow in Syracuse, New York. Pete Yorn always knew he had to go west.

It's about homecomings. Pete Yorn has checked into the newly renovated Empress, a famed hotel in Asbury Park given a new breath of life. Rooms are more than 100 dollars a night, and the lobby is packed. Asking for some peace and quiet, we're shown through this corridor. There's Asbury's leading gay bar, Paradise, which has not yet let in the first guests of the day.

Don't know if anyone has explained to Pete Yorn where he actually is, but these dimly lit surroundings with Halloween décor and walls plastered with posters from gay movie classics doesn't seem to bother him. Yorn does a soundcheck on the minidisc recorder and leans back, full of expectation before his night at the Stone Pony.

"I usually come home to Jersey a few times a year, but it's been a long time since we played the Stone Pony."

He's headlining tonight. The homecoming is at the Light of Day concert, where Gary U.S. Bonds, Soozie Tyrell, LaBamba's Big Band, and Southside Johnny are among the other crowd pleasers.

"Sounds fun. I brought my bandmates from England. We definitely won't go on before midnight. That's never how it works in California, clubs in L.A. close around midnight."

Pete Yorn is on his way. This guy is probably the Asbury scene's best selling export since the early days of Bon Jovi, and there are still ties that bind.

"Asbury Park is a cool place. The town has a history that you might not appreciate when you're younger. When I was a kid almost everything was about getting out of New Jersey."

Pete Yorn's hometown is actually Montville, about a seventy minute drive north of Asbury Park. As a kid he used to spend summers in Asbury Park or its neighboring town, Bradley Beach. Now, Yorn is walking down memory lane, laughing.

"Growing up around here, our parents would take us to Asbury, Bradley, or Deal. They actually met on the beach in Bradley Beach. Dad saw Mom in a bikini, and that was it. Damn, I can't stand looking at those old pictures."

He started out as a drummer, and put his first band together in his early teenage years. Opportunity, at the time, was to be found in Asbury Park.

"Yeah, we always came down to Asbury. I don't know why really, 'cause as I recall it this wasn't a place we dreamed of playing. I guess we just weren't getting booked anywhere else.

"I remember this one place called the Deckhouse. I don't know if it's still there, I doubt it. Anyway, I think the second show I ever played was at the Deckhouse, and about halfway through the opening song I couldn't hear the drums any more. I turn around and just see feet in the air. My drummer's throne had just collapsed, and he fell back off the stage."

Small clubs, late nights. A breakthrough seemed a long way off.

"I never played the Stone Pony until 2001, when my first album, *Musicforthemorningafter*, was already in the stores. But that was totally cool. My first time back in Jersey, having a record out. So many friends from high school, kids I hadn't seen in years, all my cousins. It was a real reunion. All of that and the Pony. This legendary dive.

"Nowadays we don't play many clubs like that. It's usually theaters."

Even at that point, Pete Yorn had traded East Coast for West Coast, Jersey for California, to stake out his claim in the rock 'n' roll world.

"New Jersey was a dead end. Most people in my generation

felt that way. It was impossible to get anywhere in a career for those who chose to stick around.

"I don't know why it was like that. I guess everybody talks about Jersey and Springsteen. And even 'Born to Run, ' Bruce's biggest song, is about wanting to get away. That's pretty much the mentality of a lot of people here."

onto the *Dawson's Creek* soundtrack, and "Strange Condition" was a hit in the Jim Carrey movie *Me, Myself, & Irene.*

The stage was set, and *Musicforthemorningafter* was a debut album that sold. Then came *Day I forgot*, and Pete Yorn had established his name for real.

This music sounds neither Asbury nor Springsteen. Yorn

"It's actually the same thing with Asbury Park. To me, Asbury is a faded flower. Days gone by, old glories and all that."

Pete Yorn grew up close to Asbury Park and the Springsteen culture.

"Maybe too close. Regardless of whatever town you come from there's an urge to get out. For me it was always a matter of romanticizing California."

Yorn continues:

"Bruce was huge at home. There was no way of getting around him. I was in my early teens and definitely more into other stuff, like punk rock.

"When *Born in the U.S.A.* was released I kind of rebelled against it. What Bruce was singing about was too close to home. I wasn't interested, I wanted something more exotic, something more under the radar.

"I guess it's like living in New York City and saying that you don't have time to go to all the great museums. Then when you move along, after about five years or so, you've missed the entire thing."

But when Pete Yorn went to college, his friend gave him a hard time: "I want you to get *The Wild, the Innocent*, and I want you to put on the headphones. If you have some weed, smoke a big joint. Lay down on the floor and listen to 'New York City Serenade.'"

"I did what he told me to do. The music hit me hard and I'm still a huge fan."

It was also during his college years in Syracuse, New York, that Yorn decided to make his move west. He was sick of the cold, long winters, and the heavy snow.

"The time had come. I left for California, and that's when I eventually found some success in music."

Pete Yorn was signed to Columbia Records, but the debut album took a year and a half to finish. During that time he wrote music for film and television. "Just Another" made it

speaks to a different, perhaps a younger, audience. But he doesn't think there's an obvious ambition to develop a particular style.

"The way I work. I don't know, the whole process is still a mystery. I kind of observe what goes on around me. The stuff I write about is usually based upon experiences of other people. I put myself in their shoes. Sometimes it's also about things I experienced myself first hand, but I easily get bored with myself.

"To me, the music's also about attitude. I would so identify with the way certain bands looked and dressed. When you're into a band, and people at the shows dress in certain ways, you identify with that. I like to feel that I'm part of some sort of scene. And when I was younger it was even more so.

"Sometimes I could forget the words and just take in the sound or image."

That's why Yorn still treasures bands such as the Smiths and the Cure.

Life in Montville, New Jersey, had nothing like that to speak of.

"It's a small town, thirty minutes west of New York City. The part of town where I grew up was developed in the '60s. There were a lot of horse stables around my house."

Pete Yorn is glad to be home again. It's been years since he last visited Montville, and he's looking forward to spending a couple of days in town.

"One of my lighting guys still has family there. So we're gonna stay at their house and enjoy his Italian grandmother's cooking."

Everything looks different in Los Angeles. But Yorn thinks that the differences are more evident on the surface.

"It's different, yes. But I had worked there over summers, during college, and that way I got to know a lot of people. It's

kind of fun, I must have twelve or fifteen old friends from Jersey who all live within ten miles from my L.A. house.

"Ninety-nine percent of everyone who goes to California to make it all happen ends up having their dreams not come true. L.A. is not just dreams and illusions. There is a crass, brutal reality.

"It's actually the same thing with Asbury Park. To me, Asbury is a faded flower. Days gone by, old glories and all that. There's always been talk of redevelopment, but I come back every now and then and see the same unfinished building."

Moving back home? Don't think so. In Los Angeles he is surrounded by friends and the entire family. Pete Yorn's oldest brother is a lawyer and serves as assistant district attorney in L.A. County.

"He prosecuted gang members for several years. Then there's Rick, my middle brother, who made it big in the entertainment industry.

"Rick was a financial guy, living in San Diego and doing

New York hours. He was getting up like four in the morning, waiting for the market to open. Then he met some people who [were] successful in entertainment, and thought: 'If these guys can do it, so can I.'

"He started as secretary, worked his way up really fast, and did very well."

Today Rick Yorn is part owner of The Firm, a powerful Hollywood talent agency on Wilshire Boulevard. Among his clients are the Dixie Chicks and Limp Bizkit, Leonardo DiCaprio, Samuel L. Jackson, and Pete Yorn.

"Rick takes care of me. But he was not all that great of a drummer, so I kicked him out of the band."

Pete Yorn made it to the charts via film. He says that today, at a time when MTV shows only a few videos, and radio is rigidly formatted, songwriters have to find new avenues.

"Film gets it out there. TV advertising is also part of the future. A few years ago, that type of thing was taboo. I still haven't put any of my songs in commercials, but that's totally OK, of course. You can even hear a Nick Drake song in the Volkswagen commercial. To survive as an artist you need to reach an audience. If commercials are the only way, then why not?"

Yorn is among the very few who made the cut. He's moving up, says that life is good in L.A. where he's close to his family and it's summer all year long.

"I spend most of my time locked into the studio. Otherwise I am not much different from anyone else. I try to be with my family and I guess that on occasions you might find me looking for trouble. That's fairly useful if you want to have inspiration for the songs."

Now he's sitting next door to the Empress Hotel in Asbury Park, with a countdown to the first of three Light of Day appearances. It's November and fall is very evident.

Yorn looks out over Ocean Avenue.

"Asbury Park should have a future. There's a beautiful beach here, and there are many beautiful beaches on either side of town.

"I actually think that Asbury, in many respects, reminds me of Venice Beach. Here, like there, you'll find so many cool places. What makes Venice a lot more jumping is that summer never seems to end."

"I try to be with my family and I guess that on occasions
you might find me looking for trouble. That's fairly useful
if you want to have inspiration for the songs."

Michael Strollo

Are we going to see the next Springsteen? Hardly. John Eddie knew the answer to that in the middle of the '80s. But the future in and around Asbury Park can be something else. A multifaceted range of songwriters who grew up with the stories from the past and music of the day. Some are already on the way. Others, like Michael Strollo of Exit 105, are beginning to learn about how the industry works.

Sunday afternoon. Michael Strollo likes a good party, but he's a Catholic and goes to church every Sunday. So when Strollo parks his jeep outside Celtic Cottage in Long Branch, it's not a rough Saturday that he's hiding behind dark sunglasses.

"My songs are about young people who either walk around being pissed off or accept their situation. No matter what, I am going to stay focused. I know who I am. No chance I'm going to get off track."

He takes a sip of ice water, plays with his napkin and says: "I have no idea how many songs I have written in this exact bar."

Michael Strollo grew up in West Long Branch. Started playing in high school, and bought his first guitar when he was sixteen.

"Saw the Dave Matthews Band on VH1. Unbelievably good. No effects, no tricks. I wanted to know if I could do the same thing. The bug bit me."

The acoustic guitar cost eighty-nine dollars at Jack's Music Shoppe in Red Bank. Strollo didn't have that much in his pocket, but the salesperson was reasonable.

"That guitar was never really so great, but it gave me a feeling. And I wrote a dozen or so good songs with it."

Strollo is still in his twenties, but years spent in bars along the Jersey Shore, and all the open mike nights, have seasoned him.

"I went out as a solo act for three years or something. I was always checking the papers, looking for different venues to play. Most of the time I got gigs here in Long Branch, or in Sea

Bright. I convinced the club owners to let me play, even though I wasn't actually of age."

He was looking to get an answer. To find an audience, get a response. To communicate.

"I've never seen anything wrong with being a cover artist, but nor does it interest me to make a few dollars by playing someone else's music. When you write your own material and notice that there's one, two, or maybe a hundred people who can identify with it, who nod, smile, understand. That's communicating, and there's nothing more beautiful in music."

Strollo talks about pride and honesty. About continuing to grow and mature, as a musician and as a person.

"The only way to get to the next level was to get a band together. I knew that my songs would gain a lot from the power that comes from electric rock 'n' roll."

He moved around in different apartments, usually living in Long Branch or Deal, Asbury Park's more upscale neighboring town.

"I put out my own ads, I met with other bands. I held auditions at home. But I never thought of going into New York. My songs don't need a big city feeling. What I write about is right here, in Jersey. This is where my life is, this is where my stories belong."

When you drive south on the Garden State Parkway, Exit 105 shows the way to Long Branch. Exit 105: A suitable band name for the next generation of local heroes. A band (Strollo, lead guitarist Art Hoffer, bassist Scott Consoli, guitarist Anthony Bagliore, drummer Steve Carter) that has seen its reputation spread quickly along the Shore. Spread in the shadow of the greats: Bruce Springsteen, Johnny Lyon, Jon Bon Jovi.

"We were in this spot called Donovan's Reef when I noticed Mr. Springsteen in the audience. I thought: No way, that can't be him, but it was actually Bruce. He was there with his family and stayed the whole way through our set."

So the reputation would start spreading even faster.

"Seriously: I have never been a fan. But I am hugely impressed by how he has managed his career and how good he is with other people. Mr. Springsteen, is without a doubt, an icon and a great visionary."

"My songs don't need a big city feeling. What I write about is right here, in Jersey. This is where my life is, this is where my stories belong."

Michael Strollo doesn't want to make a big deal out of his meetings with Springsteen, but:

"Of course, just the fact that he said that he likes our music is huge. It can open doors. We got an invitation to play on the boardwalk outside Giants Stadium when the E Street Band did their ten concerts there. We got a place in the Light of Day shows in Asbury Park, since Bruce is good friends with the organizer, Bob Benjamin. And we were also at Pittsburgh's Flood Aid benefit."

Exit 105 opened in Pittsburgh's Heinz Hall, where Bruce Springsteen headlined with Joe Grushecky's Houserockers. The evening raised 255,000 dollars for families who had had their homes destroyed in a flood disaster. The evening also gave Michael Strollo's Exit 105 eleven minutes of glory.

"Mr. Springsteen came on during our set. We played Bob Dylan's 'All Along the Watchtower' together. It was fantastic. He radiates energy, shares energy with others. You get to grow by his side, but you also know your own place."

Michael Strollo stifles a laugh. Says instead with a more careful enthusiasm:

"Others have suggested that Mr. Springsteen recognizes himself in me. But the only thing I know for sure is that he likes our music. Our meetings have been very professional, and that's the way I want it to be. I would never exploit his fame."

Musically, Strollo is often compared to one of Springsteen's friends, Pearl Jam's Eddie Vedder.

"Yeah, Vedder or bands like Stone Temple Pilots. Then there are others who draw parallels to Bruce or even Roy Orbison.

"I imagine that all music from Jersey is compared to Bruce. He is such an influential artist that he definitely shines through in many young musicians. The same is, of course, true with Dylan, U2, Led Zeppelin. That's where everything comes from. They're all artists or bands who led the way."

Strollo is cautious of labels. The only thing he wants is to play for real, from the heart.

"Bruce is Bruce, Bono is Bono. I am Mike and if what I do is good enough then my music will end up being played."

Exit 105 signed a management contract with Paramount Entertainment. The band has songs together for an album, and negotiations with record companies are underway. Strollo says that most of it seems promising.

"But I'm not in a rush. That's why I'm never going to say yes to some independent label who comes up with a ton of empty promises about being able to turn me into a rock star. I've had those offers before.

"They want you to get dolled up, dye your hair and everything. That's never going to happen if it's not what I, myself, want to do. Because, what can they do for me? One year, one hit? A few dollars? I'm never taking the band in that direction."

Michael Strollo wants to be an artist. Not a star, not just a musician.

"I live my life and want to share my experiences through music. That's why I have to continue being honest, continue trusting myself. If it so happens that the industry never lets me in . . . OK, then that's the way it's going to be."

Success, what's success? Strollo talks about maturity.

"For a young guy who winds up in the wrong crowd, success is smoking pot and stealing a bunch of stuff. That's how he'll be accepted. For others success can mean getting married, getting a job, and raising a family.

"For me, success is telling the difference between right and wrong. Being secure in myself, daring to make the right decisions. Money has never been that important, because no one can turn me into a better songwriter by throwing a bunch of dollars at me. On the contrary, I just think that you lose something along the way. Mr. Springsteen has proven that it doesn't need to be that way. He is just as passionate today, still a music lover. That's one of the reasons I, and so many others, admire him."

Michael Strollo thanks his family for giving him inner security.

"And I have a girlfriend who loves me for who I am. Not because I might turn out to be a rock star.

"That's another of those things. The girls. It's cool when they go crazy at the edge of the stage, but you have to learn to see what people are out after. We're young, it's OK to have fun. But always ask yourself: Who is it they want? Mike Strollo the real me or the guy behind the mike? Same thing with the parties. It's nice to be offered drinks, eat well, and be clapped on the back. But all that's just image, and nothing I would find myself around without the music."

The first album will contain ten to twelve songs. Then Michael Strollo wants to take the band on tour, preferably to Europe.

"Because there's a bigger chance of winning musical respect there.

"Our goal is to get out there, all the way. To capture each individual it's so important to show the audience that you're for real. Bruce succeeded in doing it, Bruce and U2. Hell, I get shivers just thinking about how Bono meets his audience. I can tell where he was in his life when he wrote those songs. That's what separates the biggest ones from all the others. Bands that follow the times. That's what I want to achieve with Exit 105."

Never look back?

"Yeah, you have to allow yourself that. Here, around Asbury Park, it's unavoidable. We're all part of something very special, and we should be proud of that. But we should never try to do what's already been done. The only chance to take this farther is to trust in oneself."

**"They want you to get dolled up, dye your hair and everything.
That's never going to happen if it's not what I, myself, want to do."**

WHEN WORLDS COLLIDE

Albie Monterrosa

There's a new sheriff in town. He doesn't look like the others. He sounds different. And no one knows how long he'll be sticking around. Albie Monterrosa puts everything in the hands of the Great Spirit.

He looks like a rock star, but the car that Albie Monterrosa drives is the type that would definitely be labeled "economy" by any rental agency.

Monterrosa manages a smile. He puts down his guitar case and greets you with his entire body. Handshake, knuckles to knuckles, shoulders to shoulders, chin to chin. It seems like some sort of ritual where he comes from.

He talks quickly and moves with sweeping gestures. What Albie Monterrosa likes is getting a chance to tell his story, the story of deSol. He is the leader of the band that might be the next big thing to come out of Asbury Park.

When they rang in the new year, 2006, at the Stone Pony, another Asbury Park sound was unveiled. A sound that seems more like it draws from Carlos Santana than from Bruce Springsteen. But if you ask Albie Monterrosa, he'll make you understand that deSol is about rock 'n' roll.

Monterrosa has his roots in Latin culture, and when deSol had just landed in Asbury, after an eternity of traveling across America, he knew how his message would be taken:

"The papers say: 'deSol plays Latin and yes, they're from Asbury Park! How can this be?'"

The band belongs to a music scene. Monterrosa and his men walk the same streets that once belonged to Springsteen, Johnny Lyon, and John Bongiovi.

"I appreciate everything that comes with this sort of belonging. It feels both large and inspiring. Sometimes it seems like I come from another part of the world than the other guys. But I guess the Great Spirit unites us."

Albie Monterrosa laughs. He is at home in a place in another part of the world.

"We've been traveling a lot over the last year. But the bonds to Asbury Park are strong. This is where deSol was formed. It was the clubs in this town, places like the Saint, that opened the doors and said: Welcome."

He has lived in or around Asbury Park for the adult part of his life. But Albie Monterrosa grew up in Hollis, Queens, in neighborhoods where it was all about LL Cool J, Run DMC, or Salt-N-Pepa.

Monterrosa soon picked up the same references.

"My mom and dad come from El Salvador, but in a place like Queens, where so many cultures melt together, no one can feel like an outsider. Everyone is different and the same nonetheless."

When the family moved to the Jersey Shore, worlds would collide.

"It was there and then I suddenly realized I was different. I can basically say that I experienced a type of racism. It wasn't anything that was said or done. Just something unpronounced, something that was always there in the way people looked at you."

Monterrosa plucks at the guitar, as though to tell his story to the music that reveals who he is. The person he discovered when worlds collided.

"Just the fact of being different opened my eyes. I started to question myself. Who am I, what am I doing with my life? What do I want from music?"

Albie Monterrosa had been in several bands in his youth. Rock bands where nothing really happened, or where various members would get tired of things and leave town. Maybe to find everyday work instead of chasing after their dreams.

"Me, I got in touch with myself and with my culture. I wanted to become a representative of my culture, of my gods. I started to realize that music had to come from what and who I truly am."

Monterrosa went looking and found the answer. He took stock of who he was, what rhythms he wanted to dance to. He opened the door to his predecessors.

"Hip hop was big where I grew up. But there was always something different as well. I loved bands like Led Zeppelin, Kiss, and Mötley Crüe."

And then he heard Rubén Blades. There it was: a sense of belonging. Spirits, role models, gods. Zeppelin and Blades. Rock 'n' roll and Latin.

"Just different seeds that had been there the entire time, but without getting the necessary water and nutrients to bloom."

Albie Monterrosa formed deSol. He found a home in clubs such as the Saint, Harry's Roadhouse, and the Stone Pony. There was an audience who wanted to listen. People of different ages and with entirely different backgrounds. A party gang between twenty-five and sixty-five.

The band scraped together a few dollars and dreamed of being able to buy a van. DeSol wanted to travel.

"Bar mitzvahs, Russian weddings. You name it, we played everywhere at any time of the year. And we noticed that music was universal. People wanted to move, they wanted to dance. They all wanted to have a party. We invited everyone to a party where anyone who wanted to join us was welcome."

DeSol was on the way, but without knowing where they were going. Then came Franke Previte, once front man in Franke & the Knockouts, and later the Oscar winner for the theme song to *Dirty Dancing*. Previte knew the industry and could point the way.

"Before we met Franke there was nothing but the music. He could do everything else. He knew bookers, agents, record company people. He taught us the legal aspects of things. Franke described the band as a business effort and explained how we could get that business to grow."

Monterrosa strums at the guitar again. Then he says:

"Franke taught us to think bigger, like on a global scale. We were in Asbury Park, yes. This is where we start. But does it end here? Franke did everything for us. He's my brother."

DeSol and Previte would eventually part ways nonetheless. Without really explaining why, Albie Monterrosa says that the band found itself "between managements."

Monterrosa thinks it sounds polished. After hitting the strings once again he says:

"Everyone who has seen and heard deSol live knows the energy there is in the band. I don't think that energy comes out on the record."

The sophomore effort, *On My Way*, will capture everything that might have been missing the first time around. Albie Monterrosa speaks fondly of the early Rolling Stones albums; he wants to create the same type of organic sound image.

"Listen to the Stones and you'll hear rock 'n' roll that bleeds, deSol is also a band that bleeds."

There have been several important radio stations to hit the repeat button on deSol's song "Karma." The band had its first album out on the Nashville label Curb, and it's doing well. Not selling in gigantic volumes, but enough to create a platform. Albie Monterrosa seems at once both satisfied and unsatisfied:

"Everything went incredibly fast. Neither I nor the others in the band had time to think things over. The album has strong songs, but the whole process felt more or less like doing a demo recording."

The journey started cautiously. DeSol was mainly to be found in the clubs along the Jersey Shore. Places with everything from fifty to several hundred listeners.

Something else happened along the way. Monterrosa got the chance to tour with Los Lonely Boys and the Wailers. He opened for R.E.M., played festivals such as Austin City Limits and Lollapalooza.

"I love the large festival format because it lets us meet an audience that we might have otherwise never got across to. But those gigs have their own limitations at the same time. You're rarely onstage for more than forty minutes.

"This is where deSol was formed. It was the clubs in this town,
places like the Saint, that opened the doors and said: Welcome."

"That's why I need the other scene as well. Small venues that are close to the audience. This is what gives us a totally different type of freedom."

Now he's back home in Asbury Park. Catching his breath after a tour that both gives and takes.

"People in Asbury have supported us. This is the audience that has made things possible for deSol. It feels good to come home and be greeted with smiles and wishes for good luck. It's really only now that I understand that so much has happened since we took off.

"On tour it's all about travel, travel, travel. And when you never stop you never have any idea of where you actually are. You sleep too little, and complain when you call home to your friends: 'Damn, now we're going to the next town to do some promoting. More TV, more radio and paper interviews.' That's when friends say: 'Get real, what are you complaining about? That sounds like a pure dream.'"

Albie Monterrosa says it's nice to be home again. He's taking a moment to reflect what's been happening to the band and also to make some plans for the future.

**"Franke taught us to think bigger, like on a global scale. We were in
Asbury Park, yes. This is where we start. But does it end here?
Franke did everything for us. He's my brother."**

"I am trying to find out where we stand, and I know it's a long way to the top. It's a long way to Giants Stadium."

He uses neither if nor when. But he promises that deSol (Monterrosa, James Guerrero, Chris Guice, Andy Letke, Ron Shields, Kevin Ansell) will be ready.

"I love this job and I pray for success."

Then Albie Monterrosa says that Asbury Park is a good place to start. There is a point to the sense of belonging. The world knows who Bruce Springsteen is, and therefore they have also heard of Asbury Park.

Monterrosa himself has never been very close to Springsteen or his music. He was a latecomer to Asbury Park, arriving in town many years after Springsteen was a regular at the clubs along Kingsley, Cookman, and Ocean Avenue.

He just notes that Asbury is good for deSol. There is culture here and still a buzzing music scene. It also provides the calm that makes Monterrosa able to keep focused. Here, in the small town, it is easier to be seen without being disturbed. Pulsing, seductive, and tempting New York City can wear down creativity. There, in the big city, most people get caught up in their anonymity.

"But life in the city is fantastic nonetheless. I never want to be completely away from it.

"At the same time I can dream about moving to the most barren parts of New Mexico. For the quiet, the stillness. I often think about that; sitting alone under the stars and listening to the howling of the coyote."

He plucks the strings a little more, then packs the guitar in its case, stands, and says goodbye with all his body. A type of ritual where Albie Monterrosa comes from.

THIS
TOO
SHALL
PASS

ALAC
A

GABE
was
here

Thom McAn

October 1, 2004

Of course we tried. After all, he's just another local hero. The guy even wrote the song.

But let's be realistic.

Why would he, the world's biggest rock star, commit to an interview session with two small-town Swedish journalists?

Why would he bother?

Another relevant question: How, exactly, would we handle such a situation?

Jörgen and I talked about it a lot between the two of us. What the hell would we do? Wouldn't it be embarrassing to pull out an LP from 1973 to have it signed?

One alternative was to have Bronson, our Swedish publisher, who is also a freelance journalist, take care of the job, together with a photographer friend. Someone who doesn't give a damn whether it's an *American Idol* wannabe or the world's greatest rock star sitting across the table.

There remained, of course, the possibility of rising to the occasion with some kind of dignity.

In the end, we got close enough to realize that it was probably best as it happened. We realized this on one extraordinary evening in October, 2004.

Outside the Wachovia Center in Philadelphia, scores of people are running around with lost looks on their faces. We know exactly how they feel, because Bruce Springsteen & the E Street Band are about to kick off the Vote for Change tour, and we're without tickets.

An arena for 20,000 feels far too small, considering the occasion. Bright Eyes and R.E.M. are the opening acts, John Fogerty is billed as special guest.

It sounds amazing, and it's going to be. We're in the middle of this lost crowd, and we stand here thinking the same thoughts: a king's ransom, or at least a few hundred dollars, for tickets.

We've driven the rental car the entire way from the hotel with the emergency brake on. The guy in the booth at the parking lot is probably wondering if he should call the south Philly fire department.

But there is more important business at hand. Because, for one thing, we do have a way into the Center. Toby Scott, who's been Springsteen's recording engineer for more than twenty-five years, has promised to talk with us for a while. "Mr. Scott will meet you at the backstage entrance," we've been told by his management.

There's a way in, sure. Probably the same one that will show us out, one hour later.

But the thing is that Toby Scott meets us with two stickers. "Here, keep these on your t-shirts. If someone tries to stop you later just give me a call."

We look at one another. What's he saying? Is he serious?

Toby Scott means exactly what he says: "Hope you enjoy the show."

So when the interview is over, we're still sitting inside the Wachovia Center. With stickers on our t-shirts and what are guaranteed to be stupidest smiles in all Philadelphia.

Lofgren comes out and joins Little Steven. Clarence sits down, seeming to have some pain in his hips. One by one they all drop in for the sound check. One by one but not . . . right, here he comes.

Bruce Springsteen is smiling from ear to ear. He wants to have fun tonight.

First he plays "The Star Spangled Banner," solo on acoustic guitar. But he sounds like a whole orchestra. Then Roy Bittan keys the opening to "Lost in the Flood." Next there's Fogerty counting down "Centerfield."

They keep it up for forty-five minutes, and it's pure magic. Even Jörgen, with all the Springsteen experience in the world, has to dry his eyes.

We look at one another and wonder if it's not just as good to leave now? Now, when everything is so magical? From the top, there's only one way to go, isn't there?

Yes, usually. But this is not your ordinary evening.

Because later on, when we are standing down at the edge

of the stage (with our stickers), strange things start to happen. Bright Eyes makes a shaky impression, as this arena is a bit too big for them. But perhaps R.E.M. can raise the temperature?

Michael Stipe, Peter Buck, and Mike Mills are passing by when the spotlight falls on their presenter. He says: "Stop this Bruuuuuuuuuuuuuuuuucing. We're gonna have a Bruce-free zone here tonight. Let me instead introduce one of the greatest American rock bands of the last twenty years: R.E.M.!"

Springsteen asks Philadelphia to show R.E.M. respect. But if a Springsteen audience has ever shown its Boss any disrespect, it's here and now. R.E.M. gets sincere applause, but then approximately 19,998 people continue chanting "Bruuuuuce."

At the left wing of the stage, there are at least two of us who obey. Because there we are. It's just him and us. He hangs out a little longer while R.E.M. is opening their set with "The One I Love." Hollers "yeah!" and shows some of the characteristic moves to the music.

Jörgen is standing right behind the man; I am just a couple of steps in front of him. I turn around about twenty-odd times, pretending to look at Jörgen or the audience. Trying to look casual. Trying to make believe that R.E.M. is the biggest thing ever to happen in rock music, because I think Bruce probably wants us to think so. Or at least to pretend.

Failure is total. Eyes popping out of the skull.

That wry neck is still a reminder of a somewhat embarrassing situation.

Jörgen loves to laugh about it. But, hey pal: I saw the same look in your eyes.

Don't know if Springsteen noticed anything. Maybe he did, maybe not. I suppose he's used to people staring. Hope so.

We at least partly maintained our dignity. We never asked him to sign anything for the wife and kids. But we got close enough to figure one thing out for sure: that interview session was never a very good idea.

The concert?

Amazing.

If we're biased?

As much as anyone else would be.

It's easy to let your feelings start running away on an extraordinary evening in the Wachovia Center.

EPILOGUE—CITY OF DREAMS REVISITED

March 31, 2007

Standing at that same intersection. This is where the whole journey began, where Cookman Avenue meets Kingsley Street. Two years and six months have passed and we're still the out-of-towners, the outsiders looking in. Nonetheless, returning to Asbury Park, this city of dreams, always brings a feeling of belonging.

A lot happened as time went by. For better or for worse? Can't really tell. It's true that the oceanfront developers are breathing new life into town, and let's hope that fresh tax money can help improve its welfare. But who can be certain that the population on the West Side of the railroad tracks will benefit from a bunch of rich people moving into million dollar condos along Ocean Avenue?

While meeting former City Council woman Kate Mellina in the fall of 2004, we learned that Asbury Park's survival depends on a lot of things, rock 'n' roll tourism included. She took us on a tour along Springwood Avenue and while guiding us through the poorest parts of town, Mellina said:

"To tell you what is important to the future of Asbury Park I have to get you to understand how people live here. Tourists come to town, Springsteen fans who want to save Tillie and complain about the fact that Palace Amusements isn't there anymore. I regret that too, but I also know that the survival of these people is more important.

"Kids' test scores are horrible. We have so many of them dropping out of high school it's unbelievable. The median income is somewhere around 23,000 dollars. That's not even enough to pay for your houses. The streets and the buildings are in bad shape. You name it, and it's broken."

Kate Mellina wasn't claiming to have all the answers, but her message was clear: the oceanfront development is bringing hope to a city of ruins.

"What it really means to me, outside of having a pretty and neat beachfront, is that the tax money from these units will be spent on the parts of town that need it [most]."

She seemed convinced that the developers, the Asbury Partners, are here to make things happen. This time it's for real; this time Asbury Park will see a new "rising," even though signs spreading that word had to be taken down. A certain Boss made it clear that his song, and record, was sending out a message that really had nothing to do with the revitalization of this city.

"The Asbury Partners are the master developers which basically means that they're the central organizers," said Kate Mellina. "They pay all the money for legal fees and the engineers. They make the deals with subdevelopers and different companies. What happened before was that this one guy developed it all by himself, and when he went bankrupt the whole project just fell apart. The way things are planned this time around means that if one project isn't doing well, we can put a different subdeveloper in there."

After listening to a rock 'n' roll tourist questioning condominiums and fearing an insecure future for historic landmarks, such as the Wonder Bar and the Fastlane, Mellina said:

"Well, you can't get in the retail and the amusement, all the fun stuff, if nothing gets done. We need to bring in some tax money and people won't come here until they see that it's a safe area. It has to be OK to live here. But I'm gonna do whatever it takes to save the Stone Pony.

"Each of these battles, we have to fight them one by one. There are so many details, it's just mind blowing."

No matter what the future might bring, things will never be quite the same again; not without the Upstage Club, the Student Prince, and the Sunshine In. And most certainly not if the Wonder Bar and the Fastlane won't be allowed to stay open. These properties, along with the beautiful Baronet Theatre and the house of punk rock, the Asbury Lanes, were sold to the Asbury Partners who, in turn, signed an agreement which put a company called Madison Marquette in charge of the oceanfront retail and entertainment development.

In a news release, dated May 22, 2006, Madison Marquette stated: "The retail and entertainment plan includes a boardwalk redevelopment, a lakeside retail promenade, and a major new hotel. The plan preserves the area's historic character and celebrates its musical heritage."

But how is all this possible if the efforts to reopen the Fastlane won't pay off, and if Lance and Debbie's Wonder Bar, the most historic of all local clubs that survived into the 2000s, will no longer be there to serve and provide good music?

The Stone Pony still ranks high among the East Coast venues. This is indeed the house that Bruce built, but it was the Upstage Club and the Student Prince that built Bruce. None of these places will ever reopen, and that's why the town needs the Wonder Bar—and the Fastlane—to hang on to the dreams and promises of those who made things happen back in the 1960s.

Don Stine is a well-known and respected Asbury Park native. He used to run Antic Hay on Cookman Avenue, a bookstore where Bruce Springsteen stopped by for a signing event after the release of a revised edition of his book, *Songs*.

"Springsteen visited one day and offered to do a book signing. We had previously had Clarence Clemons do a CD signing and people were lined up down the stairwells, so I knew there was no way I could accommodate the number of people that would want to come to such a Springsteen event. I told Bruce my concern and he said: 'Maybe we can keep it low key,' to which I just laughed and declined.

"I then became known as the only person ever to say 'no' to Bruce Springsteen and was pretty much taken to task by my friends for refusing the offer. I eventually saw Bruce a few more times and I suggested that a contest be held that would have people come to downtown Asbury Park to enter a contest with a limited number of winners, an amount I could handle. That was eventually what was decided and Springsteen subsequently did his only book signing in my store with 200 winners allowed entry."

As the building on Cookman Avenue was sold, Don Stine decided to close down his business, but he remains active in town as a trustee for the Asbury Park Historical Society. He tells us about growing up in Asbury, then leaving for college and married life, and returning in the mid '80s to once more get involved in the local music scene.

"While still in my teens I attended places like the Upstage and the Sunshine In. I actually saw Springsteen for the first time at the Sunshine In, performing with Steel Mill. But since I left in the late '60s I missed most of the early years of Springsteen, Southside Johnny, and Bon Jovi.

"I certainly enjoyed the concerts in Convention Hall and I remember being unexpectedly confronted by the Rolling Stones next to their limo. Young women were screaming and tearing at my clothes so I quickly opened the limo door and Jagger and the band jumped in and took off. My only time being assaulted by hoards of young, horny women. I highly recommend it!"

Coming back in the 1980s things had changed.

"I was dancing at the Stone Pony one Sunday night and suddenly everyone stopped dancing. I couldn't understand why until someone told me it was Bruce Springsteen up onstage. I said: 'Who?' My friend couldn't believe I didn't know who Springsteen was but, anyway, that was my first introduction to him after he became famous. I have since always enjoyed his music and I have attended concerts or seen him at 'surprise' appearances.

"I also became involved and helped spearhead the effort to save the Stone Pony from demolition. I hope we have succeeded but I feel that it's still very much up in the air for various reasons."

Don Stine says that the musical heritage of Asbury Park remains one of the town's most important components; from the early days of John Philip Sousa and Arthur Prior, to the big bands and swing era, to the jazz and blues clubs on the West Side, to the sounds of Asbury Park rock 'n' roll bands.

"One of my incentives for saving the Stone Pony was to create an entertainment district at the southern end of the beachfront which would be free from residential development. However, I don't think this is going to happen and I fear the days of the legendary clubs may be limited. Residential development and musical venues do not necessarily go hand in hand, alas.

"However, Asbury Park is still a city in redevelopment and the future may hold anything. Hopefully the city's vast musical heritage will live on."

Downtown Asbury might not be the most frequented business area in Monmouth County. But things are shaping up. Right before Christmas, 2004, Harry's Roadhouse on Cookman was the talk of the town. That's when Springsteen moved his Holiday shows from Convention Hall to Harry's, next to the dive where it all began.

Sadly, as 2004 turned into 2005, a dispute ended with a change of locks and a liquor license revoked. Harry's sign was taken down before anyone even knew what happened. The good news is that the Red Fusion Bar was later opened on the very spot where Harry's used to stand. John Eddie, deSol, and Exit 105 were among the artists booked during 2006.

It's a fact, though, that waning public interest forced the house of blues, known as the Crossroads Bar, to close down on Main Street. But along the same street, you'll find one of the area's liveliest rock clubs: the Saint, operated by Scott Stamper, who is also organizer of the Asbury Music Awards.

As we stop by the Saint is hosting a singer/songwriter night. Onstage we'll find Bobby Strange, a short guy with a funny hat and a large voice. He has made a few trips to Europe with Boccigalupe & the Bad Boys, but spends most of his time playing clubs throughout Monmouth County. He is a modern local hero.

Down by the Shore, punk rock has its own home at the Asbury Lanes, and keeping the Stone Pony open seems to be among the developers' priorities. The Fastlane and Lance and Debbie's Wonder Bar don't seem to be so high on the list, and it's indeed a depressing thought not to have the Wonder Bar open, hosting local top acts such as Bob Burger, deSol, John Eddie, and, of course, Lance Larson himself.

"I'm trying to look at things this way," says co-manager Debbie Delisa. "They're bringing the amusements back, and that's good because it proves that they want the entertainment. They knocked down parts of the Casino and I think they might put the Stone Pony there, overlooking the ocean. Also, they're gonna redo the Berkeley Carteret Hotel and there's gonna be more than 300 rooms."

Wonder Bar partner and Jersey Shore legend Lance Larson adds:

"The developers have been here for the last five years. They own these places now, and I think with the Madison Marquette on board we're going in the right direction. I'm certain they realize that without places like the Pony and the Wonder Bar you're just another Manasquan, you're just another Shore town. So let's just see what happens down the line."

Then there is another very special place. You won't find it in Asbury Park, but rather a short drive away, in Belmar.

A few blocks south of E Street, down by the marina, there's a tiny little house. Outside there's a sign that says: 'Ragin' Cajun established in 1992.' Check it out some Sunday evening. Bring a bottle of red or a six-pack, because they don't serve their own. The food, on the other hand, might be the spiciest along the Jersey Shore.

Ragin' Cajun is neither a nightclub nor a rock 'n' roll venue. Ragin Cajun' is a Creole restaurant with blues on the Sunday menu. And not just any blues.

Every Sunday since 1996, Ken Sorensen comes here from Ocean Grove. At around seven PM he packs up his little case, the one that holds a few Hohner harmonicas. In the same corner of the room sits Sonny Kenn, with either a Gibson or his white Stratocaster. Vic Bayers is most likely already behind the drums, and Dave Meyers has definitely plugged in his bass by now.

This is Stringbean & the Stalkers, and a whole book's worth of Asbury history.

Sorensen (who has Norwegian roots) has nothing to do with the Upstage or the Student Prince. He took his share of lessons starting in the British 1960s and 1970s blues to wind up at some crossroads way down South. He plays the blues like he feels it: soft, melodious, ravishing.

"Preferably at the Ragin' Cajun," he says. "'Cause here it's mostly friends who come by, and then we can play it just as we please. It has even happened that we have written new songs during gigs."

The Stalkers are Ken Sorensen's band, and a continuation of the blues that he and Dave Meyers used to play with Big Danny Gallagher.

Meyers is original. Once upon a time he was a member of the Blackberry Booze Band, which later morphed into the Asbury Jukes. Vic Bayers, the drummer, is also original. He was part of the house band at the Student Prince.

Sonny Kenn was once the first rock 'n' roll star along the Shore, and these days he goes to the Ragin' Cajun to take a break one day a week. Or maybe just to get back the feeling of things that used to be.

ABOUT THE AUTHORS

Anders Mårtensson has worked as a journalist since 1993, for most of that time as entertainment editor for the Swedish newspaper *Kristianstadsbladet*.

At the age of 11 he heard Bruce Springsteen for the first time—"Born to Run." A fan was born, both of the music and the lyrics. This admiration developed into a general interest in the music scene that emerged from the clubs in and around Asbury Park.

Jörgen Johansson is a photographer who received his training at the New England School of Photography. Has has worked for Swedish newspapers *Norra Skåne* and *Skånska Dagbladet*, and won awards for best news picture of the year.

Jörgen discovered the music of Bruce Springsteen around the time that *Born in the U.S.A.* was released, and later developed a great passion for the music—both historic and contemporary—from Asbury Park, New Jersey.